This library edition published in 2015 by Walter Foster Publishing,
a division of Quarto Publishing Group USA Inc.
3 Wrigley, Suite A
Irvine, CA 92618

Distributed in the United States and Canada by
Lerner Publisher Services
241 First Avenue North
Minneapolis, MN 55401 U.S.A.
www.lernerbooks.com

First Library Edition

Library of Congress Cataloging-in-Publication Data

Foster, Walter T. (Walter Thomas), 1891-1981.
  Horses. -- First Library Edition.
     pages cm
  ISBN 978-1-939581-39-6
  1. Horses in art. 2. Drawing--Technique. I. Title.
  NC783.8.H65F673 2015
  704.9'43296655--dc23

2013046830

012015
18582

9 8 7 6 5 4 3 2 1

Horses

From the earliest cave drawings to the modern masters, artists have long been inspired by the horse as a subject. Horses have an elegance and spirit that we're naturally attracted to and intrigued by. With their fluid lines, powerful muscles, and graceful motions, it's no wonder that these extraordinary creatures have frequently been celebrated by artists throughout the ages. And now you can learn to draw horses too, even if you've never picked up a drawing pencil. In this book, you'll find the basics of horse anatomy and correct proportion, as well as special tips for drawing facial features, ears, hooves, and manes. You'll also learn how to render these beautiful and expressive animals in exciting action poses—racing, jumping, and galloping. Just follow the simple steps in this book, and soon you'll develop your own style for drawing these magnificent animals.

CONTENTS

Walter Foster

Getting Started

Drawing is just like writing your name. You use lines to make shapes. In the art of drawing, you carry it a bit further, using shading techniques to create the illusion of three-dimensional form.

Only a few basic tools are needed in the art of drawing. The tools necessary to create the drawings in this book are all shown here.

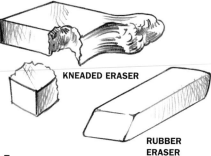

KNEADED ERASER

RUBBER ERASER

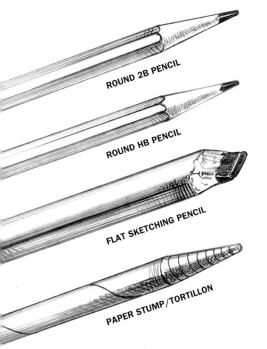

ROUND 2B PENCIL

ROUND HB PENCIL

FLAT SKETCHING PENCIL

PAPER STUMP/TORTILLON

Pencils

Pencils come in varying degrees of lead, from very soft to hard (e.g., 6B, 4B, 2B, and HB, respectively). Harder leads create lighter lines and are used to make preliminary sketches. Softer leads are usually used for shading.

Flat sketching pencils are very helpful; they can create wide or thin lines, and even dots. Find one with a B lead, the degree of softness between HB and 2B.

Although pencil is the primary tool used for drawing, don't limit yourself. Try using charcoal, Conté crayons, brush and ink, or pastels—they can add color and dimension to your work.

Erasers

Erasers are not only useful for correcting mistakes, they are also fine drawing tools. Choose from several types: kneaded, vinyl, gum, or rubber, depending on how you want to use the eraser. For example, you can mold a kneaded eraser into a point or break off smaller pieces to lift out highlights or create texture. A gum or rubber eraser works well for erasing larger areas.

Paper

Paper varies according to color, thickness, and surface quality (e.g., smooth or rough). Use a sketch pad for practice. For finer renderings, try illustration or Bristol board. As you become more comfortable with drawing techniques, experiment with better quality paper to see how it affects your work.

Other Helpful Materials

You should have a paper blending stump (also known as a *tortillon*) for creating textures and blends in your drawing. It enhances certain effects and, once covered with lead, can be used to draw smeared lines.

In order to conserve your lead, have some sandpaper on hand so you can sharpen the lead without wearing down the pencil. You may want to buy a metal ruler as well, for drawing straight lines. Finally, a sturdy drawing board provides a stable surface for your drawing.

Final Preparations

Before you begin drawing, set up a spacious work area that has plenty of natural light. Make sure all your tools and materials are easily accessible from where you're sitting. Since you might be sitting for hours at a time, find a comfortable chair.

If you wish, tape the paper at the corners to your drawing board or surface to prevent it from moving while you work. You can also use a ruler to make a light border around the edge of the paper; this will help you use the space on your paper wisely, especially if you want to frame or mat the finished product.

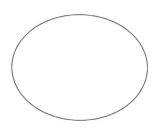

This is an oval *shape*.

This has a three-dimensional, ball-like *form*.

As you read through this book, carefully note how the words *shape* and *form* are used. *Shape* refers to the actual outline of an object, while *form* refers to its three-dimensional appearance.

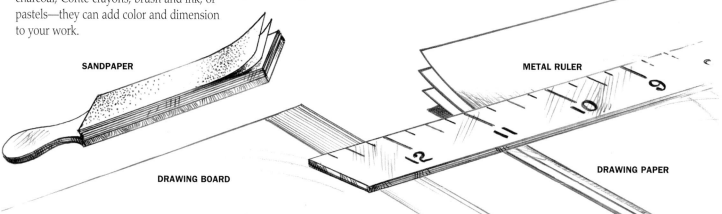

SANDPAPER

DRAWING BOARD

METAL RULER

DRAWING PAPER

Shading Techniques

The drawing tools described on the previous page will allow you to shade skillfully and effectively, giving your subject form and texture. Shading creates the illusion of depth and form of an object through the use of variations in *values*—the relative lightness or darkness of a color or of black.

You can also create different textures by varying the kind of strokes, tools, drawing surfaces, and techniques you use. A pencil sharpened to a chisel point will create thick strokes, and one with a sharp point will produce narrower strokes. The side of the lead can be used for large, broad shading, and the point for fine details. Choose a softer lead and add more pressure for the dark areas, and leave lighter areas for contrast.

Break a Conté crayon or piece of charcoal in half, and use the side to shade large areas of your drawing.

The watercolor brush makes bold, solid lines, while the paper stump creates smooth, blended areas.

#3 ROUND WATERCOLOR BRUSH

PAPER STUMP

Sharpen pencils on a sandpaper pad.

6B PENCIL

SANDPAPER PAD

CHARCOAL STICK

CONTÉ CRAYON

CHARCOAL PENCIL

Use an HB pencil for the first steps of your drawing, when you block in the basic shapes of the horse. Softer lead pencils are good for shading. Brush and India ink is another option. Experiment with your tools and materials to see what kinds of textures and effects you can produce.

Anatomy & Proportion

Some knowledge of the horse's anatomy and proportion is important for correctly blocking in the basic shape of the subject at the beginning of each drawing.

Proportion refers to the proper relation of one part to another or to the whole, particularly in terms of size or shape. Proportion is a key factor in achieving a likeness of a subject. For drawing animals and people, artists often use head size as a measuring unit for determining the length of other body parts. For example, the body of the horse is about four times the length of its head. Utilizing this kind of approximation will help you draw the horse in correct proportion.

SKELETON

SPINE **VERTEBRAE**

SCAPULA

The horse's large eye is set high on its elongated head. Notice the width of the skull from the forehead to the lower jaw and the long, tapered nose.

To make realistic drawings, keep in mind that the horse's structure is determined by its skeleton. You don't need to learn the names of all the parts of the horse's anatomy, or even how to draw them; just keep the basic sizes and shapes in mind as you draw. For example, note the triangular shape of the skull, the depth of the rib cage, and the joints in the legs. The vertebrae are slightly higher in the area over the rib cage, forming the base of the horse's withers.

SKULL

The hoof is a hard protective covering for the single toe of each foot.

HOOF

HEAD

HEAD

HEAD

HEAD

½ HEAD

HEAD

½ HEAD

4 HEADS

HEAD

HEAD

Bone and Muscle Structure

W. F.

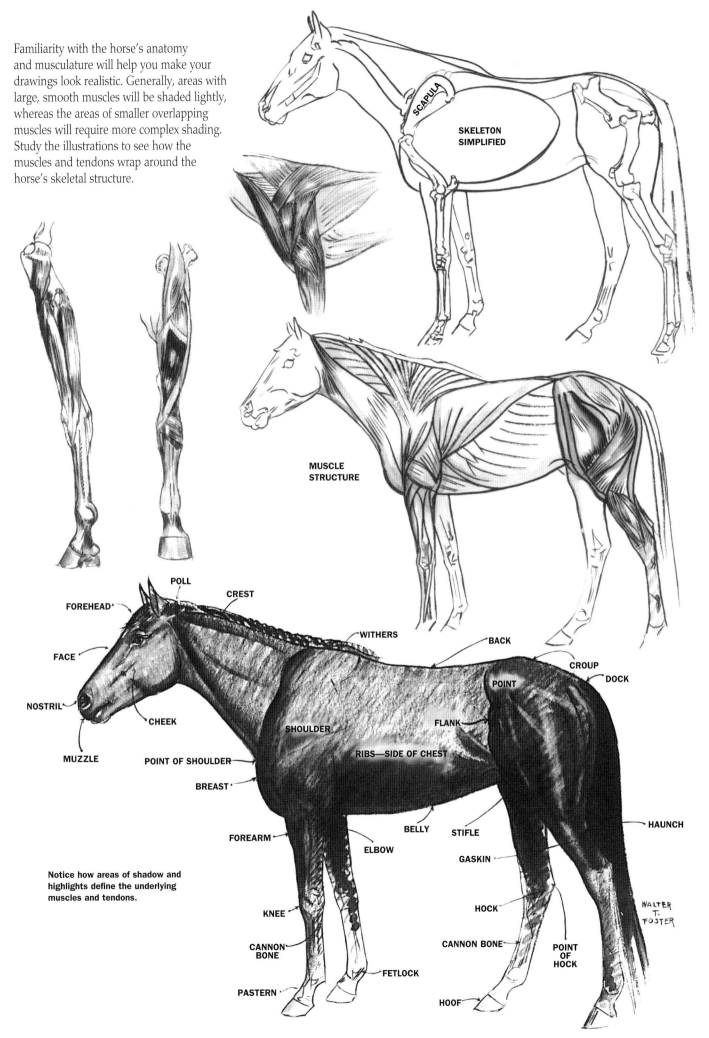

Familiarity with the horse's anatomy and musculature will help you make your drawings look realistic. Generally, areas with large, smooth muscles will be shaded lightly, whereas the areas of smaller overlapping muscles will require more complex shading. Study the illustrations to see how the muscles and tendons wrap around the horse's skeletal structure.

SCAPULA

SKELETON SIMPLIFIED

MUSCLE STRUCTURE

Notice how areas of shadow and highlights define the underlying muscles and tendons.

POLL

FOREHEAD

CREST

WITHERS

BACK

CROUP

DOCK

FACE

POINT

NOSTRIL

FLANK

SHOULDER

CHEEK

RIBS—SIDE OF CHEST

MUZZLE

POINT OF SHOULDER

BREAST

HAUNCH

BELLY

STIFLE

FOREARM

ELBOW

GASKIN

HOCK

KNEE

CANNON BONE

CANNON BONE

POINT OF HOCK

WALTER T. FOSTER

FETLOCK

PASTERN

HOOF

5

Eyes & Muzzles

Facial features, such as eyes and muzzles, are a good place to start learning to draw horses. If you are a beginner, you might want to practice drawing the parts separately before attempting a complete rendering. Study the drawings on this page, and look at the way the shapes and forms change as the viewing angle changes.

Practice by making many sketches of these features from several different angles. Copy the examples here, or use your own models. Often, details, such as the expression in the eye or the shading around the nostril, are what separate an average drawing from a remarkable one. Start by sketching the general shape with an HB pencil, and then refine the lines until you are satisfied.

Remember that the eyeball is a sphere, so the eyelid covering it will also be spherical in shape.

As is true for all mammals, horses' eyes reveal their emotions and personality.

When drawing horses—or any subject— it is best to work from live models or photographs. Trying to draw from memory or imagination is much more difficult. Collect photographs of horses and foals from catalogs, magazines, and books, and keep them in a file for reference. Such a file is commonly called an *artist's morgue.*

Horse's faces are not very fleshy, so the planes of the face are quite distinct, revealing the underlying structure of the skull.

The forms of the muscles, veins, and tendons are also easily discernible under the surface of the horse's skin and sleek coat.

Changes in values and in pencil stroke direction help make your drawings look three-dimensional.

Horses have a few large teeth in the front of their mouth, with a gap on either side between the front incisors and the rear molars.

Ears & Hooves

The position of the horse's ears reveals its mood. For example, ears pricked forward usually indicate alert interest, whereas ears laid back are a sign of anger, discomfort, or fear. As you practice drawing the ears in different positions, note how shading is used to define the form.

Use parallel strokes (hatching) to emphasize the upright position of these alert ears.

Vary the direction of your pencil strokes to delineate the round form of the ear.

Reserve the darkest values for the inner ear.

The hoof is a hard covering that encloses the underlying toe bone. The frog is the softer, more tender area in the bottom of the hoof. Notice that the hoof is longer in front and shorter in back; make sure your drawings reflect the proper angle of the hoof.

Horseshoes are nailed into the outer hoof wall, but the horse feels no pain because the wall has no nerve endings—just as it doesn't hurt when you trim your fingernails.

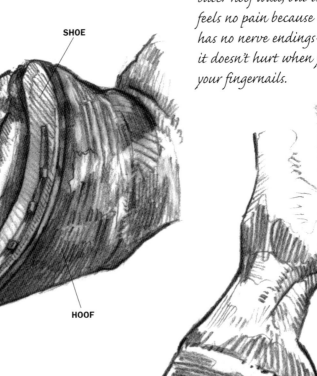

SHOE

FROG

HOOF

To show the curvature of the hoof, use varying values of light and dark. Be sure to leave a highlight where the light strikes the hoof.

Basic Heads

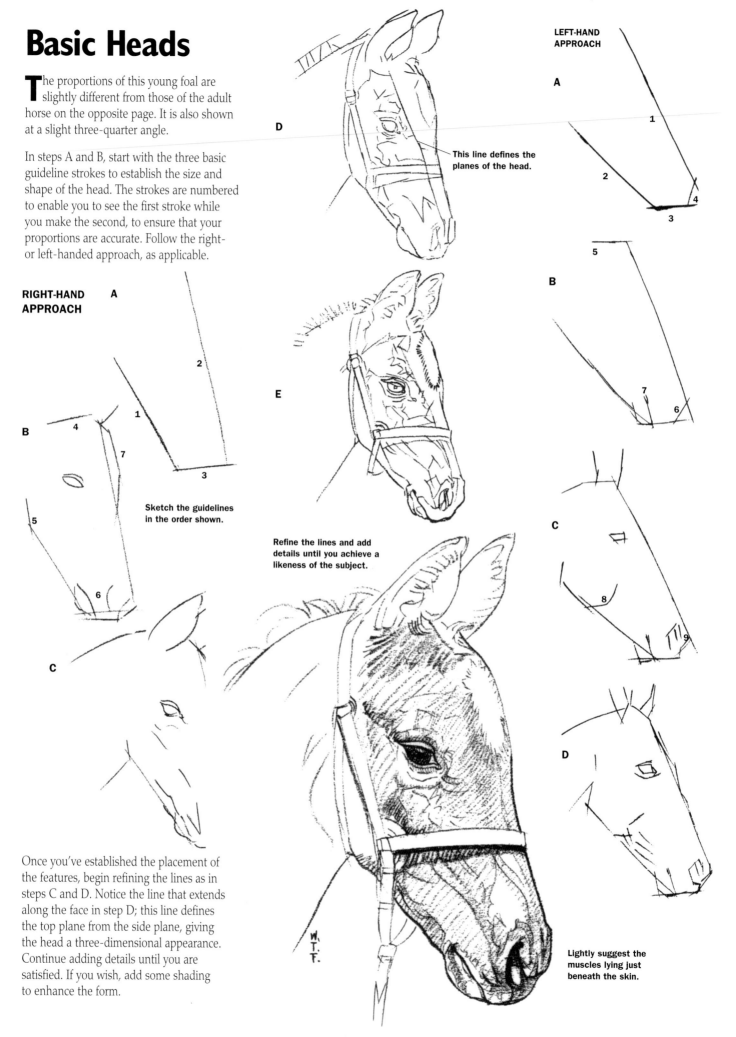

The proportions of this young foal are slightly different from those of the adult horse on the opposite page. It is also shown at a slight three-quarter angle.

In steps A and B, start with the three basic guideline strokes to establish the size and shape of the head. The strokes are numbered to enable you to see the first stroke while you make the second, to ensure that your proportions are accurate. Follow the right- or left-handed approach, as applicable.

RIGHT-HAND APPROACH

Sketch the guidelines in the order shown.

Refine the lines and add details until you achieve a likeness of the subject.

LEFT-HAND APPROACH

This line defines the planes of the head.

Lightly suggest the muscles lying just beneath the skin.

Once you've established the placement of the features, begin refining the lines as in steps C and D. Notice the line that extends along the face in step D; this line defines the top plane from the side plane, giving the head a three-dimensional appearance. Continue adding details until you are satisfied. If you wish, add some shading to enhance the form.

Although horses' heads all have a similar basic shape, there are variations among breeds and between individual horses. The drawing here is of a classic thoroughbred profile, with a straight nose and slightly tapered muzzle. Practice drawing many different profiles, and see if you can bring out the unique characteristics in each one.

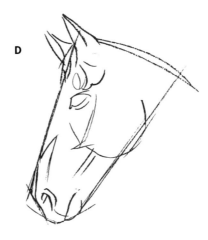

D

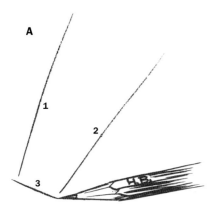

A

In steps A and B, use an HB pencil to block in a few basic guidelines to establish the placement and general proportion of the head. Then sketch in the outline of the ears and cheek, and block in the position of the eye, nostril, and mouth, as in step C. When you're comfortable with the outline, round out the muzzle, define the features, and suggest the underlying muscles, as shown in steps D and E.

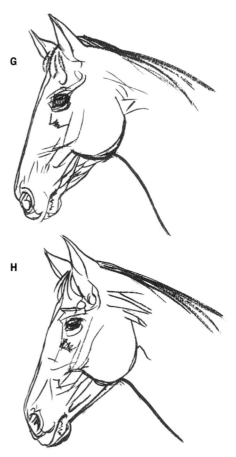

G

H

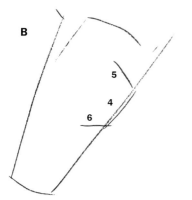

B

E

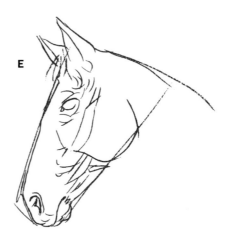

In the final steps, study your reference before further refining the shapes and adding the details. Make note of the length and position of the ears, the angle of the neck, and the curve of the nose and lower lip. Look for the point where the lines of the neck and lower jaw meet the cheek. As your observation skills improve, so will your drawings!

Don't worry about making a final rendering at this point. While working out proportions and improving your observation skills, keep the drawings loose and sketchy. You can focus on shading techniques later.

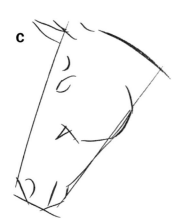

C

F

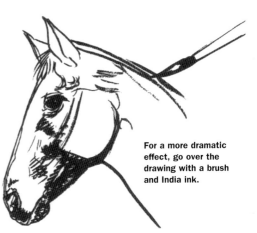

For a more dramatic effect, go over the drawing with a brush and India ink.

Advanced Heads

This profile has been developed a little further than the previous examples were. You will follow the same steps as before, but be more careful and deliberate with your lines and shading strokes. Remember to observe your subject closely so you can render a good likeness.

B

HB PENCIL

A

After blocking in the shape of the head in step A, take your time to refine the outlines, being sure to emphasize the protruding lip and the graceful curves of the neck. Mark the major muscle areas around the eye, above the cheek, and along the muzzle in step B. Then follow these guidelines to apply varying values of shading on the face and neck, using the side of a soft lead pencil.

Use long, thick strokes with a chisel point or the side of a soft lead pencil.

Apply short, light strokes for the shading on the face and neck, with a few thick, perpendicular lines for the muscles on the jaw and around the eye. Try blending some areas with a paper stump for a softer effect.

Don't be afraid to experiment and fail—remember, there's no substitute for practice!

Here are some slightly more complex examples to help you practice shading techniques. Notice the differences in the viewing angles, mane treatments, and tack (the bridles and halter). As always, start with a few block-in lines, refine your outlines, and then add the shading.

BRAIDED MANE

ROACHED MANE

Show horses often have braided manes, and roached manes have been shaved to a few inches in length so they stand straight up. These two mane styles show off the horses' necks and give you the opportunity to practice shading the muscles in the head and neck. Because there are so many differences among breeds, your observation skills will be well tested drawing horses!

Use short horizontal strokes for the front of the neck, and vary the angle of the strokes on the side to follow the curve of the neck.

As you shade these heads, look carefully at the way the contrast between light and dark values gives form to the horses. Dark and middle values add depth, and the highlights make those areas "pop out." Vary the kinds of strokes you use to emphasize the different textures in the sleek coats, the coarser manes, and the smooth leather of the horses' tack.

For a soft effect, select a 6B pencil and use a chisel point or the side of the lead to create wide, even strokes.

Foal's Body

Foals have a great zest for living and a fine sense of fun. They love to run and kick, and they are as fond of showing off as children are. Try to capture this playfulness in your drawings.

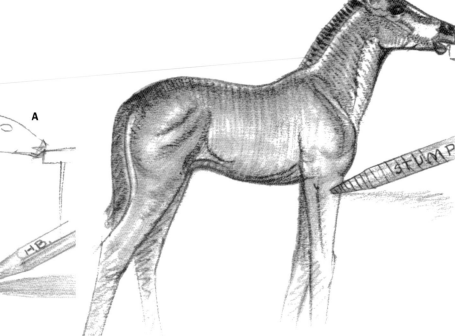

A

To sketch the foal above, start by drawing an oval with an HB pencil. Block in the body parts around this shape, making sure all the elements are drawn in correct proportion. Notice how long the foal's legs are in relation to its body. Then use a 6B pencil to shade the foal, blending out some areas with a paper stump for a soft, rounded effect.

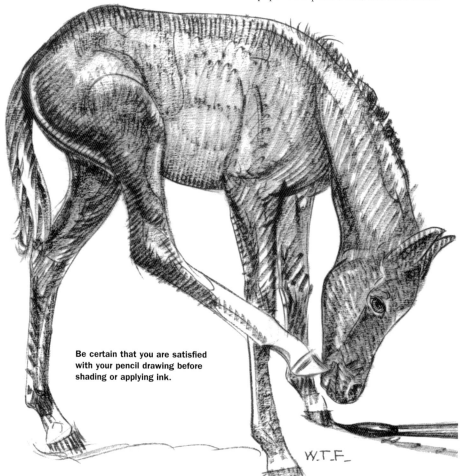

A

This drawing was made on rough-textured paper and finished using a *drybrush* technique. After working out the outline of the foal in pencil, apply the light and middle values with washes of India ink or black watercolor paint. Then use a dry brush and undiluted ink to lay in the darkest shadows and details. The drybrush technique produces rough, broken lines with feathered edges and is an easy way to create texture.

Be certain that you are satisfied with your pencil drawing before shading or applying ink.

W.T.F.

12

Here again, layers of ink washes are used to achieve a more solid rendering. After blocking in the basic shape of the body with an HB pencil, refine the lines until you are satisfied with the proportions and outline. Then use a clean brush to apply plain water over the foal's body, being careful to stay within the outlines. Next load the brush with diluted ink, and wash it over the body in smooth, even layers. This technique is called *wet-on-wet*, and it produces soft, loose blends. Note, however, that the washes are more difficult to control with this method than when painting wet-on-dry or with the drybrush technique.

Experiment with either painting wet-on-wet or allowing the paper to dry between washes. As you apply your washes, leave some areas lighter for highlights, and brush on extra layers of ink for the dark areas on the neck and belly. Use the tip of a dry brush to draw the fine outlines and details.

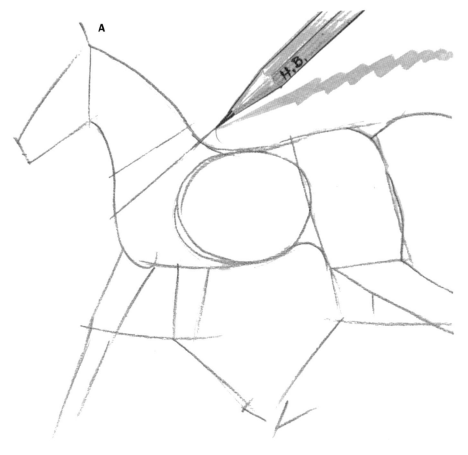

A

In a trot, this frisky foal's diagonal legs work in unison at a brisk, two-beat gait.

Apply multiple layers of diluted ink for the darkest areas.

Add water to the ink for the gray areas.

Leave some areas white for contrast.

#3 ROUND WATERCOLOR BRUSH

W.T.F.

Adult Horse's Body

Gaited horses, such as the Hackney, have an extremely high action, or leg carriage. Study your subject carefully to make sure that you draw the leg positions correctly. As you block in this high-stepping horse, begin with an oval for the midsection, and add circular forms for the rump and chest. Then rough in the head, legs, and tail, and start suggesting the major muscle areas, as in step A.

A

B

C

Start to indicate the darkest areas with short, parallel strokes, called *hatching*.

Use the side of the lead or a paper stump to shade the darkest areas.

Vary the direction of the hatching to suggest changes in the horse's form.

Leave white areas for highlights and contrast.

In steps B and C, shade the darkest areas of the horse with thick hatching, following the direction of the different planes and muscles of the horse's face and body. Then use a paper stump to blend some of the middle and dark values. Finally, use the sharp point of a 2B pencil to redefine the outline and some of the hatching.

It's important to get the pose right when you draw a horse rearing up on its hind legs. Remember that the horse's center of gravity is over its shoulders. If you draw the horse leaning too far forward or too far back, the horse will look unsteady.

A

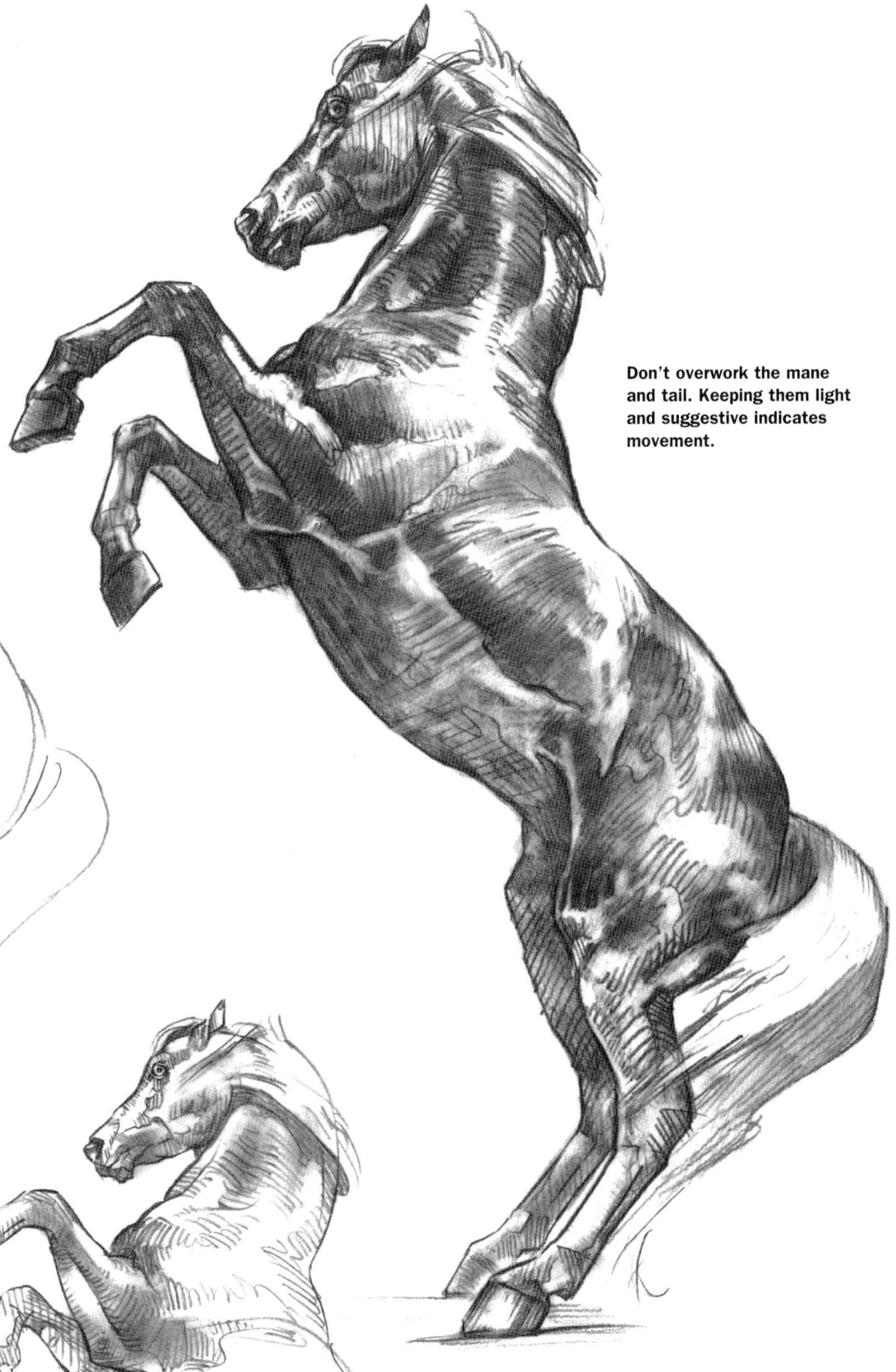

Don't overwork the mane and tail. Keeping them light and suggestive indicates movement.

This type of pose can be difficult, but don't give up! Keep practicing until you get it right!

B

C

Be sure the pose and proportions are correct before you begin shading.

As for all body drawings, start with an oval for the horse's midsection, and add ovals for the hindquarters and shoulders. Then block in the lines for the legs, tail, neck, and head, as shown in step A. Your strokes should be quick and loose to give the pose a spontaneous, natural feel.

Follow the steps to complete the drawing. Remember the horse's skeletal and muscular structures when shading.

15

Quarter Horse

The quarter horse is a powerfully built, muscular breed, known for its agility and superior cattle-cutting abilities. The name *quarter horse* is derived from the breed's capacity to run at high speed for distances up to a quarter of a mile. Emphasize the strong hindquarters and muscular neck when you draw this horse.

This pose represents another challenge. Here the horse is viewed from the rear and at an angle, so you will need to use foreshortening techniques in your drawing. *Foreshortening* means to reduce or distort parts of a drawing in order to convey the illusion of depth as perceived by the human eye. In this case, the horse's side is shortened to show that the front of the horse is farthest from the viewer. As a consequence, the rump and hindquarters appear larger in relation to the horse's front end, because that area is closest to the viewer.

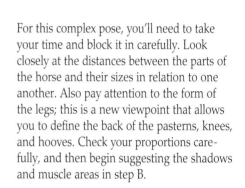

A

For this complex pose, you'll need to take your time and block it in carefully. Look closely at the distances between the parts of the horse and their sizes in relation to one another. Also pay attention to the form of the legs; this is a new viewpoint that allows you to define the back of the pasterns, knees, and hooves. Check your proportions carefully, and then begin suggesting the shadows and muscle areas in step B.

B

C

Use a paper stump to soften some of your shading strokes to produce middle values; then build the form by applying darker values over this layer.

This area has been foreshortened to create the illusion that the hindquarters are closest to the viewer.

As you lay in the dark and middle values in step C, vary the angle of the hatching to follow the planes of the muscles, face, and leg joints. For your final shading, use a soft 2B pencil and paper stump to smooth out the strokes, leaving strong highlights to bring out the sheen of the horse's coat. Take care not to overwork the legs in your final shading; the light areas show the horse's white "socks."

Keep a strong contrast between the dark values and the highlights to emphasize the well-developed muscles.

A horse's height, measured from the ground to the withers, is generally given in "hands." One hand is equal to 4 inches, the approximate width of a human hand.

Clydesdale

The Clydesdale, a large draft horse bred for heavy farm work, is now a popular parade horse, easily recognized by its "feathers"— the long hairs around its lower legs. The pose shown here is similar to the pose of the quarter horse, and this draft horse is also a muscular breed. To distinguish the two in your drawings, notice that the larger Clydesdale has a rounder rump, heavier legs, thicker and more arched neck, and a Roman (arched) nose.

A

B

Be sure to emphasize this horse's massive proportions as you block it in.

Block in this horse carefully, just as you did for the quarter horse on pages 16 and 17, keeping the principle of foreshortening in mind. Use a soft lead, such as a 2B, to establish the areas of light and dark in step C, and, for contrast, use heavy, straight strokes for the mane and tail.

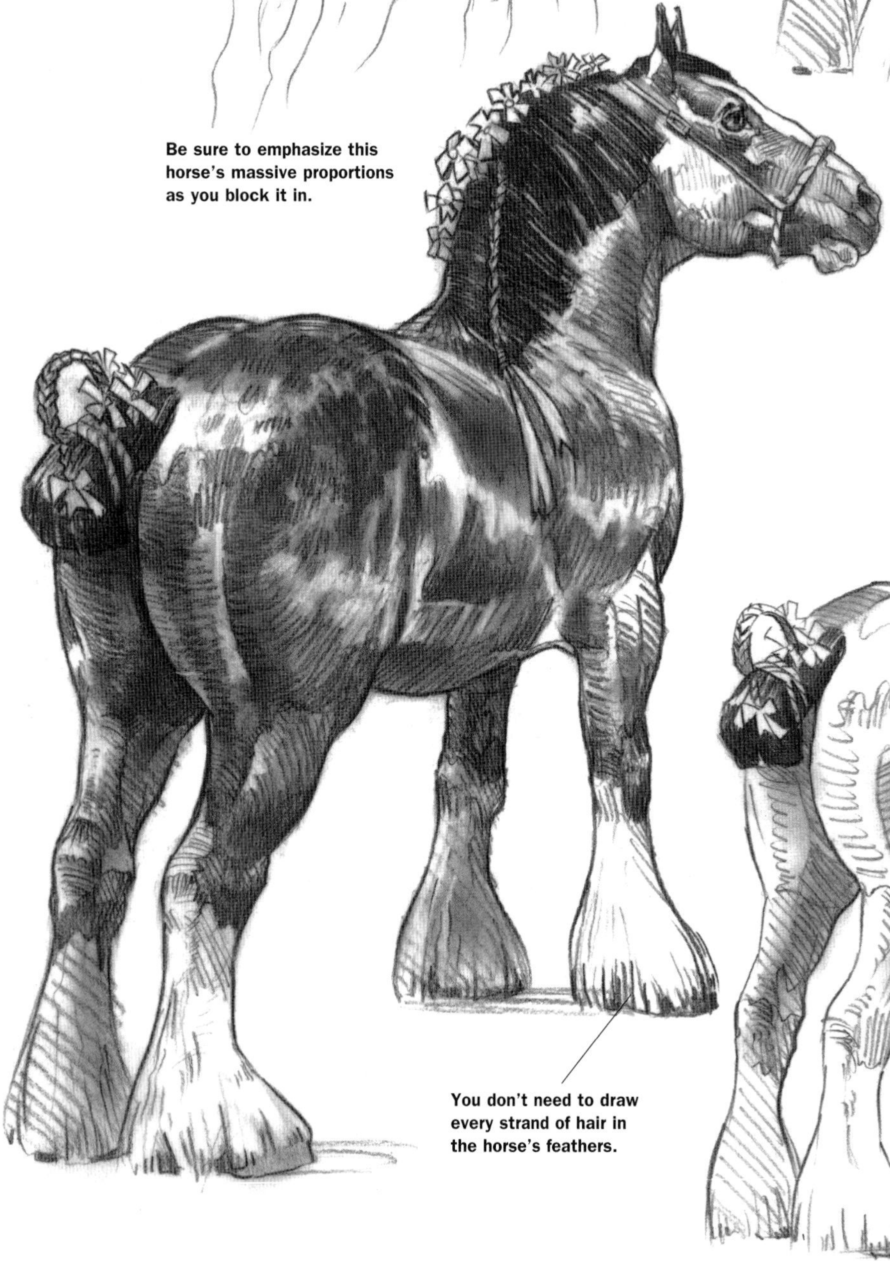

C

You don't need to draw every strand of hair in the horse's feathers.

Study your subject carefully so you can depict its unique characteristics, such as the decorated mane and tail of this parade horse.

Circus Horse

Horses used in the circus are large-boned breeds such as European warmbloods. These breeds have broad backs and strong builds combined with an elegant, graceful carriage. This striking pinto provides good practice for your shading techniques because its coat has both light- and dark-colored areas.

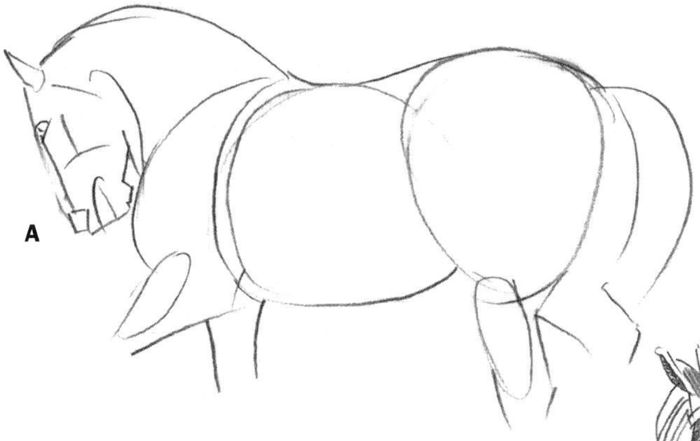

A

B

Use large ovals and circles when blocking in this horse to establish its size and strength. The reins are attached to the surcingle around the horse's body, so the head needs to be angled sharply toward the horse's chest, and the neck is greatly arched. In your final rendering, shade the white areas lightly, and use an eraser to pull out the highlights in the dark patches and in the tail.

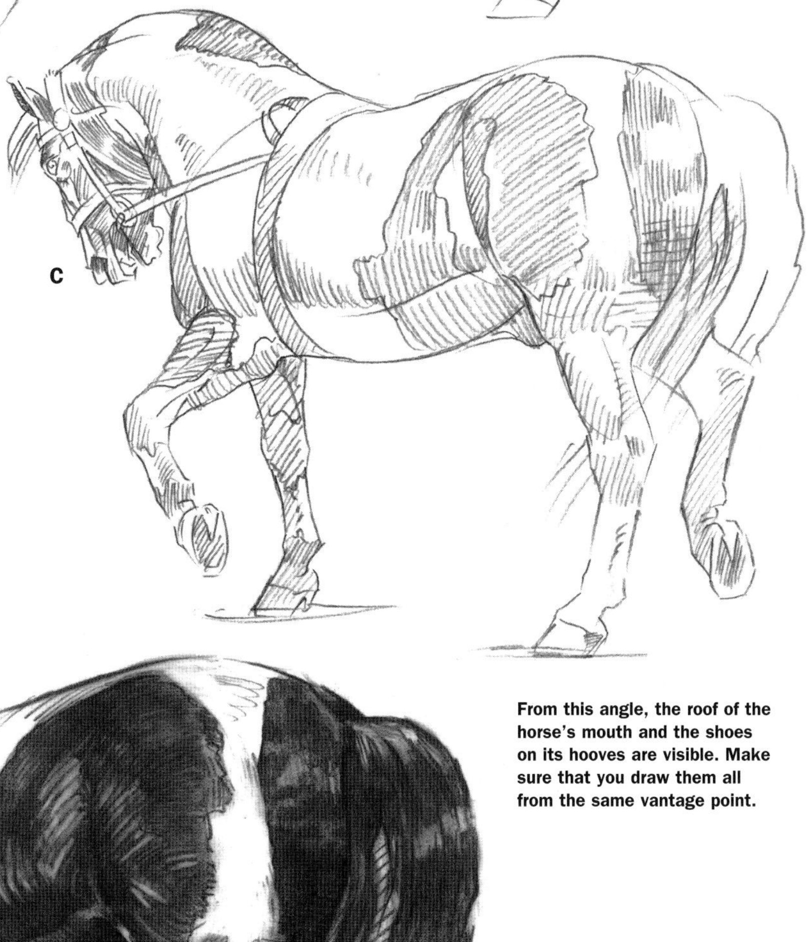

C

From this angle, the roof of the horse's mouth and the shoes on its hooves are visible. Make sure that you draw them all from the same vantage point.

See page 7 for tips on drawing hooves.

19

Arabian

The Arabian is a high-spirited horse with a flamboyant tail carriage and distinctive dished profile. Though relatively small in stature, this breed is known for its stamina, graceful build, intelligence, and energy. Try to capture the Arabian's slender physique and high spirit in your drawing.

Block in the body with an HB pencil, placing the oval for the body at a slight angle to indicate that the body will be foreshortened. Take care when blocking in the head to stress the concave nose, large nostrils, and small muzzle. As you start shading in steps B and C, keep the lines for the tail and mane loose and free, and accent the graceful arch of the neck.

A

B

Be sure to emphasize this horse's narrow chest and face to convey its more delicate build.

From this angle, the line of the spine is visible. Add subtle shading here and along the withers to give your drawing a three-dimensional quality.

Refine your shading with a soft lead pencil and paper stump, leaving large areas of white for the highlights. These highlights show the shine on the horse's coat and indicate the direction of the light source.

C

Arabians were highly prized by the desert Bedouins for their stamina and speed.

Shetland Pony

One of the smallest of the pony breeds, the Shetland is a hardy animal originally from the Shetland Islands off of northern Britain. This pony exhibits the characteristic small head, thick neck, and stocky build of the breed.

A pony is designated as any breed that stands less than 15 hands, or 60 inches tall. The little Shetland is only about 42 inches at the withers.

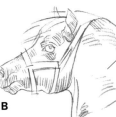

A

As you block in the pony's body, carefully observe its proportions; the length of its body is about two and a half times the length of its head. In step A, start with large circles and ovals to capture the pony's solid build. Use hatching strokes to start indicating the middle values as shown in step B, using a paper stump for the darkest areas in step C.

Notice the pony's relatively short, thick neck.

B

C

Use the side of the lead and a paper stump for light, wispy strokes to finish off this light-colored pony.

Horse & Rider in Action

When you depict a horse with a rider, the two should should be drawn as if they are one entity. Develop them both at the same time as you draw. The rider's body, leg, and hand position are important elements that, when drawn correctly, will make your drawings realistic.

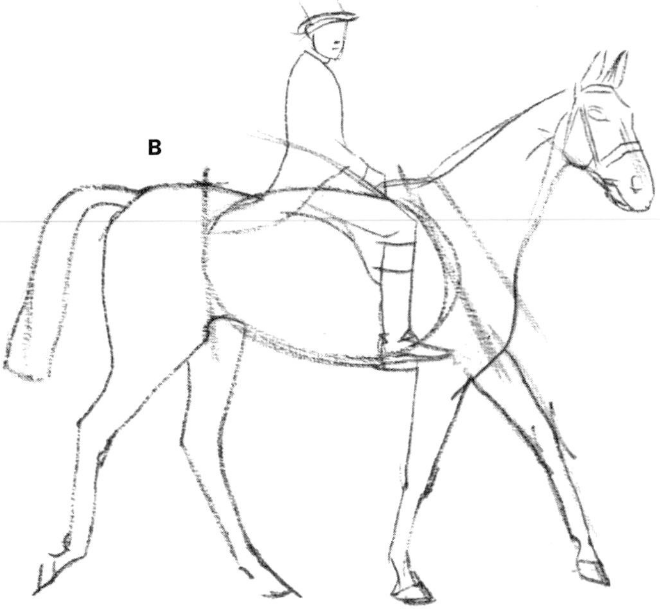

A

B

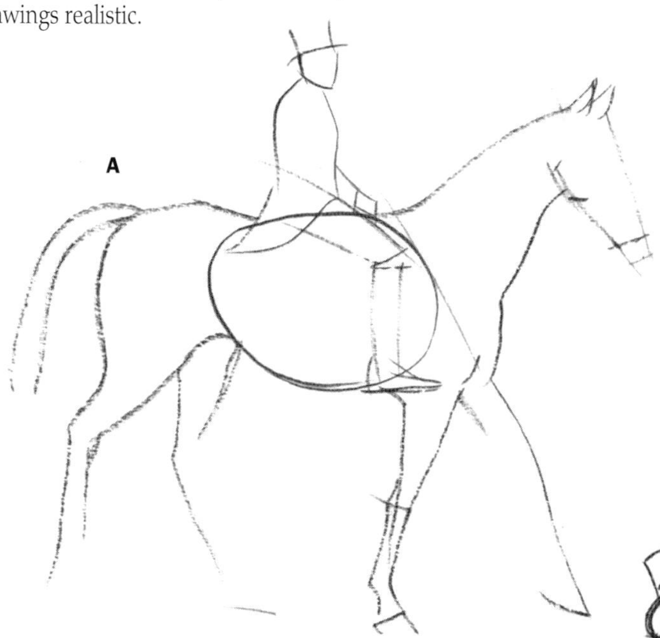

Practice drawing the horse's various gaits, as in this series of sketches. Take note of the rider's position. At a walk, the horse's head is upright, and the rider's body is perpendicular to the horse's.

In step A, begin with a horizontal oval shape for the horse's body, and block in the rider and the horse's head, neck, and legs. Mark the angle of the horse's shoulder line to help you establish the correct angle of the right foreleg. Notice how the horse's hind foot turns backward as it is lifted off the ground.

Keep in mind that the size of the rider and the size of the horse must be kept in correct proportion to one another.

The slow, loping gait of a horse is called a canter. At this moderate pace, the horse's center of gravity is shifted slightly forward, evident in the forward thrust of the head and body. Notice that the rider is leaning forward toward the horse's head, following the horse's motion with his own body. Keep your lines fluid and loose to convey the sense of movement.

Don't forget that the most important thing about drawing is having fun.

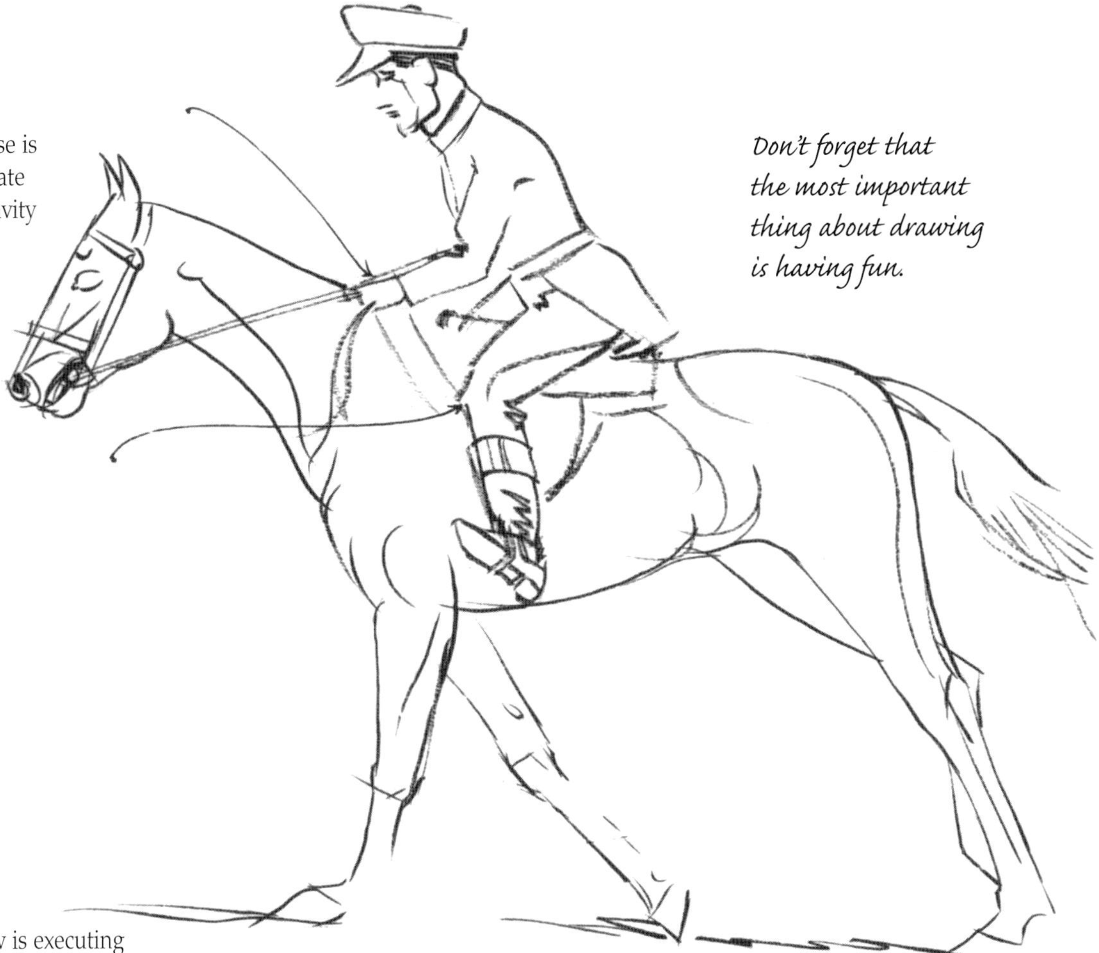

The horse in the sketch below is executing the kind of controlled movement required in the precise training style of *dressage*, the French term for "training."

Note the more upright posture and closed arm angle of the rider below. The taut reins act as an aid to help the horse keep its body movements precise and collected. Show this in your drawing by emphasizing the vertical and horizontal lines of this prancing action.

In this example, the foreleg is parallel to the ground plane. A horizontal guideline will help ensure that the pose is correct.

23

The Gallop

The gallop is the horse's fastest gait; some horses can reach a speed of 35 miles per hour at a full gallop. At one point in this three-beat gait, all four legs are off the ground at the same time; at another point, all the horse's weight is supported by only one leg, as shown here.

B

A

Because this horse is viewed at an angle, the oval for the body must be angled. Block in the chest and hindquarters with circles, and use angular lines for the knees and face, as in step A. Keep the lines for the tail free-flowing.

Don't overwork your final shading; use just enough to suggest the form. The large area of white indicates a strong light source but also gives this horse in flight a light, airborne quality.

C

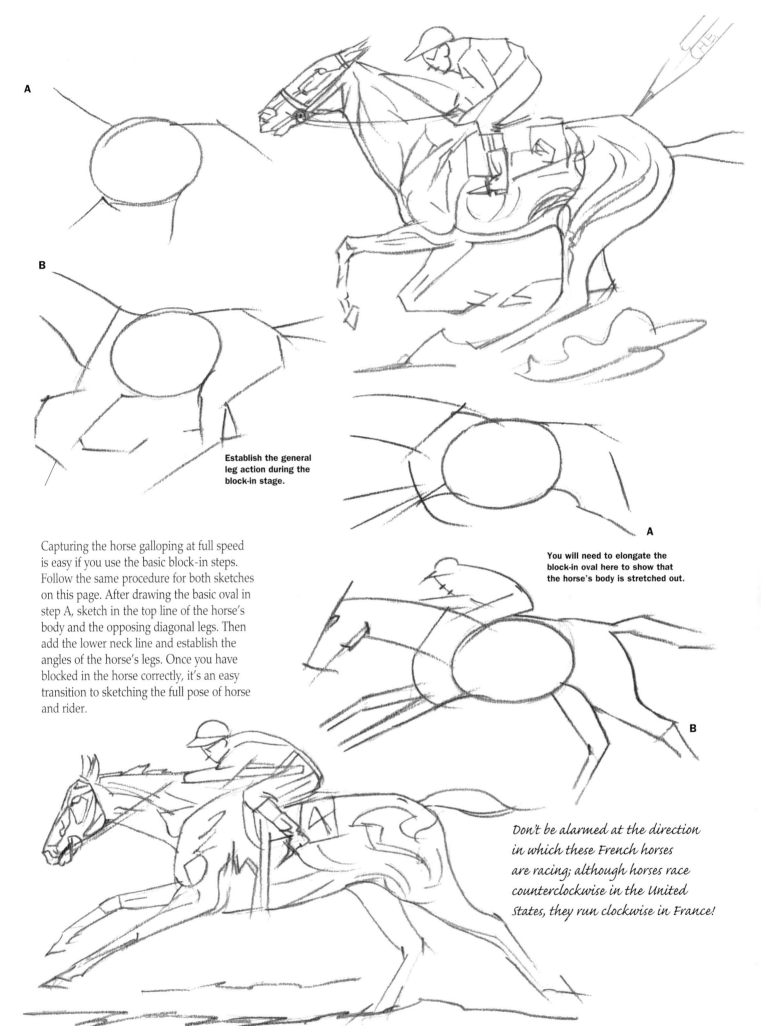

A

B

Establish the general leg action during the block-in stage.

A

You will need to elongate the block-in oval here to show that the horse's body is stretched out.

B

Capturing the horse galloping at full speed is easy if you use the basic block-in steps. Follow the same procedure for both sketches on this page. After drawing the basic oval in step A, sketch in the top line of the horse's body and the opposing diagonal legs. Then add the lower neck line and establish the angles of the horse's legs. Once you have blocked in the horse correctly, it's an easy transition to sketching the full pose of horse and rider.

Don't be alarmed at the direction in which these French horses are racing; although horses race counterclockwise in the United States, they run clockwise in France!

A

The Jump

Jumping is an exciting horse sport, whether it's stadium show jumping, cross-country racing, or steeplechasing. Notice how dramatically the rider shifts body position to follow the horse's movement. The rider must remain over the horse's center of gravity to help the horse maintain its balance and to keep from hindering the horse's effort. Being aware of these details will help keep your drawings accurate.

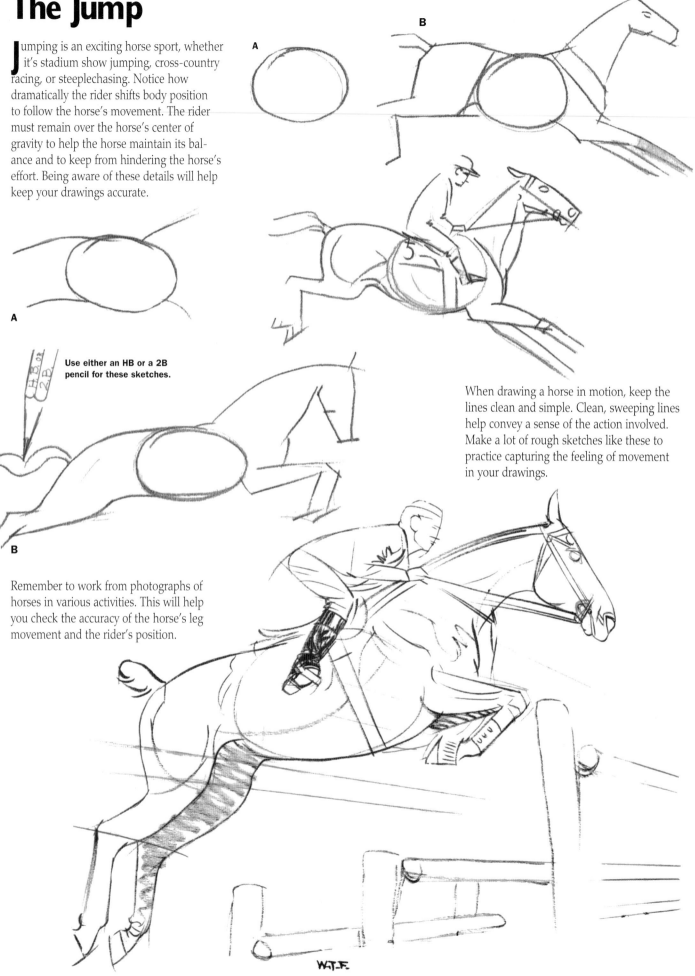

A

B

A

Use either an HB or a 2B pencil for these sketches.

B

When drawing a horse in motion, keep the lines clean and simple. Clean, sweeping lines help convey a sense of the action involved. Make a lot of rough sketches like these to practice capturing the feeling of movement in your drawings.

Remember to work from photographs of horses in various activities. This will help you check the accuracy of the horse's leg movement and the rider's position.

WTF.

Polo Pony & Player

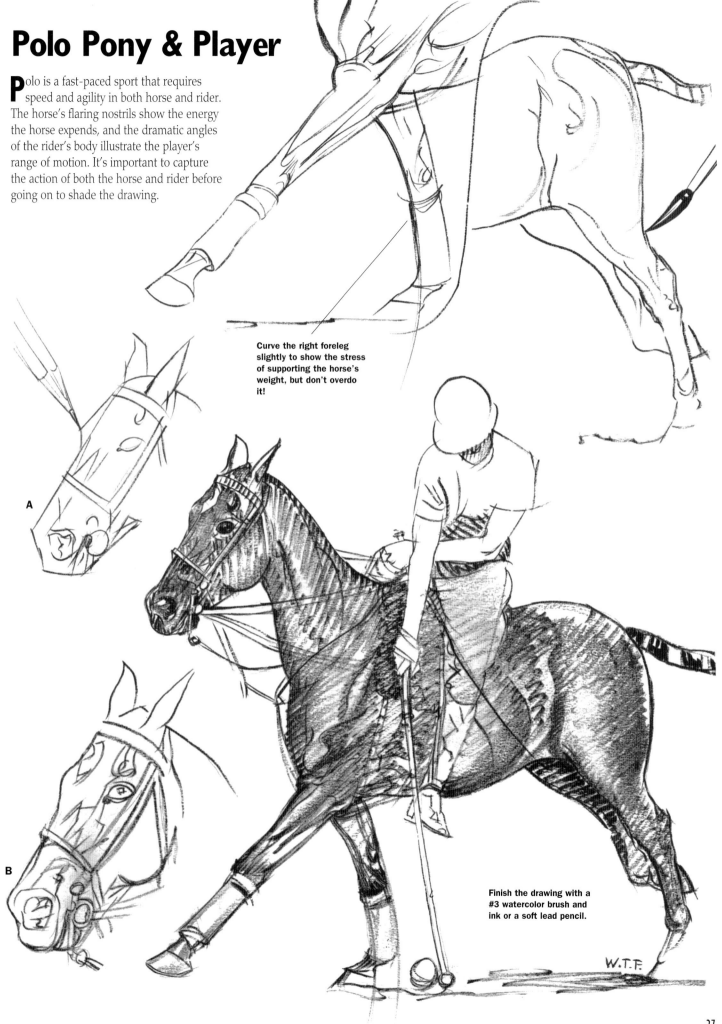

Polo is a fast-paced sport that requires speed and agility in both horse and rider. The horse's flaring nostrils show the energy the horse expends, and the dramatic angles of the rider's body illustrate the player's range of motion. It's important to capture the action of both the horse and rider before going on to shade the drawing.

Curve the right foreleg slightly to show the stress of supporting the horse's weight, but don't overdo it!

A

B

Finish the drawing with a #3 watercolor brush and ink or a soft lead pencil.

W.T.F.

Racehorse & Jockey

This closeup drawing of a horse and jockey was completed with brush and ink. First use an HB pencil to block in the horse's head, and then develop the jockey's pose. Be sure to correctly establish the action and rhythm of the horse and rider, as well as the horse's expression, before applying the ink.

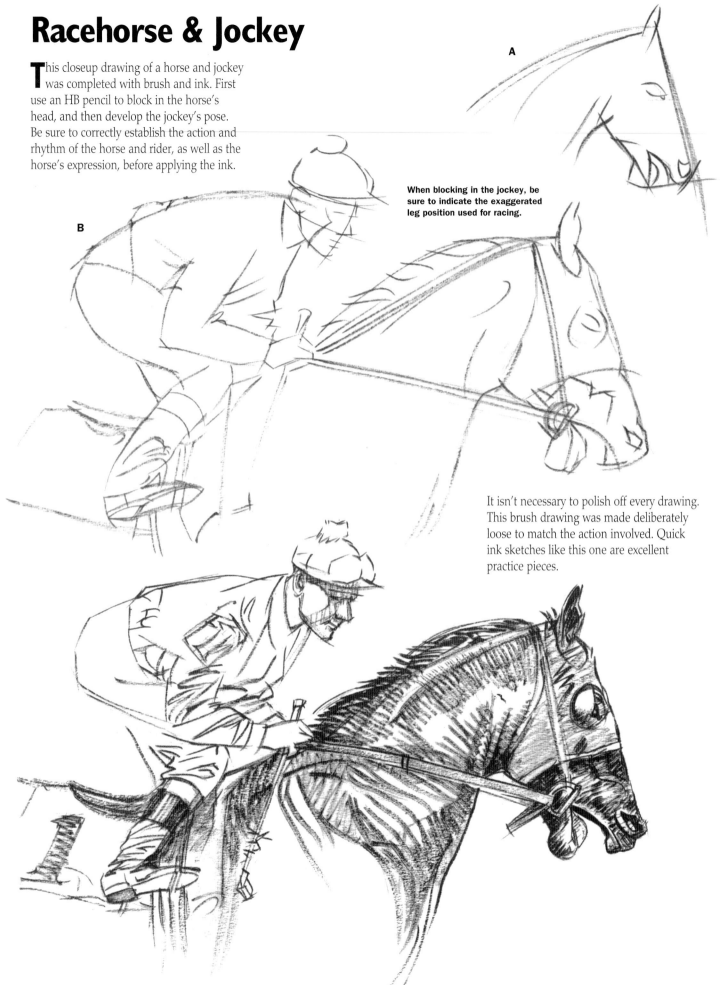

A

When blocking in the jockey, be sure to indicate the exaggerated leg position used for racing.

B

It isn't necessary to polish off every drawing. This brush drawing was made deliberately loose to match the action involved. Quick ink sketches like this one are excellent practice pieces.

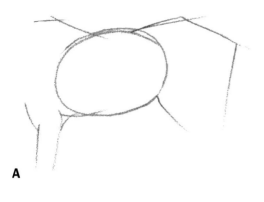

A

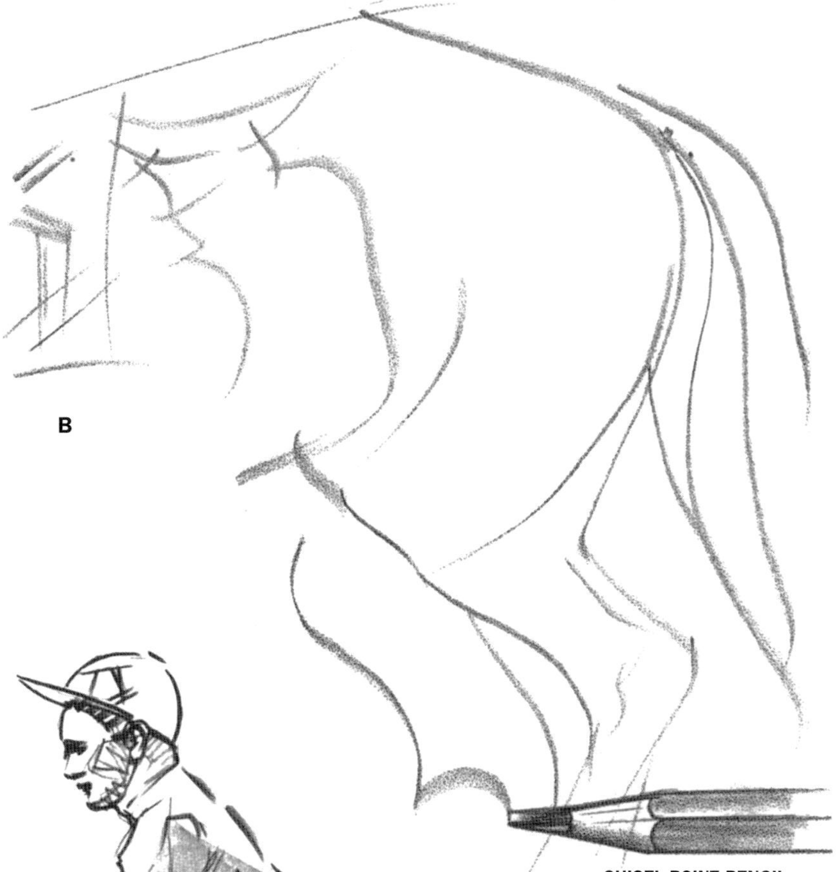

B

This racehorse shows the high-strung character typical of young thoroughbreds. Concentrate on the prancing feet and the pulled mouth to illustrate this horse's eagerness—it is literally champing at the bit!

Try drawing this pair on a large piece of paper. Break off a Conté crayon, or use the side of a pencil lead to develop the form with wide strokes that follow the shape of the horse. Experiment with a chisel point, and vary the angle of your strokes. Use a variety of textures to keep the look of the drawing loose and spontaneous.

CHISEL POINT PENCIL

CONTÉ CRAYON

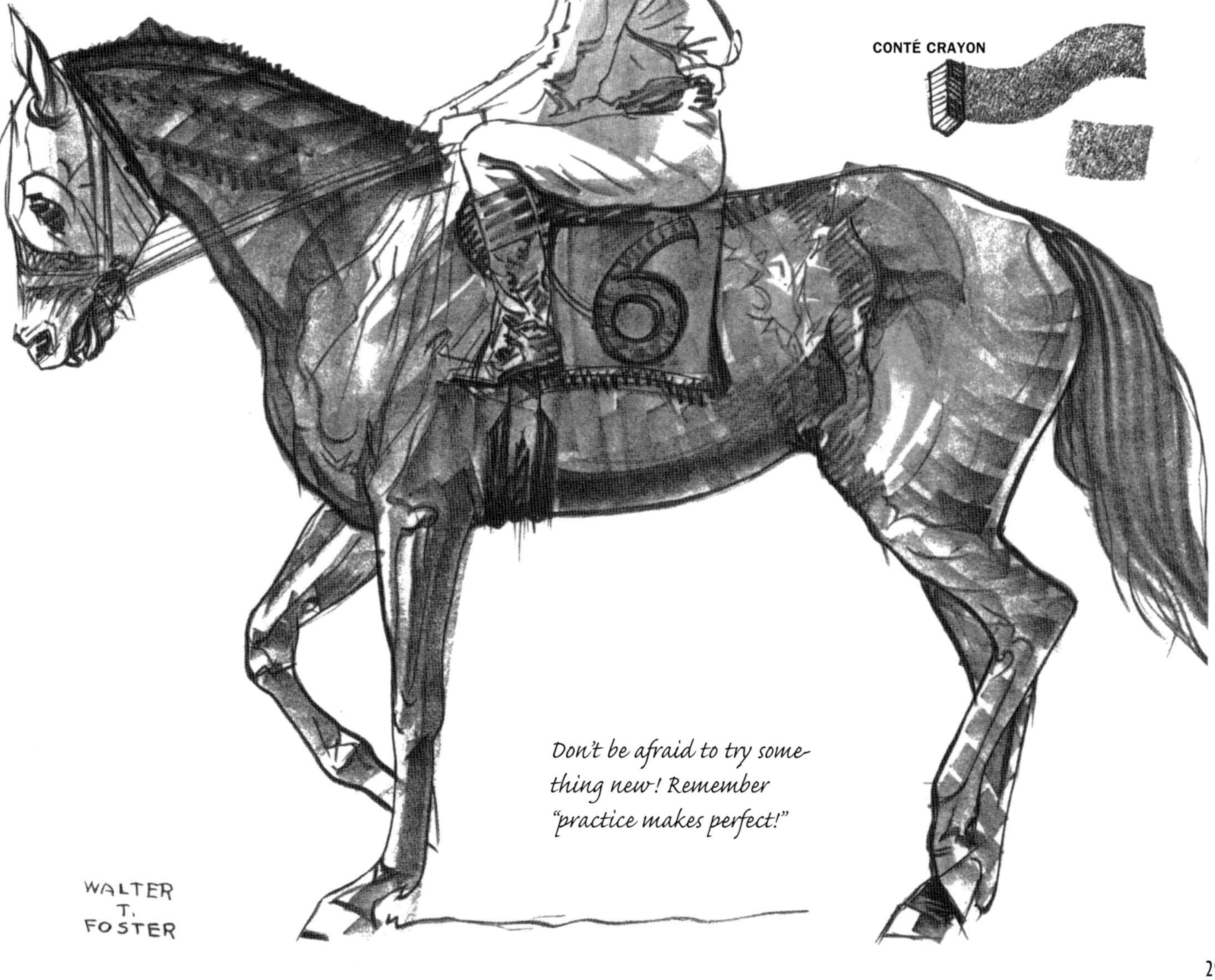

Don't be afraid to try some-thing new! Remember "practice makes perfect!"

WALTER T. FOSTER

Western Horse & Rider

The western rider's attire and horse's tack reflect their cowhand heritage. The western stock saddle is larger and deeper than the flat racing or jumping saddles. Cowhands need to be firmly and comfortably seated while executing the quick maneuvers required for cutting cattle. Also notice that the western stirrup is worn longer, so the rider's leg has a straighter angle than that of English riders.

Take care when you block in the horse's right hind leg, and study the shape of the muscles and joints; this is a bit of a tricky angle.

A

B

This pair has a lot of detail, so take care when blocking in. Distort the oval for the horse's body to show the viewing angle, and place circles for the horse's shoulders and hindquarters in step A. Don't forget to block in the saddle horn as well. When you sketch in the rider, pay careful attention to his foreshortened arm and the angle of his boot.

C

Check your proportions carefully as you begin developing your drawing in step B, and note the rider's hand position. Western riders hold both reins in one hand, so one hand is free for other work. Make the horse's neck arched and relaxed, and study the placement of the horse's legs. Then begin laying in the shadows in step C.

Notice that the rider's hat casts a shadow on his chest as well as on his face.

In your final drawing, apply the shading techniques you've learned so far to make the drawing appear three-dimensional. Now is the time to add the details on the saddle and the rider's clothing. The rider's belt buckle, the tooling on the saddle, and the intricacies on the horse's bridle are important components that make this pair unique. Now all your drawing practice and observation training will really pay off!

The next time you study a horse, think about what makes it special, and try to capture that quality in your drawings. Happy drawing!

About the Artist

Walter T. Foster was born in Woodland Park, Colorado, in 1891. In his younger years, he worked as a sign painter and a hog medicine salesman. He also performed in a singing and drawing vaudeville act. Walter invented the first postage-stamp vending machine and drew political caricatures for several large newspapers. He's well known as an accomplished artist, art instructor, and art collector. In the 1920s, while running his own advertising agency and instructing young artists, Walter began writing self-help art instruction books. The books were first produced in his home in Laguna Beach, California, where he wrote, illustrated, and printed them himself. In the 1960s, as the product line grew, he moved the operation to a commercial facility, which allowed him to expand the company and achieve worldwide distribution. Walter Foster was a truly dominant force in the development of art instruction books that make it possible for many people to improve their art skills easily and economically. Walter passed away in 1981, but he is fondly remembered for his warmth, dedication, and unique instruction books.

NAUTICAL ANTIQUES

With Value Guide

Robert W.D. Ball

77 Lower Valley Road, Atglen, PA 19310

Printed in the United States of America
ISBN: 0-88740-602-5

Published by Schiffer Publishing, Ltd.
77 Lower Valley Road
Atglen, PA 19310
Please write for a free catalog.
This book may be purchased from the publisher.
Please include $2.95 postage.
Try your bookstore first.

We are interested in hearing from authors
with book ideas on related subjects.

DEDICATION

My mother, Emily Lewis (Hathaway) Ball, born and raised at 498 Cottage Street, New Bedford, Massachusetts, would have loved this book! She'd have had something interesting to add about almost every entry, for she grew up surrounded by them and they were, quite naturally, an important part of her life...and memories. Mom's nautical heritage ran deep...in fact, one of her ancestors, Colonel Claghorn, was the designer of that famous early warship, The Constitution. God bless her, she never forgot a thing that happened during her 91 years on this earth, and was as sharp as a tack to the very end. She would have been 94 this year, but she went to join the rest of her family several years ago. Too bad, Mom... sure could have used your help to make certain I got everything right! Your children and grandchildren miss you, and my personal wish would be to send you a review copy...my deadline should have been five years ago!

ACKNOWLEGMENT

To my old, dear friends, Dick and Claudia Bourne, for allowing me full access to the photo files of the Richard A. Bourne Co., Hyannis, Massachusetts, as well as providing me with as much information about nautical memorabilia as they have learned in their many years in business. May success and good fortune follow them in all of their endeavors.

CONTENTS

GLOSSARY

ARTIFICIAL HORIZON: A level mirror, as the surface of mercury in a shallow basin, used in measuring the altitude of a celestial body.

BAROMETER: An instrument for measuring atmospheric pressure, especially an aneroid barometer or an evacuated and graduated glass tube (mercury barometer) in which a column of mercury rises or falls as the pressure of the atmosphere increases or decreases.

BALEEN: Sections of whalebone; i.e., the horny, elastic material that hangs in fringed, parallel, plate-like sheets from the upper jaw or palate of whalebone whales and serves to strain plankton.

BECKETS: A contrivance, as a looped rope, hook and eye, or grommet used for securing items. For example, the rope handles on a sailor's sea chest.

BINNACLE: The upright cylindrical stand holding a ship's compass, usually located near the helm.

BLUBBER: The fat of the whale, from which oil is obtained.

BODKIN: A pointed instrument for making holes in cloth.

CHRONOMETER: An instrument for precisely measuring time.

CIRCUMFERENTOR: An astronomical instrument with a part in the form of a calibrated circle.

CORSET BUSK: A shaped piece of highly decorated whalebone, whale ivory, or baleen that was inserted into the front of a woman's corset, with the tip resting under the breast bone. This was done to improve the individual's posture and carriage.

DITTY BOX: A small box used by sailors for holding sewing equipment, toilet articles, and miscellaneous personal gear.

FID: A round, pointed wooden tool for separating the strands of rope in splicing. Also refers to a wooden or metal bar for supporting a top mast.

FIDDLEHEAD: A carved decoration on a ship's bow, curved like the scroll of a violin head.

FLENSING KNIFE: A specially made knife used for cutting blubber from a whale.

GADROON: A small cup without handle, a bowl, various decorations used on molding; i.e., beading, flutings, reeding, etc.

GAM: A congregating or coming together of whales; also a visit between crews of whaling ships.

HELIOGRAPH: A device for sending messages or signaling by flashing the sun's rays from a mirror.

JAGGING WHEEL: Also known as a pie crimper. Usually made of scrimshawed whalebone or whale ivory in the shape of a handle with posts at one end to support a rotating wheel, carved in such a manner as to produce a crimping effect in the outer edge of a pie dough lid. Highly decorative and much sought after.

OOSIK: An Eskimo spear throwing device, giving greater distance and penetration.

POLARIS: A navigational device; i.e., the North or Pole Star is the closest star to the north celestial pole and remains nearly stationary througout the night.

QUADRANT: An instrument similar to the sextant in design and function, and superseded by it.

SCRIBE: A pointed instrument for scoring wood, etc. to show where it is to be cut.

SCRIMSHAW: The intricate carving and decoration of bone, ivory, etc. as of whales and walruses, done by sailors on long voyages.

SEAM RUBBER: A device made of wood or whalebone for the purpose of flattening and disguising, as much as possible, stitched and/or glued seams.

SEXTANT: An instrument used by navigators for measuring the angular distance of the sun, a star, etc. from the horizon, as in finding the position of a ship.

SHIP'S TELEGRAPH: A signaling apparatus for the ship's officers on the bridge to inform the Engine Room of any changes in propulsion, i.e., a repeater mechanism in the Engine room shows "Slow," "Full Ahead," and so on.

SWIFT: A scrimshawed expanding reel used to hold skeins of silk or wool that are being wound off.

TRYPOT: A large cast iron pot used aboard whaling vessels to render the oil from pieces of blubber boiled in the pots.

INTRODUCTION

Ships that sail the sea hold a fascination for most of us. From small sailing dinghies, to whaling ships, to the largest passenger steamers that ply the seas...and yes, for those of us old enough to remember, even the troop transports that represented our first "ocean cruise," we are enchanted by things nautical.

I have a host of other memories involving ships, including an especially chilling one of a wide-eyed youngster sitting on a desolate Martha's Vineyard beach during the early years of World War II and watching the results of German submarines firing on U.S. merchant ship convoys in the distance. Although I couldn't see the ships, the explosions after the torpedoes hit their targets sent ominous columns of smoke skyward...and the chilling discovery, days later, of the sad remnants of debris that washed ashore from these sunken ships will be with me forever.

But there were other, more pleasant memories. Growing up in the 1930s allowed me to see other types of vessels that had sailed those same seas many years before. I often visited my mother's hometown of New Bedford, Massachusetts for weeks at a time, staying in the old family house at 498 Cottage Street that my grandfather had built. There I frequently spent the day making a nuisance of myself at the family carpentry shop on Center Street, which was located near the docks and adjacent to the Whaling Museum.

There was nothing more fascinating for a inquisitive youngster than to roam the dock area. At that time old two and three masted ships were still tied to the docks at the foot of the street. When I tired of soaking up as much atmosphere (as well as the smell of dead fish!) as I could handle, I would haunt the Whaling Museum, just blocks away. There I'd scout the halls for hours on end, lusting after the model ships on display, imagining going around the Horn to the Pacific in one of these ships, and wondering what kind of life it must have been for those men who went down to the sea in ships.

In my grandmother's house were examples of most of the items that were part and parcel of living in one of this country's great whaling ports. Scrimshaw pieces were everywhere and meals were served on plates brought back from China. In one room was the leather bound, hand-painted camphor wood chest, studded with brass nails for which my grandmother traded her $5.00 tin trunk when she went off to college in the 1880s. Her best friend had just received the chest from her father, a whaling captain, on his return from China but, thankfully for us, she preferred my grandmother's to the beautiful one that now sits proudly in our hall!

While much of the family business was involved with building dwellings, there was a sideline of ship's chandlery work that was also done from the shop. Located in what is now part of a National Historical site, the shop was in the family for many generations going back to the early 1800s, if not earlier. In fact, I often uncovered, in some dusty drawer, ship's cabinetry hardware in the original boxes and dated in the 1830s and 1840s.

When I was bored with hanging around the shop or the docks, I often trudged to the head of the street where all the many cluttered and musty-smelling antique shops of the day were congregated. My mother was well acquainted with the proprietors, so I was allowed to wander almost at will! The things you could find back then would drive today's antique dealer wild with desire! Whaling tools, carved ship sternboards, harpoon guns, ship's flintlock rifles, try pots, scrimshaw work; all could be had for less than the cost of a carton of cigarettes in today's economy! One particularly vivid memory is of ship's lanterns and lights filling the entire wall of a local shop...there must have been over one hundred to choose from.

Yesterday's memories are today's highly sought-after collectibles, with a thriving trade in old nautical items fueled by the continuing fascination of one generation after another. The selection is endless, with many avenues of collecting to pursue, limited only by the contents of your wallet and your patience in tracking down that very special piece that's lurking in a dusty attic or a forgotten corner of some antique shop.

On the following pages, I've attempted to share some of the feelings for our nautical past that I was fortunate enough to experience at an age when memories and appreciation become ingrained in our consciousness and remain there forever. May you receive as much from this book as it has been my pleasure to give...a respect and love of our seagoing heritage and a glimpse of those hearty men who made it all happen!

SCRIMSHAW

Scrimshaw is a virtually untranslatable word that is used to describe objects made of the ivory from walrus and sperm-whale teeth. It also encompasses, in the broad sense of the word, the arts and crafts that occupied the lonely hours of whalers aboard ship. It would appear that scrimshaw became popular when whaleships took to the high seas in the early 1700s. Hacked from the jaws of sperm-whales by a cold chisel, the teeth became prized possessions that were planed smooth, polished, usually with shark skin, engraved with a sailmaker's needle and colored with different shades of ink and wax to enhance the art work.

The art of scrimshaw became a passion among sailors, occupying every spare moment. They created familiar scenes ...ships, whales and whale catching, landscapes from home or foreign ports, and, of course, portraits of the women left behind. Many a piece of scrimshaw contains verses from the gospels, while those sailors not so godly indulged themselves in the erotica, much of which was highly daring, especially for the period! Besides whale's teeth, many useful and artful objects were fashioned from pieces of whalebone...clothes pins, bobbins, needle cases, thimbles, bodkins, personal possession jars, tongs, yardsticks, blocks, dipper handles; the list is endless and imaginative.

One of the most desired and highly prized of these was a jagging wheel, or pie crimper, used to give that distinctive look to the edges of a pie crust. Imagination ran riot, with forms varying from that of a unicorn with 1,2,3, or 4 wheels, incorporating a fork and sharpened straight piece for piercing the pie crust, and inlaid with exotic woods, coin silver or baleen, to the mundane, utilitarian wheel and handle piece that was merely functional. In form and design, many of these jagging wheels can best be described as beautiful, both in concept and function, a tribute to the scrimshander's patience, skill and imagination.

Swifts are a notable contribution to the art of scrimshaw. These folding contraptions had clamps, were held together with tiny rivets, and were designed to make the rolling of a ball of yarn a simple, one-person operation. Many a wife, daughter or loved one waiting at home had their man at sea foremost in their thoughts while doing the homely but necessary task of yarn winding. On observation, think of the countless hours of painstaking labor that were required to produce a masterpiece of precision such as a swift demands!

Close to the heart - both literally and figuratively - of the sailor's beloved was the corset busk, a piece of highly engraved and decorated whalebone or baleen approximately 12" long, that was inserted into milady's corset in the front, below the bust, for the purpose of providing proper carriage of the upper body. Picture, if you will, a modern woman subjecting herself to such torture in the name of fashion! Although, truth to tell, the stiletto heels of today would appear to be torture enough! Seldom seen other than by the wearer or her husband, corset busks had much artistic talent lavished upon them. Heraldic devices, patriotic motifs and geometric and foliate designs, were among many motives used to produce a beautiful albeit useful, if masochistic, object.

A great adjunct to the male fashion plate of the period was the cane, and if there was one item sailors enjoyed making in all their infinite varieties, it was canes! They came in all shapes and materials, limited only by the imagination of the maker. There were canes of foreign exotic woods with scrimshawed handles, and others made of shark vertebrae threaded onto a steel rod with spacers of rings of bone, baleen and exotic woods. There were fluted, spiral and rope-carved whalebone canes, with stylized handles, in designs as varied as a clenched fist, a dog's body, a fish, or a Turk's head knot. A collector's category unto itself, the beauty and ingenuity to be found in what was formerly a simple walking stick, are endless.

During the Revolutionary and Napoleonic Wars, seafaring captives of all the involved countries languished, for the most part, in ancient warships converted into prisoner-of-war hulks. Demasted and permanently grounded in harbor, these fearsome prisons offered nothing to its inmates but perpetual drudgery and utter boredom. In England, Napoleonic war prisoners were incarcerated in prisons, under similar conditions, at Dartmoor, Portchester Castle and Norman's Cross. English captors proved apt pupils of their French guests, and, when captured by Americans during the War of 1812, utilized these talents to great avail. In an effort to obtain whatever they could beyond the bare necessities of life, the more artistic of the prisoners made artifacts from old bones, straw, glass, wood and whatever else they could beg or barter from their warders. As museums in England, France, Portugal, Spain and the United States will testify, the prison officers were the first to pay tribute to the exquisite skill and imagination of these men who worked under the most dismal conditions to render such objects of great beauty. Intricately woven straw-work often was used to showcase an elaborately constructed ship model, religious scene, or simple carved bone memento. We are fortunate that pieces of history such as these have been preserved for our own and future generations to admire.

Finally, the sailor-artisan would turn his talents into the realm of imagination, where nothing was too difficult to translate into whalebone or ivory, be it an escutcheoned coat rack with walrus teeth pegs, tool handles, tongs, ditty boxes and all manner of kitchen utensils, to inlays of whale ivory in the most plebeian of tools and other articles. Read on and enjoy!

The opposite sides of the previous two whale's teeth.

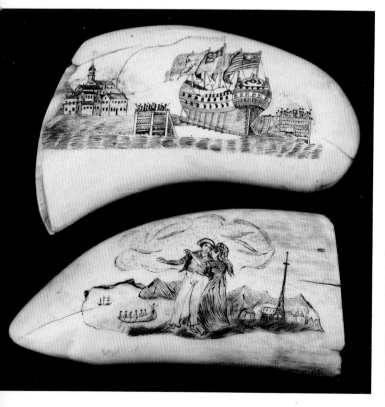

Whale's Teeth

Two wonderful scrimshaw whale's teeth. *Top:* Early scrimshaw whale's tooth engraved on one side with an American ship launching, a highly unusual subject for scrimshaw. On the opposite side is a very fine whaling scene, including the stoving of a boat. American, ca. mid-nineteenth century. Length 5.13".
Bottom: a deeply engraved early scrimshaw whale's tooth; on the one side, a Naval officer with two ladies who appear to be Spanish, while on the opposite side, a sailor bids farewell to a native girl, while a boat waits to take him to his waiting ship. Both scenes appear to be in South America. Ca. mid-nineteenth century. Length 5.38".

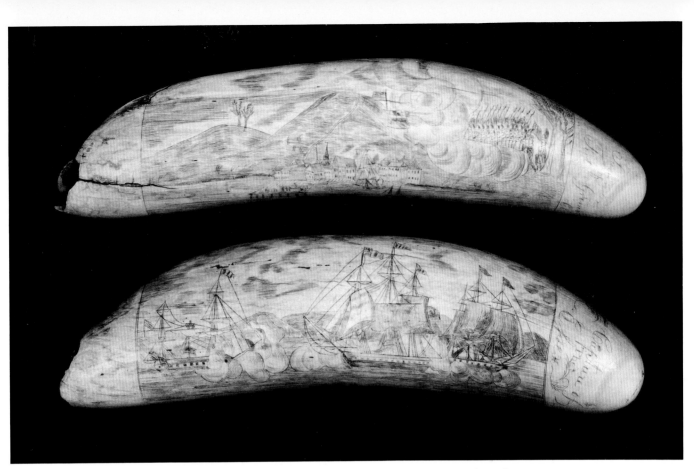

Pair of rare and exceptional large scrimshaw whale's teeth, with engravings on all four sides depicting "The surrender of Fort Griswold, Ct.," "Abolition Meeting," "Enterprise and Boxer," and "Capture of the Essex." Signed "H. Comings." The engraving "Abolition Meeting" identifies each of the six figures represented. American, ca. mid-nineteenth century. Lengths 10" and 9.75".

Reverse view of the pair of scrimshaw whales teeth.

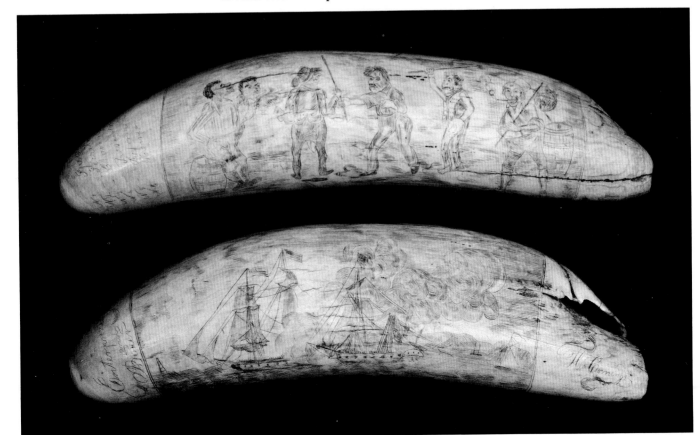

Left: an exceptional scrimshaw broad bull whale's tooth, engraved in color, featuring a colorful American ship under sail, above which is an eagle flying over a trophy of American flags, emblem, crossed cannons, and cannonballs. American, ca. mid-nineteenth century. Length 6.50".

Center: A walrus tusk with very fine engraved and colored images which are, from bottom to top: the full figure portrait of a lady in ball gown, a saddled stallion by a tower flying the American flag, the figure of a sailor on a pedestal holding the American flag, and a flowering plant encircled with a wreath at the top. American, ca. mid-nineteenth century. Length 15.25".
Right: A large bull whale's tooth, beautifully engraved with the full-figure portrait of a young woman wearing an elaborate and colorful gown standing on a black and white tiled floor. Ca. mid-nineteenth century. Length 8.13".

Left: An important scrimshaw whale's tooth originally used as a seal killing club, and later engraved by its owner upon retirement. Engraved on one side is an arctic seal hunt scene entitled "Sea Lion Hunting Pacific 1890." On the reverse are engraved the initials "LW." Note the brass ring with attached line. Length 5.88". *Center:* Early scrimshaw whale's tooth with an engraving dedicated to sailors' rights and free trade. The tooth has a full figure portrait of a sailor by an anchor with an eagle behind him, the initials "WP" above him, and surrounded by a banner which reads "Free Trade and Sailor's Rights." At the bottom left are the initials "AM," and on the lower right, the words "Free Trade U.S.A." At the top of the tooth is a ship under full sail. Ca. 2nd quarter nineteenth century. Length 6.38". *Right:* Exquisite scrimshaw whale's tooth with a portrait of Capt. Howes done in superb pinpoint work. The subject of the work is a bearded whaling captain shown in half figure wearing a heavy beard. The pinpoint or stipple engraving is an unusual technique in scrimshaw engraving, reminiscent of early mezzotint engraving which allows the engraver to produce a superbly detailed portrait. Ca. 3rd quarter nineteenth century. Length 6".

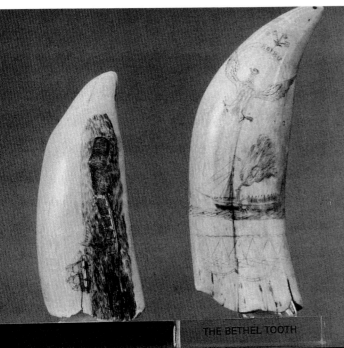

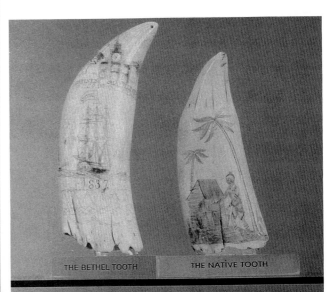

THE BETHEL TOOTH

THE BETHEL TOOTH   THE NATIVE TOOTH

Top left: Scrimshaw whale's tooth, known as the "Bethel" tooth. Engraved on the one side with a ship flying the flag "Bethel" in the center with the date "1837" below her; near the tip is a church with a large clock under which are the words "Mariners Chappel for Them/That Go Down to the Sea." The church flies a banner with the letters "BL." On the reverse is engraved an early paddle wheel steamship above which is an American eagle with a banner reading "Union." All engravings involved the use of colored inks. Ca. 2nd quarter nineteenth century. Length 7.88". *Top right:* Scrimshaw whale's tooth engraved with the use of color depicting a South Sea native, two palm trees, and a primitive building on one side; on the other is a finely detailed whaling scene. Ca. mid-nineteenth century. Length 6.50".

Bottom left: Large scrimshaw whale's tooth engraved and colored on one side with a large eagle with flag shield, American flags, and trophy of arms, drums, etc., and a marine scene below. On the reverse, is a full-figure portrait of a lady. Ca. mid-nineteenth century. Length 6.75". *Bottom right:* Early scrimshaw whale's tooth engraved with some color depicting a scene of an American ship passing a fortification on one side, with an early paddle wheel steamship on the bottom edge, and on the reverse, a panoramic view of a small town with green trees. Ca. 2nd quarter nineteenth century. Length 7.38".

The reverse view of the four scrimshaw whale's teeth.

Left: Excellent scrimshaw whale's tooth with a presentation that reads: "J. Jackson, to Jane Hotchkins." On one side is the figure of a sailor embracing a girl, on one narrow side an American ship, and on the reverse, an eagle with harp and flowers. Ca. mid-nineteenth century. Length 6.50". *Right:* Beautiful scrimshaw whale's tooth engraved on one side with an eagle holding a banner which reads "E Pluribus Unum." Beneath this is a portrait of Liberty within a wreath, below which is a banner that reads "Liberty and Equality," and under this is a running dog. On the opposite side is a portrait of Napoleon on horseback, with a hunter and a bear underneath. Ca. 2nd quarter nineteenth century. Length 5.63".

Very rare scrimshaw whale's tooth by C.F. Tousey. On one side is a panoramic view of "Monghyer Hyndoostan," and on the opposite side, from top to bottom, a half-figure portrait of a woman identified "L. Lashuir;" beneath the portrait is a lion, and under it, an elephant. Ca. mid-nineteenth century. Length 6.50".

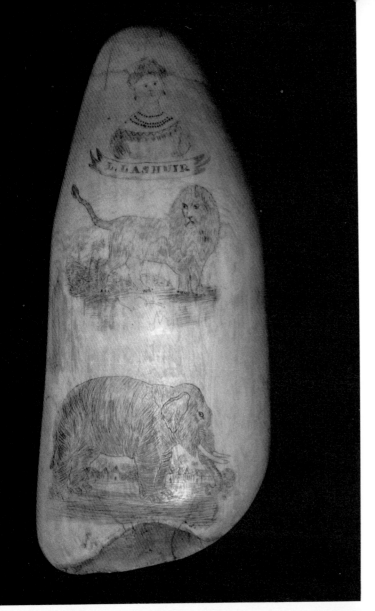

Opposite view of the Tousey whale's tooth, showing portrait, lion and elephant.

Left: A very fine scrimshaw whale's tooth engraved on one side with a man's portrait, and on the opposite with a finely engraved three figural scene. Ca. 2nd quarter nineteenth century. Length 6.06". *Center:* Pair of scrimshaw whale's teeth mounted on a wooden pedestal. The teeth feature portraits of American and English whaleships, and each tooth has a whaling scene that encircles its circumference at the base. On the back are crossed British flags. English, ca. 3rd quarter nineteenth century. Length 6". *Right:* Scrimshaw whale's tooth on a simple wood mount, engraved with the portraits of two women in conversation. Ca. mid-nineteenth century. Length 4.38".

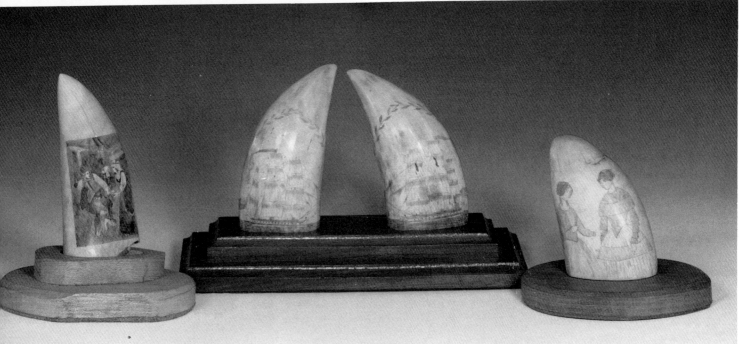

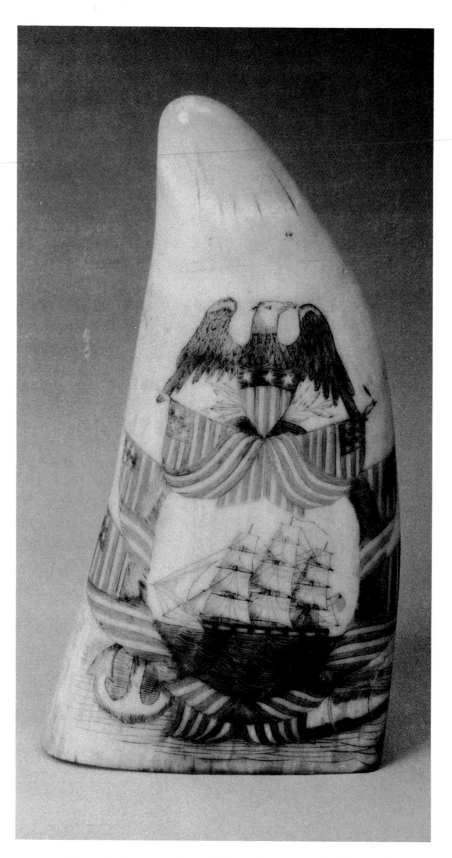

Unusually fine scrimshaw whale's tooth, engraved and colored appropriately with an American ship under full sail enclosed within a circular trophy of American flags, with eagle and flag shield at the top, and an anchor, cannon, and cannonballs beneath. This tooth represents the best possible use of color and patriotic symbolism in scrimshaw. Length 5.50".

Very fine large scrimshaw whale's tooth deeply engraved on one side with an eagle with flag shield and banner, the flag and an arch of stars above, and on the reverse the initials "TA" encircled in a wreath held by a dove over a willow tree. Vines and berries form an arch over the entire scene. A flaming star is at the tip of the tooth. Ca. 2nd quarter nineteenth century. Length 7".

The opposite side of the scrimshaw whale's tooth.

Left and right: Very rare scrimshaw vases made from two whales teeth mounted on whale ivory bases. Each vase is engraved on one side with a sailing ship. Ca. 3rd quarter nineteenth century. Height 6.75". *Center:* Large piece of curved panbone with an oversized engraving of a girl holding a basket filled with fish and lobster entitled "The Italian Fisher Girl." Ca. 3rd quarter nineteenth century. Overall height 12.63".

Top: Exceptional large bull whale's tooth engraved on one side with a scene of a ship and whales entitled "Ship Eagle Homeward Bound"; on the reverse is a very detailed whaling scene. Ca. early to mid-nineteenth century. Length 9.25". *Bottom:* Large early scrimshaw whale's tooth engraved on one side with a panoramic shipwreck scene and on the opposite side with an early view of the U.S. Capitol and a ship. Ca. 2nd quarter nineteenth century. Length 6.50".

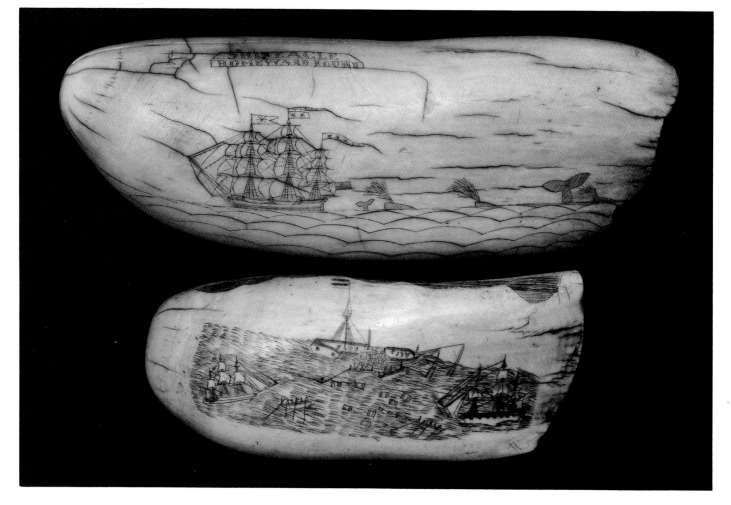

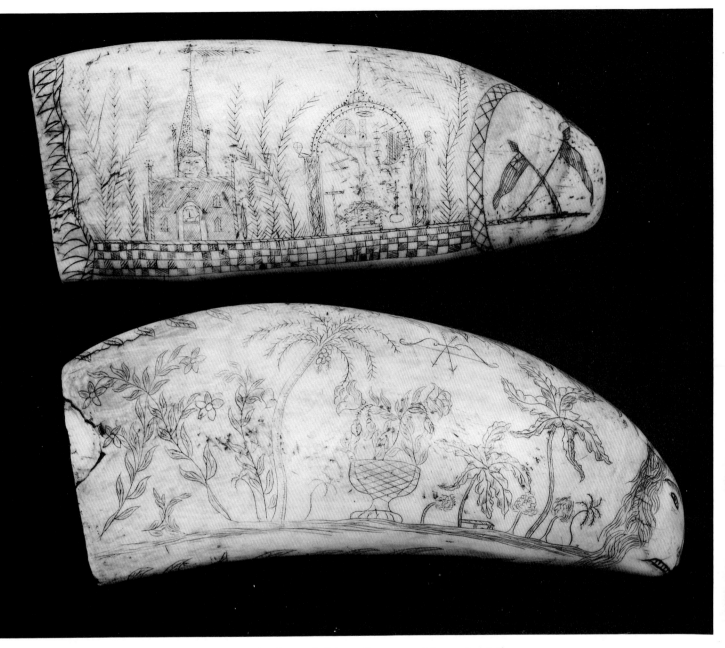

Top: Large scrimshaw whale's tooth engraved in great detail. On this side is a church or temple with two faces worked into the details of the building. Next to this is an arch under which are seen various Masonic symbols. Atop the arch is a clock showing 10 minutes past 6 o'clock, and at the tip are crossed flags done in color. The other side features a ship in a storm entitled "BK. Sussex off Cape Horn." A bird among shrubs on the tip, probably a pheasant. Presumably British, ca. 2nd quarter nineteenth century. Length 7.25". *Bottom:* Unquestionably done by the same hand, this very fine early scrimshaw whale's tooth very similar to, but not a match for, the one above. On this side is a variety of trees and bushes. Engraved on the other side is a British ship at anchor with palm tree nearby and a wreath encircling entwined hearts. At the tip, visible from both sides, is a lion's head. Ca. 2nd quarter nineteenth century. Length 7.25".

A lovely pair of scrimshaw whale's teeth engraved in color with various ships, a whaling scene, steamboat, and several vessels flying colored flags, two of which are American. Ca. 2nd quarter nineteenth century. Length 9".

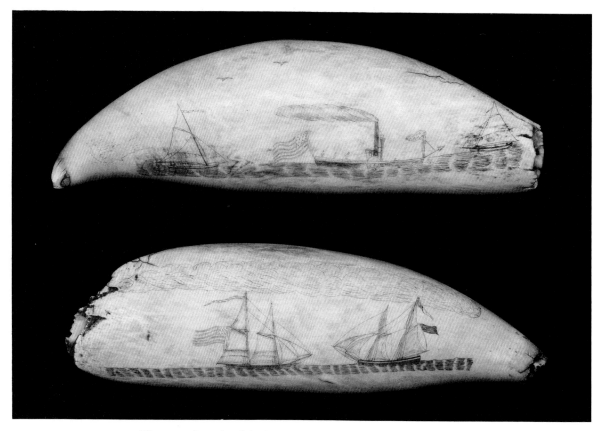

The opposite side of the lovely pair of scrimshaw whale's teeth.

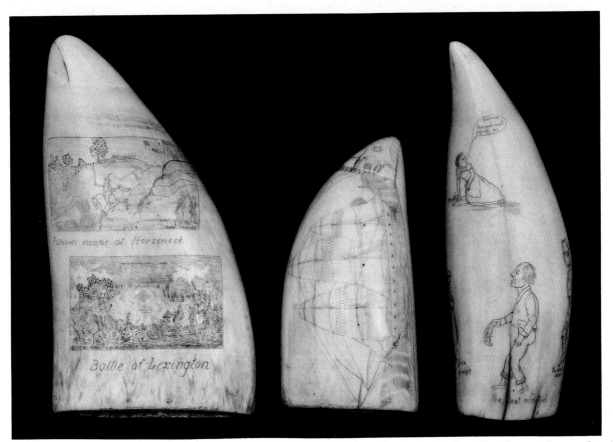

Left: Rare large bull whale's tooth engraved with four scenes, two on each side, entitled "Putnam's Escape at Horseneck," "Battle of Lexington," "Battle of New Orleans," and "Surrender of Cornwallis." Signed on the side "By W.H.Lyon." Length 5.75".
Middle: Fine scrimshaw whale's tooth engraved on one side with the half figure portrait of a sailor, flags and an eagle within an arch; on the opposite side, an American frigate. Length 4.63".
Right: Scrimshaw whale's tooth engraved with six humorous scenes of humans, all of which are titled. Ca. mid-nineteenth century. Length 6".

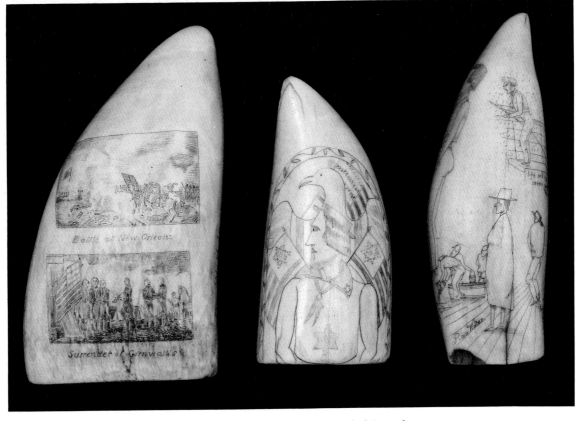

The reverse of the preceding three whale's teeth.

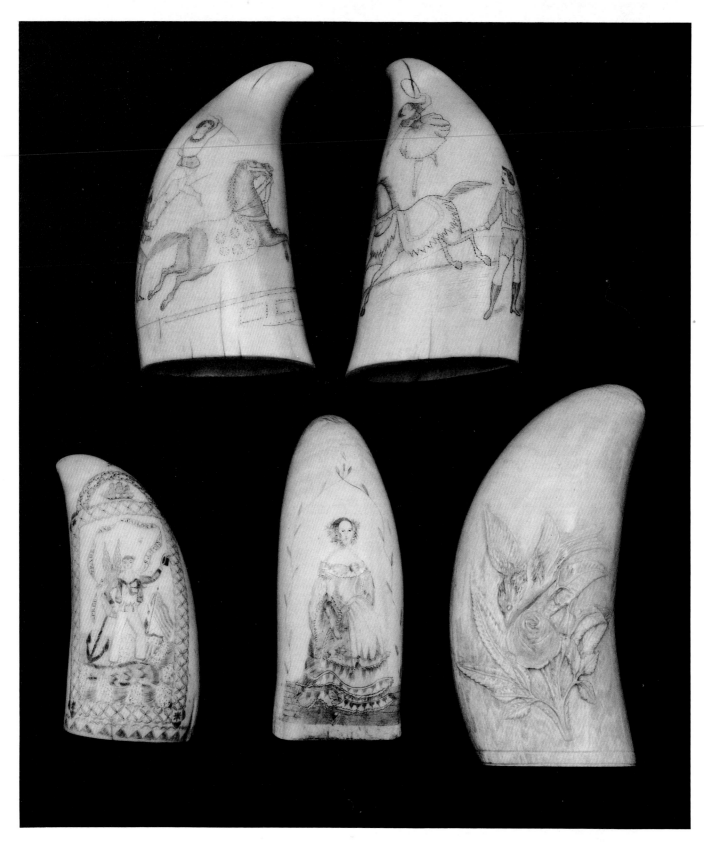

Top: A pair of exceptional whale's teeth, each engraved with early circus scenes of bareback riders. Ca. 3rd quarter nineteenth century. Length 5.88". *Bottom:* **1.** Rare scrimshaw whale's tooth engraved in color with an American flag, shield, anchor and eagle. The eagle holds a banner reading "Free Trade and Sailor's Rights." In an arch over the engraving is a fully rigged sailing ship. Ca. 2nd quarter nineteenth century. Length 4.63". **2.** A fine scrimshaw whale's tooth beautifully engraved with the full-figure portrait of a Victorian lady in regal ball gown. Ca. mid-nineteenth century. Length 5.13". **3.** Rare early sculptured whale's tooth with relief carving of a single rose with a bird perched on one leaf. On the reverse is a later engraving of a young woman with a bird encircled by a banner with roses around it. Ca. mid-nineteenth century. Length 6".

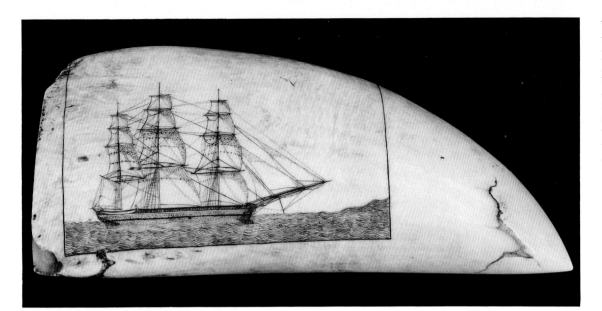

Wonderful scrimshaw whale's tooth with superb engraving. Engraved on one side with a picture of a ship, and on the opposite side with a portrait of a lady gazing out of a window. Ca. mid-nineteenth century. Length 6.88".

A pair of large, vertically mounted bull whale's teeth with wooden bases. Both are engraved in color with four portraits of children, one entitled "The Swinging Girl." Ca. mid-nineteenth century. Length 7.13", overall height 8.75".

The opposite side of the bull whale's teeth.

Left: Fine large scrimshaw whale's tooth engraved in color with the full figure portrait of a Victorian lady on one side, while on the opposite side is a seated nude lady brushing her hair. Ca. mid-nineteenth century. Length 7". *Center:* Another fine scrimshaw whale's tooth engraved in color on one side with the half-figure portrait of a lady sewing, while on the opposite side is the full figure portrait of a costumed dancing lady. Ca. mid-nineteenth century. Length 7". *Right:* Scrimshaw whale's tooth engraved on one side picturing a sailor with eagle, emblem and symbols of trade, while on the other side is an American ship under sail. Ca. 2nd quarter nineteenth century. Length 5.25".

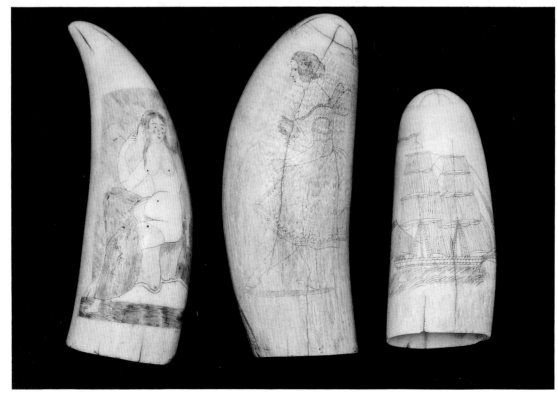

The opposite sides of the previous three whale's teeth.

Top left: Scrimshaw whale's tooth engraved in color on one side with an American ship, and on the opposite side with an eagle and a pair of American flags. Ca. mid-nineteenth century. Length 4.63". *Top right:* A pair of fine scrimshaw whale's teeth, one engraved with the figure of Liberty on one side and a small boy on the opposite side. The second tooth engraved with the figure of Justice on one side, another representing American Commerce on the opposite. Ca. mid-nineteenth century. Length 4.50". *Bottom left:* A very rare early scrimshaw whale's tooth dated 1845 on one side, and engraved in exceptional detail with the full-figure portrait of a lady surrounded by fanciful floral and geometric designs. Ca. 2nd quarter nineteenth century. Length 5.63". *Bottom right:* Fine scrimshaw whale's tooth engraved around its entire circumference with an ancient garden scene including two figures, entitled: "St.John chap iv. 6.7." Ca. mid-nineteenth century. Length 5.50".

The reverse view of the preceding group of scrimshaw whale's teeth.

Superb scrimshaw whale's tooth, engraved and colored with
an eagle and banner, as well as a trophy of flags, cannon, drum
and emblem on one side; the opposite side features an elaborate basket of fruit and flowers, while the entire tip is in the
form of an eagle's head. C. 3rd quarter nineteenth century.
Length 5".

The reverse side of the whale's tooth.

Top, left to right: **1.** Fine scrimshaw whale's tooth engraved with a bird on a branch. Ca. mid-nineteenth century. Length 4.50". **2.** Scrimshaw whale's tooth engraved in color with the excellent rendition of a tropical bird. Ca. mid-nineteenth century. Length 3.50". **3.** Scrimshaw sea elephant tooth engraved on one side with an American ship, on the opposite with a bending willow tree. Ca. 2nd quarter nineteenth century. Length 4". **4.** Early scrimshaw whale's tooth engraved in color with a portrait of "Eliza" encircled with a wreath under the words "Forget Me Not." Ca. mid-nineteenth century. Length 5.25".

Bottom, left to right: **1.** Very fine scrimshaw whale's tooth engraved overall with ships, scenes, foliage, etc., and on a banner the following: "60 Blls. 1849," probably referring to the whale from which the tooth was taken. A rare piece of dated scrimshaw. Length 4.88". **2.** Early scrimshaw whale's tooth entitled "Sweet Home" beneath which is an imposing building by a river. Continuing the scene on the other side is the maker's ship viewed at anchor with intertwining hearts above it. Mounted on a turned pine base that has an old label reading "Mr. Pennell." Ca. mid-nineteenth century. Length 6.50". **3.** Pair of rare scrimshaw whale's teeth engraved in color with the figure of Liberty with eagle and flag shield, and a Viking boat on the reverse, above which are the words "U.S. Ship Swatara on the Transit of Venus Expedition Dec. 9 1874." On the side in script are "Kerguelen" and "Crozets." The second tooth has a figure of a sailor standing by an anchor, a ship with eagle, flag and banner above him; engraved above with the following: "U.S.S. Swatara Hobertowen Tasmania Dec 9 1874." Signed by the engraver "O. Lindboarms." Also marked with other locations. An outstanding pair of historic teeth. Ca. 3rd quarter nineteenth century. Length 5.38".

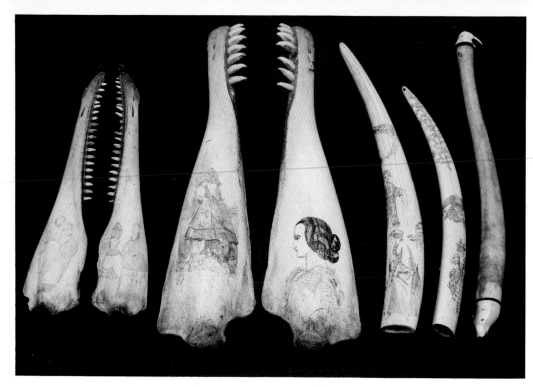

Left: Pair of porpoise jaw bones engraved on one jaw with a man holding a baby, while on the other are two Victorian ladies in elaborate gowns of the period. Ca. 3rd quarter nineteenth century. Length 17". *Center:* Pair of blackfish jaws, engraved on one jaw with the head and shoulders portrait of a Victorian lady, while the other jaw has the exquisite engraving of an elaborately gowned Victorian lady with two children playing at her feet. Ca. 3rd quarter nineteenth century. Length 22". *Right:* **1.** A very fine scrimshaw walrus tusk engraved on one side from top to bottom with a mountain lion in a tree watching a ship depart, a small boy, and a Victorian lady; on the other side, from top to bottom, an American flag, a church with graveyard, portrait of a young woman, and a kicking mule. Further embellished with leaves, an eagle and a rose. Ca. 3rd quarter nineteenth century. Length 20". **2.** Fine scrimshaw walrus tusk engraved on one side from top to bottom with a tall flowering plant, an eagle with a shield and banner, and a Victorian lady. Ca. 3rd quarter nineteenth century. Length 17". **3.** Eskimo Oosik, fitted at one end with a walrus ivory bear's head, and at the opposite end with a walrus ivory head. Ca. early twentieth century. Length 21.25".

Top left: Pair of extremely fine scrimshaw whale's teeth, one engraved with a nude hunter, the other with two nude women. Ca. mid-nineteenth century. Length 6.13". *Top center:* Small piece of blackfish jaw bone engraved with full-figure portraits of two elaborately dressed Victorian ladies. Ca. 3rd quarter nineteenth century. Length 5". *Top right:* Rare scrimshaw whale's tooth engraved in color on one side with a figure of the Statue of Liberty in her familiar position with flaming torch held aloft, and on the opposite with the famous Civil War eagle "Old Abe" perched on the flag. Ca. 3rd quarter nineteenth Century. Length 5.75". *Bottom left:* Very large scrimshaw whale's tooth engraved on one side with a ship, and on the opposite with the full figure of a Victorian mother and child. Ca. mid-nineteenth century. Length 8.88". *Bottom right:* Fine scrimshaw double ship's block made entirely of whalebone. Ca. 3rd quarter nineteenth century. Length 3.25".

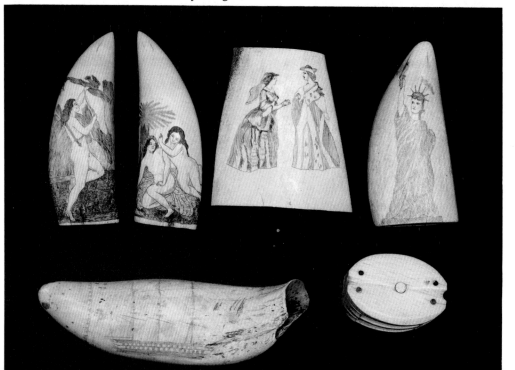

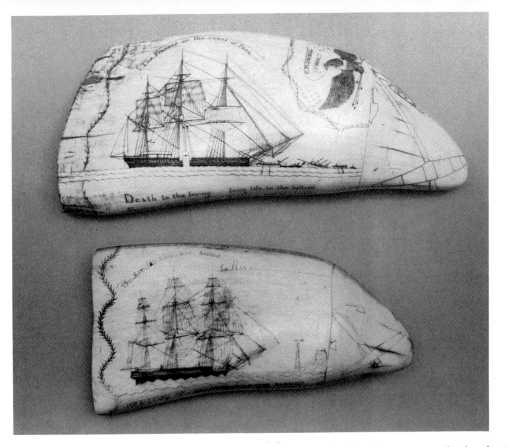

Top: An exceedingly rare large scrimshaw tooth, by Frederick Myrick of the whaleship "Susan." On the one side is depicted the ship "Frances" of New Bedford off the coast of Peru, and on the other, her homeward passage. The tip of the tooth is engraved with crossed flags, a fouled anchor and heraldic eagle. This tooth is larger than the average "Susan's" tooth, and is considered by some to be among the best pieces produced by Myrick. Starbuck shows that there is a high likelihood that the "Susan" and the "Frances" were in the same approximate area at the same time, and in fact returned home to their respective

ports within less than one month of each other. Length 8".

Bottom: Another rare scrimshaw whale's tooth by Frederick Myrick depicting the ship "Barclay" off the coast of Peru on one side, and on her homeward bound voyage on the other. Engraved with crossed American flags, a fouled anchor and a heraldic eagle near the tip. Like the ship "Frances," the "Barclay" was also at sea at the same time as the "Susan," and according to Starbuck, they arrived home within less than a month of each other. Length 6".

A view of the reverse side of the two Myrick whale's teeth.

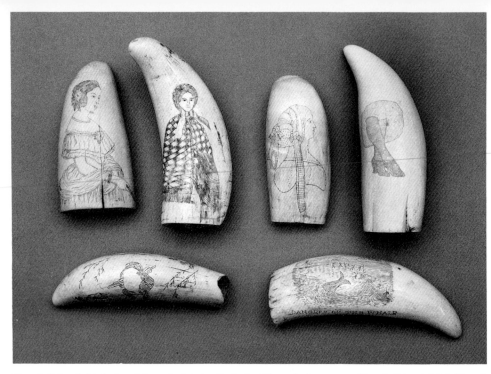

Top, left to right: **1.** An older whale's tooth, but with early twentieth century scrimshaw work. Engraved on one side with the 3/4-figure portrait of a young Victorian lady; on the opposite, with a ship on the lower half and an eagle with cannons and the American flag in color, cannon balls, anchor and drum. Length 5". **2.** Large scrimshaw whale's tooth engraved on one side with a 3/4-figure portrait of a Victorian lady wearing a plaid cape. Ca. mid-nineteenth century. Length 5.88". **3.** Scrimshaw whale's tooth engraved in pinpoint work with the head and shoulders portrait of a Victorian lady. Ca. mid-nineteenth century. Length 4.75". **4.** Interesting large scrimshaw whale's tooth engraved on one side with a lady's leg in very fine pinpoint work. Ca. midnineteenth century. Length 6.38".

Bottom, left to right: **1.** Scrimshaw whale's tooth engraved on one side with a humorous study of a frog carrying what appears to be a parasol while being watched by a fish; on the opposite side is a pine tree, a bucking horse and a coiled rattlesnake. Ca. mid-nineteenth century. Length 5.75". **2.** Scrimshaw whale's tooth engraved on one side with deep engraving of a whaling scene entitled "Dangers of the Whale Fishery." Ca. 3rd quarter nineteenth century. Length 6.25".

Top, left to right: **1.** Fine large scrimshaw whale's tooth engraved on one side with the head and shoulders portrait of a Naval officer, and on the opposite with a violent Naval battle involving three ships; beneath this scene is a nesting bird. Ca. midnineteenth century. Length 7". **2.** Old scrimshaw whale's tooth engraved with three different ships on one side and a cross on the opposite. Ca. 1840-1860. Length 6.50". **3.** Large scrimshaw whale's tooth engraved with a portrait of an American sailing ship. Ca. mid-nineteenth century. Length 6". **4.** Old scrimshaw whale's tooth with an early twentieth century engraving of a ship and anchor, engraved band around the lower circumference of the tooth. Length 5".

Bottom, left to right: **1.** Scrimshaw whale's tooth engraved with a storm-tossed ship approaching a lighthouse on one side, and the head and shoulders of a Victorian lady on the opposite. Ca. 3rd quarter nineteenth century. Length 5.25". **2.** Scrimshaw whale's tooth with unusually fine early 20th century engraving showing a whaling scene on one side, with decorative wreaths and bands, and a heraldic eagle on the opposite. The date "1841" is beneath the eagle, and around the bottom "The Whaling Ship Kutusoff out of New Bedford." Length 5.50".

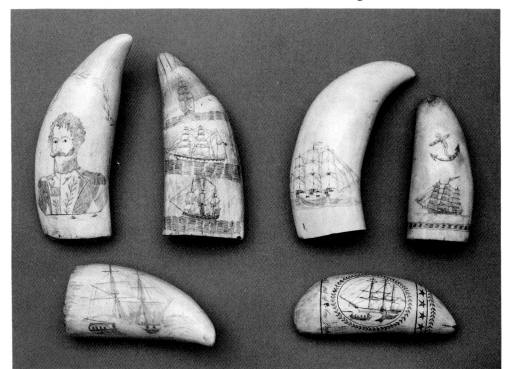

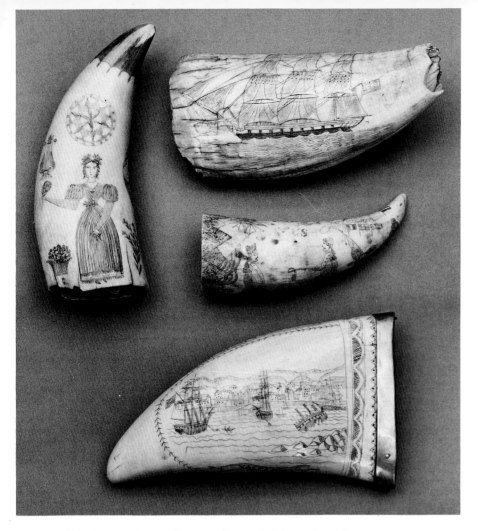

Top left: Outstanding early scrimshaw whale's tooth with exceptional fine overall engraving with delicate and extensive use of color featuring full-figures of ladies, flowers, wreaths, rosettes, a lyre and geometric designs. Done in a style reminiscent of the work of the Pennsylvania Dutch. Ca. 2nd quarter nineteenth century. Length 6.38". *Top right:* Very fine early British scrimshaw whale's tooth with typical deep engraving of a whaling scene on one side, and a ship on the opposite. Ca. first half nineteenth century. Length 7".

Bottom left: Fine early scrimshaw whale's tooth engraved in color with a scene of an American ship at anchor on one side, the other depicts the surrender of Cornwallis at Yorktown, together with a cannon, stacked cannon balls, flags, the letters "US" and the signature "T. Johnson." Ca. early nineteenth century. Length 5.75". *Bottom right:* Important scrimshaw whale's tooth engraved on one side with an elaborate whaling scene, and on the opposite with a view of Valpariso with an American ship in the left foreground. Tooth is banded at its base in silver. Ca. mid-nineteenth century. Length 7.25".

Pair of exceptional scrimshaw whale's teeth, one engraved with the portrait of a ship, the other with the portrait of a lady viewed through an arch; both mounted on identical solid brass bases. Ca. 2nd quarter nineteenth century. Length (teeth) 6.25".

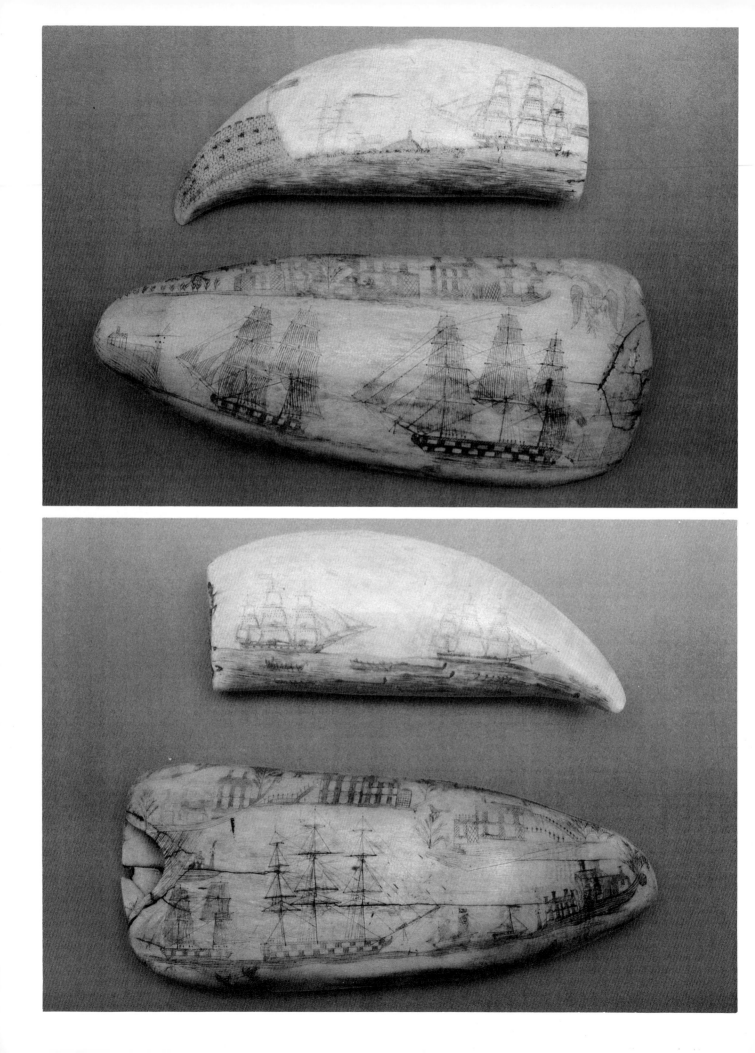

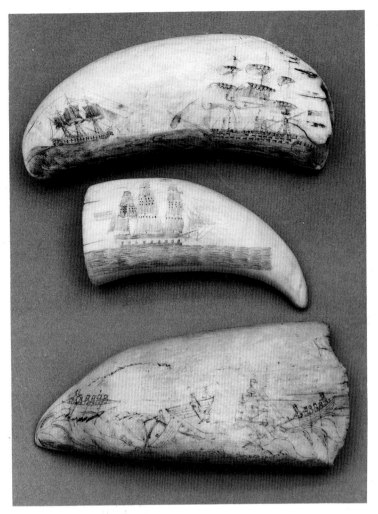

Opposite page, top:
Top: Rare scrimshaw whale's tooth, engraved and colored with a whaling scene on one side, and an American ship passing a fort on the other. Ca. 2nd quarter nineteenth century. Length 6".
Bottom: Early rare scrimshaw whale's tooth, engraved overall with ships, port scenes, buildings, eagles and a sperm whale. American, 2nd quarter nineteenth century. Length 7.63".

Opposite page, bottom
The reverse view of the preceding scrimshawed whale's teeth.

Top: Very fine early scrimshaw whale's tooth, elaborately engraved on one side showing ships attacking one another; between the war ships are two diving whales. On the opposite side are two ships preparing for battle with their guns run out. Ca. first third nineteenth century. Length 6.75". *Center:* Rare scrimshaw whale's tooth engraved on either side with a full-rigged American ship under sail. While not rigged as whalers, it is interesting to note the house flag of Joshua Richmond and Son, whaleship agents in New Bedford in the 1860s, and that their only ship was the "Lancer." On the opposite side, the second vessel flies the flag of Joshua Slocum, agent for the whaleship "Montezuma" and so listed in the 1850 New Bedford Whaling Directory. Length 5". *Bottom:* Fine early scrimshaw whale's tooth engraved on one side with a panoramic whaling scene depicting a sperm whale biting a whaleboat in half while two other whaleboats approach, the whaleship visible nearby. On the opposite is an engraving of a ship under sail plunging into a large wave. Imaginative and interesting! Ca. mid-nineteenth century. Length 6.63".

Pair of large scrimshaw bull whale's teeth, each engraved with a scene depicting first, the attack by a whaleboat on a pod of whales, and second, the "Nantucket Sleigh Ride" that follows. Ca. mid-nineteenth century. Length 8.31".

Top, left to right: **1.** Deeply engraved scrimshaw whale's tooth with a scene of the sailor's farewell on one side, and his ship on the opposite. Ca. 3rd quarter nineteenth century. Length 4.75". **2.** Napoleonic period scrimshaw whale's tooth engraved in color with a soldier holding a musket and carrying a knapsack on one side. Ca. early nineteenth century. Length 5". **3.** Scrimshaw whale's tooth engraved around its circumference with an active marine scene showing four vessels, one of which is the "Quail," an early British steamship. Ca. mid-nineteenth century. Length 5.75". **4.** Sculptured whale's tooth deeply carved with the half-figure portrait of a nude lady. Ca. 3rd quarter nineteenth century. Length 5.25". **5.** Fine small scrimshaw whale's tooth engraved in color with a portrait of a small girl holding a parrot, and the name "Elaine" on one side; on the opposite, the portrait of a man in riding clothes with the name "Pedro V." Ca. 3rd quarter nineteenth century. Length 3.50". **6.** Early scrimshaw whale's tooth engraved on one side with the portrait of a large three decker warship. Ca. 2nd quarter nineteenth century. Length 4.38".

Bottom, left to right: **1.** Large scrimshaw whale's tooth dated July 21, 1877, with a banner containing three lines of Spanish and signed "E.C. Kittle." Deeply engraved overall with crossed American and Chilean flags above the banner and a thistle between. The date "1877" is repeated on the side; on the opposite, an altar with cross and medallion, with elaborate scrolled foliage and flowers around the tip and base. Length 6.25". **2.** Fine large scrimshaw whale's tooth beautifully engraved on one side with the full figure portrait of an elaborately dressed lady holding a scrimshaw walking stick, and on the opposite, a gentleman in Elizabethan costume with a dog at his feet. Ca. mid-nineteenth century. Length 6.50". **3.** Engraved scrimshaw whale's tooth showing, in color, the head and shoulders portrait of a soldier. This tooth was possibly intended as a memorial to the person represented, since there are two large colorful flowers beneath the portrait. Ca. 3rd quarter nineteenth century. Length 5.50". **4.** Pair of large scrimshaw whale's teeth, each engraved on one side with equestrian figures, one of whom appears to be a Roman mounted on a large white horse and the other with a scene depicting an Indian with spear attacking a herd of horses. Ca. mid-nineteenth century. Length 6.50".

Four views of an extremely rare scrimshaw whale's tooth, attributed to Frederick Myrick, showing the very early date "December 26, 1828" on one side; the name of the vessel "The Ann of London/Samuel Barney Master" on the opposite. Another side shows the ship cutting in entitled "The Ann on the Coast of Japan," the other scene is of a ship approaching a point of land with a lighthouse entitled "The Ann of London on Her Passage Home." On the tip crossed British flags are engraved on one side, the ship at anchor on the opposite. Samuel Barney was a Nantucket whaling captain hired as commander of the ship by the owners of "The Ann of London." Length 5.88".

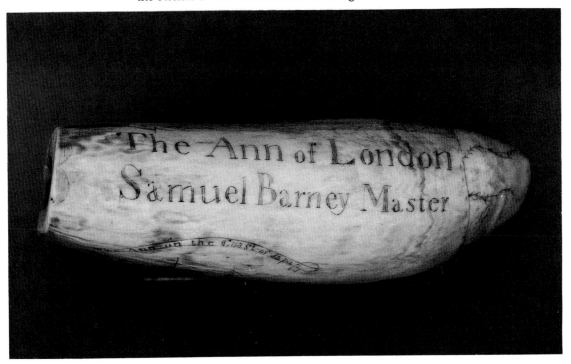

Another view of "The Ann of London/Samuel Barney Master" tooth.

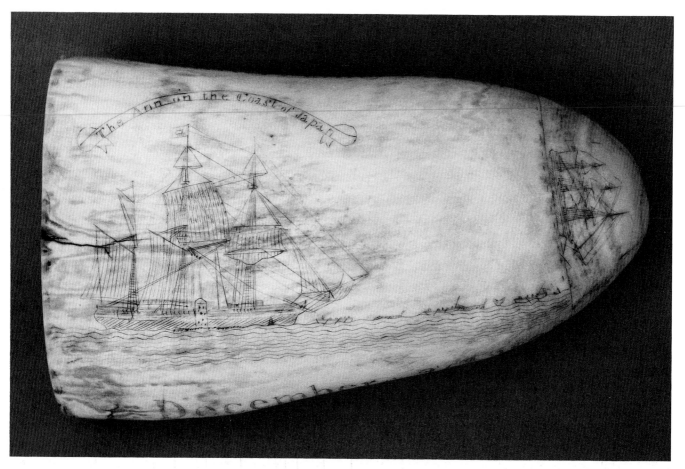

"The Ann of London" off the coast of Japan.

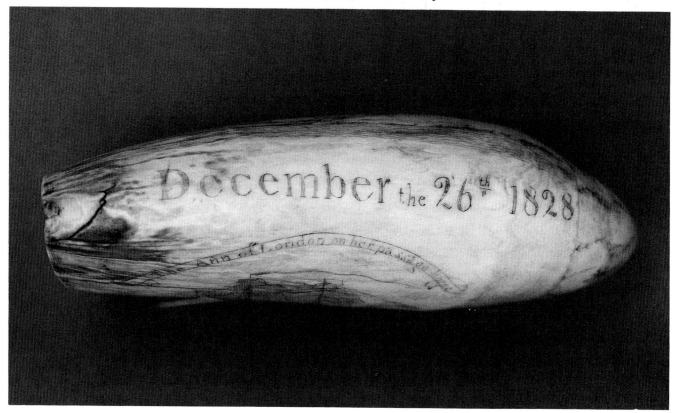

Showing the date "December 26, 1828" on "The Ann of London" tooth.

This extremely rare and highly valued scrimshaw whale's tooth is engraved with lavishly colored whaling scenes on both sides, including a stove boat. American, ca. early to mid-nineteenth century. Length 7.25".

Reverse view of the whale's tooth.

Opposite page:

Left: Rare and unusually large scrimshaw walrus tusk engraved in color with an American ship, a figure of Liberty, an eagle with flag shield, anchor, Liberty, an eye, and at the top, an eagle with trophy of flags. Ca. mid-nineteenth century. Length 29.75".

Center: Pair of walrus tusks engraved with the use of some color on both sides with figures, flowers, eagles, birds and the initials "LHC" on the one, and "RB" on the other. Ca. mid-Nineteenth century. Length 17". *Right:* Exceptional large walrus tusk engraved with two ships, an eagle with a trophy of flags, figure of Hope, Liberty, an attractive woman, birds and flowers. Ca. mid-nineteenth century. Length 30.75".

Left:

Extremely rare scrimshaw whale's tooth with elaborate engravings on both sides. On one side a trophy of arms with a banner entitled "Naval Coat Arms," an eagle with a trophy of arms, flags with anchor to the right, a sunburst above and a banner that reads "Ultim in Porvo." The bottom half of the tooth has a humorous primitive portrait of a lady and on a banner beneath her "L. Celeist." On the opposite is an elaborate waterfront scene with ships, boats, barges and buildings entitled "MONGHYER IN HINDOOSTAN." The tooth is signed "C.C. Tousey." Ca. mid-nineteenth century. Length 6".

The waterfront view on the previous tooth by Tousey.

Top left: Exceptional scrimshaw whale's tooth deeply incised with a stove boat whaling scene on one side, and on the opposite a scene of "The Ship Charles of London Whaling." Ca. 2nd quarter nineteenth century. Length 5.38". *Top right:* Very rare large scrimshaw whale's tooth engraved on one side, in color, with a scene of a whaleboat approaching a huge, blood-spouting sperm whale, and on the opposite, an American ship under full sail. Ca. 2nd quarter nineteenth century. Length 9.25". *Bottom left:* Pair of very rare scrimshaw whale's teeth beautifully engraved with half-figure portraits of well dressed young women. Interestingly, one young lady is seated in a bow-back Windsor chair, a rarity in scrimshaw. Narrowest sides of teeth are engraved with colored potted plants. American, ca. 1840-1850. Length 6.75". *Bottom right:* Large scrimshaw whale's tooth engraved and inked in black on one side with a shipwreck scene; on the opposite is a whaling scene. Mounted in silver at its broad end, with a hinged lid. Ca. mid-nineteenth century. Length 6.75".

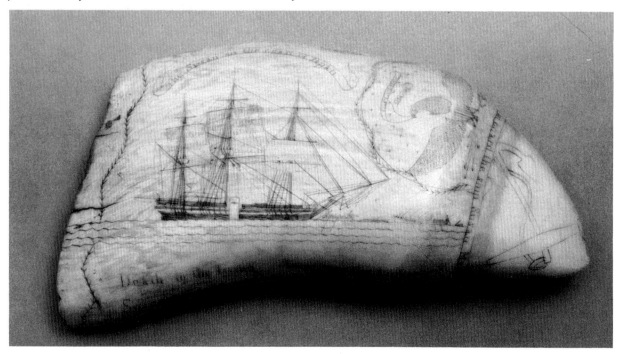

Susan's tooth engraved by Frederick Myrick, depicting "The Susan Boiling and Killing Sperm Whales" on the one side, and "The Susan on the Coast of Japan" on the other. On the edges of the tooth, between the two engravings, are "Ship Susan of Nan-tucket/Frederick Swain/Master" on the one edge, and on the other "Death to the Living Long Live the Killers/Success to Sailor's Wives & Greasy Luck to Whalers." Signed and dated March 4, 1829. Length 6.75".

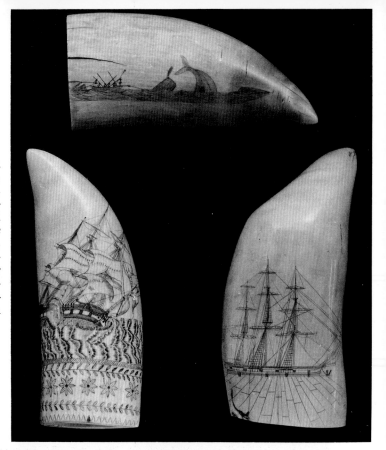

Top: Fine early scrimshaw whale's tooth engraved and inked in black with some color, showing a whaling scene on one side, and on the opposite, a scene of a sailor on a dock, with flag, boats and an eagle above him. American, ca. 2nd quarter nineteenth century. Length 6.38". *Bottom left:* Superbly engraved and colored scrimshaw whale's tooth with a panoramic marine scene encircling the tooth, depicting two ships in rough seas, one ship heeled over far enough to reveal her copper sheathing. Ca. mid-nineteenth century. Length 6.63". *Bottom right:* Very large, broad scrimshaw whale's tooth, engraved and colored with the scene of a ship at dock. An interesting use of perspective by the engraver. Ca. mid-nineteenth century. Length 6.88".

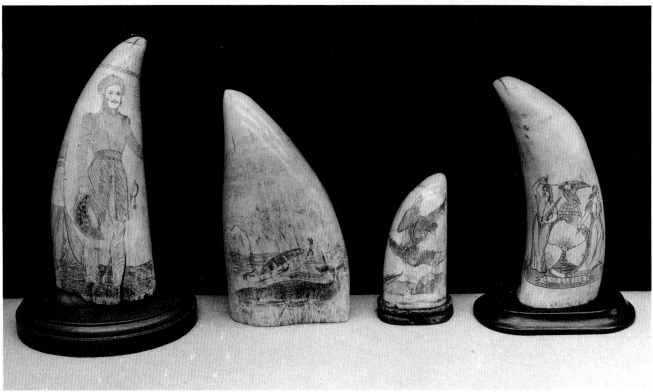

Left to right: **1.** Fine early mounted scrimshaw whale's tooth engraved and colored with the portrait of an American Army officer standing beside a tent, with the American flag to one side, and on the opposite an eagle with trophy of flags and a gathering of flowers. Ca. 1840. Length 8". **2.** Very large, broad scrimshaw whale's tooth engraved with an arctic whaling scene on each side. Ca. mid-nineteenth century. Length 6.88"; width 3.75". **3.** Scrimshaw whale's tooth showing an eagle attacking an osprey, forcing the osprey to drop a fish. Mounted on its original lead base. Ca. mid-nineteenth century. Length 4". **4.** Fine mounted scrimshaw whale's tooth engraved and colored with the full-figure portrait of a woman on one side. On the opposite are the figures of Hope and Justice, with an eagle perched on a globe and a rising sun entitled "Excelsior." Ca. 1840-1850. Length 7.38".

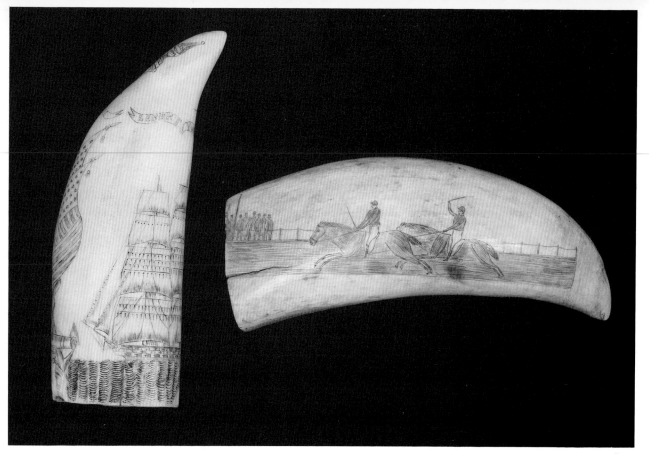

Left: Wonderful scrimshaw whale's tooth engraved all around with full-figure portrait of Liberty with eagle, flags, flag shield and banner that reads "Liberty and Freedom." The scene is continuous to the back side, which features an American frigate under sail. Ca. 2nd quarter nineteenth century. Length 6". *Right:* Fine early scrimshaw whale's tooth engraved with a panoramic whaling scene on one side; on the opposite, a horse racing scene. American, ca. mid-nineteenth century. Length 6".

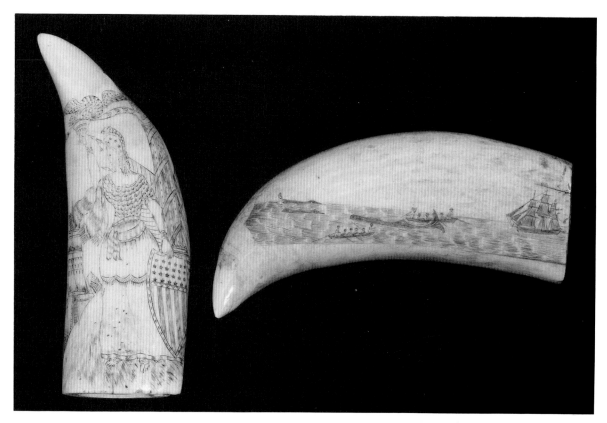

Views of the opposite sides of the preceding whale teeth.

Left: Large scrimshaw bull whale's tooth engraved with the portrait of a regal female seated on a throne. Done in blue and black tones with pinpoint work to simulate facial shadows. Ca. 1840-1860. Length 7.13". *Center:* Unusual scrimshaw whale's tooth engraved with the figure of a dancing, winged female in three colors. Base of the tooth is cut with regularly spaced triangular-shaped notches. Ca. mid-nineteenth century. Length 5". *Right:* Pair of tiny scrimshaw whale's teeth, each nicely engraved with the half-figure portraits of stylishly dressed ladies. Ca. mid-nineteenth Century. Length 3.25".

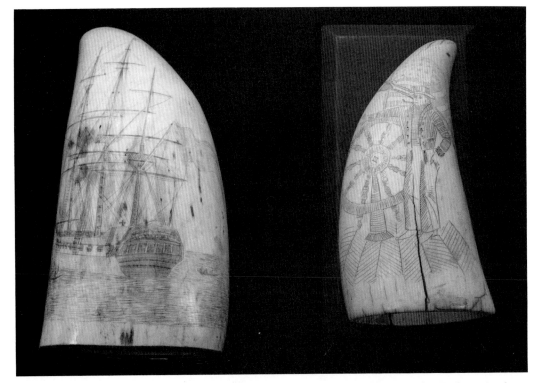

Left: Excellent large scrimshaw whale's tooth with engraving around its entire circumference of a large sailing ship with native canoes nearby, and on the opposite, the island from which the natives are seen coming in a canoe. Ca. mid-nineteenth century. Length 6.50". *Right:* Early scrimshaw whale's tooth engraved with a sailor at the ship's wheel with an American flag behind him. Ca. mid-nineteenth century. Length 5.38".

Historically rare and important scrimshaw whale's tooth, engraved by Caleb J. Albro of Portsmouth, Rhode Island, and bearing his name. Tooth is engraved on the one side with a detailed whaling scene that is entitled "Coast of New Zealand Ship John Coggeshall Newport R.I./Sperm Whale Fishery in the South Pacific Ocean." On the bottom side is the figure of a sperm whale with a harpoon and lance entitled "Sperm Whale." On the opposite side, with some use of color, and the sun half set on the horizon, is an engraved Naval battle between an American and British ship, entitled "The Constitution and Guerrier." American, ca. 1835-1845. Length 7.50".

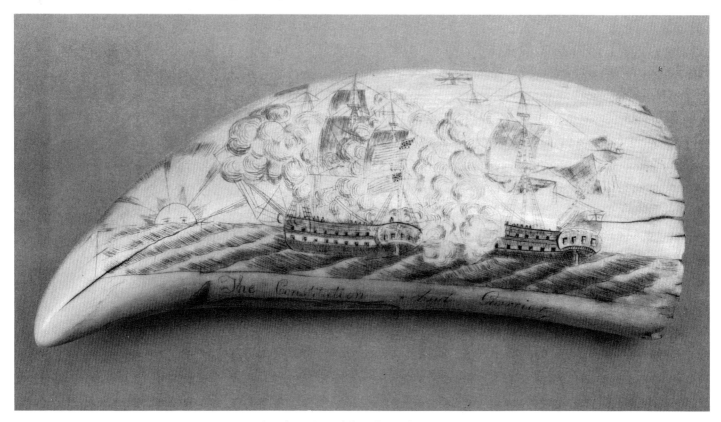

Another view of the Albro whale tooth.

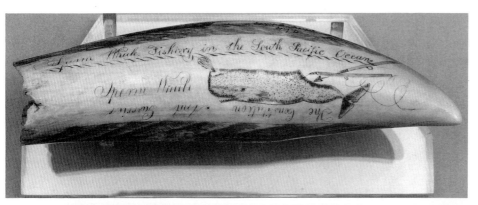

A further view of the Albro whale's tooth.

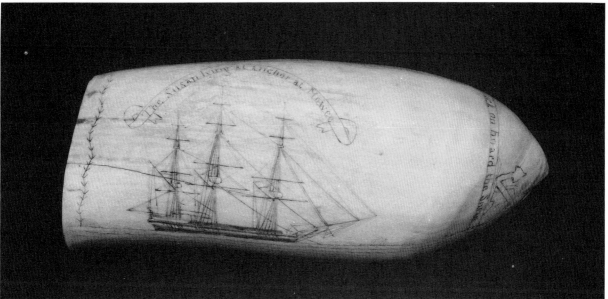

"Susan's Tooth." A very rare and important scrimshaw whale's tooth, engraved on one side with the ship at anchor and banner above that reads "The Susan Lying at Anchor at Mowee"; on the opposite, the ship is shown with all sails set and a banner reading "The Susan Cruising for Sperm Whales." On one narrow side of the tooth is engraved "Ship Susan of Nantucket/Frederick Swain/Master," and around the tip of the tooth is engraved "En-

graved by Fred'k Myrick on board Susan Feby 7th 1829." On the very tip is an engraved anchor opposite crossed American flags; below, in reversed position, an American eagle with flag shield on the breast, clutching arrows and an olive branch, and holding a banner with "E Pluribus Unum." Length 5.50". This tooth originally belonged to Nathaniel Bowditch.

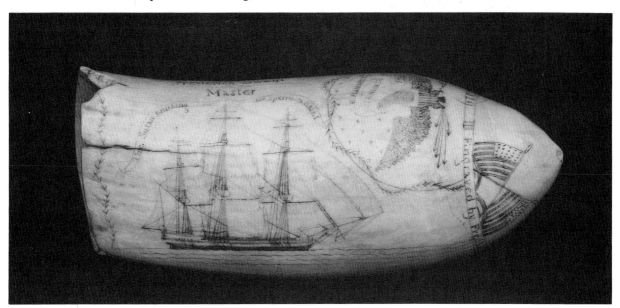

The opposite side of the "Susan Tooth."

Jagging Wheels

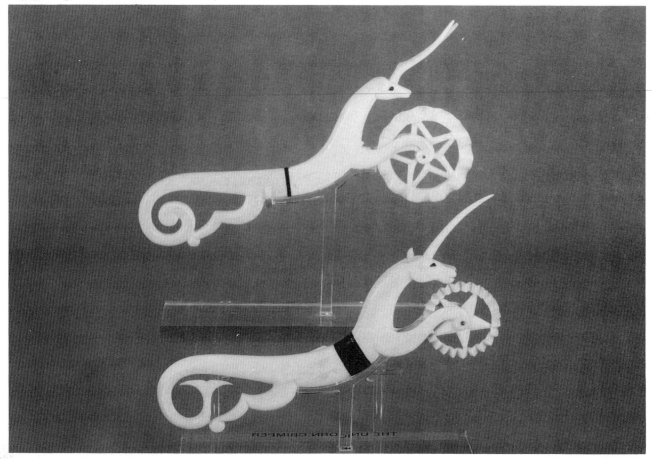

Top: Extremely rare Unicorn pie crimper, or jagging wheel, with unusual double horns. Made entirely of whale ivory with ebony band and eyes, the wheel being larger than normal. Beautifully carved with a five pointed star. Ca. 1860-1870. Length 7.75".

Bottom: Rare pie Unicorn crimper or jagging wheel, made of whale ivory with ebony connector in the center and ebony eyes. A very graceful crimper with delicate carving overall and ending in a whale's tail. Ca. 1870. 8.25" long.

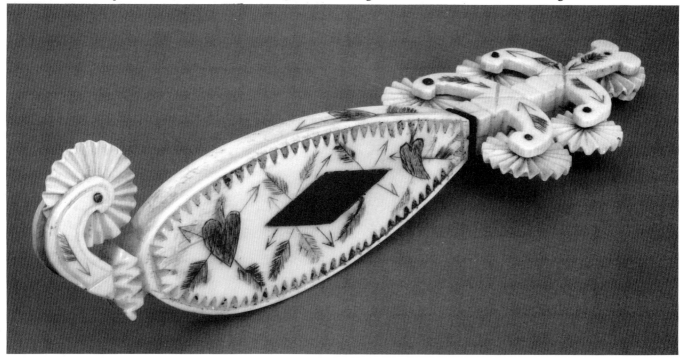

Exceptionally rare pie crimper/jagging wheel, with six wheels, tortoiseshell inlays, and engraved and colored hearts and arrows pierced by Cupid's arrows. Such wheels were usually made by scrimshanders to enter in a competition. 7" long.

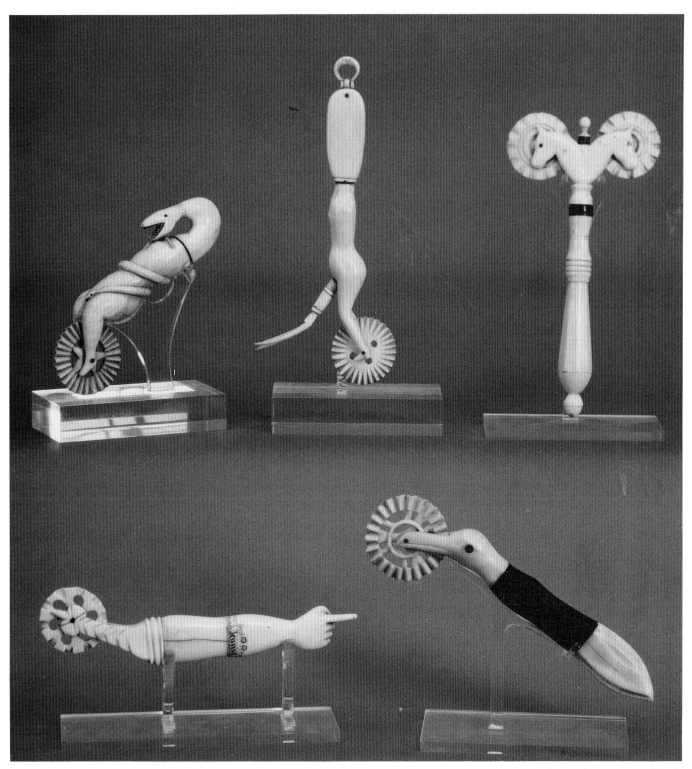

Top left: Erotic jagging wheel, made of whale ivory in the form of a nude female body with a serpent's head, and encircled by a separate serpent. To quote Flayderman, "the piece was intended to be a personal message from the sailor who carved it. The snake here representing temptation (or the devil), the wheel (or cutting tool) between the legs may indicate fear of castration." An exceptional and superbly carved wheel, American, ca. mid-nineteenth century. Length 6.50". *Top center:* Another erotic scrimshaw jagging wheel, made entirely of whale ivory in the form of a female body with a three tined fork obtruding from the pelvic area, and with the wheel held between her ankles. A flat curved handle commences at the neck. Ca. mid-nineteenth century. Length 8.63". *Top right:* Rare, unusual scrimshaw jag-

ging wheel, made of whale ivory with wood connectors. Nicely formed 8-sided tapering handle with double wheels held between horses' heads. Ca. mid-nineteenth century. Length 8". *Bottom left:* Excellent scrimshaw jagging wheel, made of whale ivory with a single wheel, the handle in the form of an arm and hand, with forefinger extended. Engraved with a garter around the elbow area, on which is the name "Jennie." Ca. 3rd quarter nineteenth century. Length 7.50". *Bottom right:* Fine scrimshaw jagging wheel, made of whale ivory and dark hardwood, with nicely formed handle terminating in the head of an albatross holding the elaborately carved wheel in its bill. Ca. early to mid-nineteenth century. Length 8".

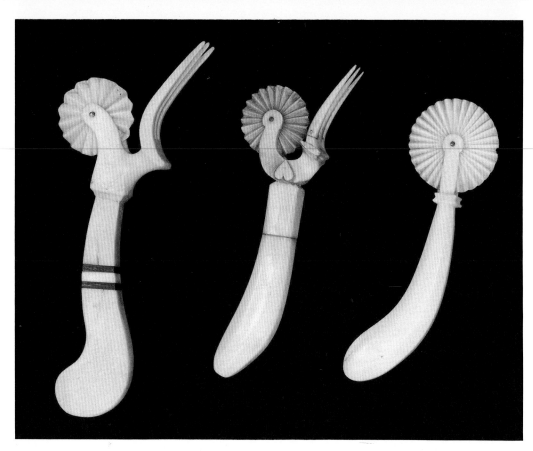

Left: Early scrimshaw jagging wheel of whale ivory with baleen inlays, featuring a scrolled handle and an excellent three-tined fork. Ca. 2nd quarter nineteenth century. Length 7.25".
Center: Fine scrimshaw jagging wheel of whale ivory with three-tined fork and carved hearts. Ca. 2nd quarter nineteenth century. Length 6.25". **Right:** Early scrimshaw jagging wheel of whale ivory with curved handle and finely carved wheel. Ca. 2nd quarter nineteenth century. Length 5.63".

Top: A rare fine open carved whale ivory jagging wheel, with heart-shaped handle, delicate carving and finely carved wheel. Ca. mid-nineteenth century. Length 4.75". **Center:** Unusual and rare jagging wheel made from whale ivory, tortoiseshell and coin silver. Most unusual. Nantucket, Mass., ca. 1840s. Length 6". **Bottom:** Fine scrimshaw jagging wheel made of whale ivory and tortoiseshell, featuring a 4-tined fork and a eight-pointed star as a wheel hub. Ca. early to mid-nineteenth century. Length 7".

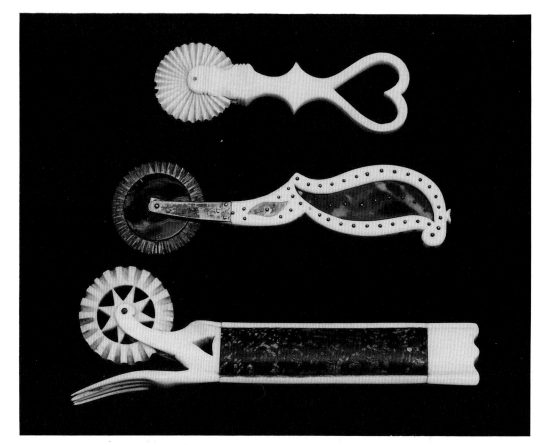

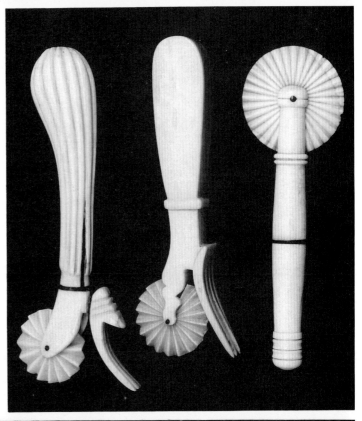

Left: Early jagging wheel with unusual pistol grip, fluted walrus ivory handle with whale ivory fork and wheel. Ca. mid-nineteenth century. Length 6.50". *Center:* Scrimshaw jagging wheel with handle and fork made of walrus ivory, and the wheel made of whale ivory. Ca. 3rd quarter nineteenth century. Length 6". *Right:* Simple Nantucket-style whale ivory jagging wheel with two-part turned handle with baleen connector. Ca. early to mid-Nineteenth Century. Length 5.88".

Lovely aged whale ivory jagging wheel belonging to the author, with open-carved handle ending in an open heart finial. Ca. mid-nineteenth century. Length 6.88".

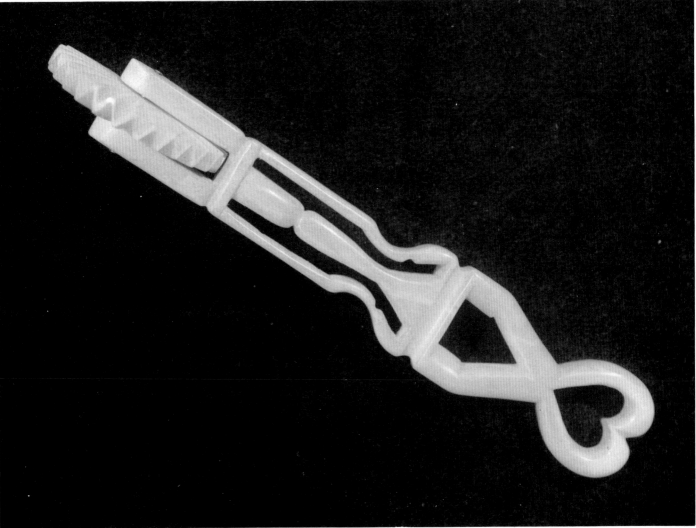

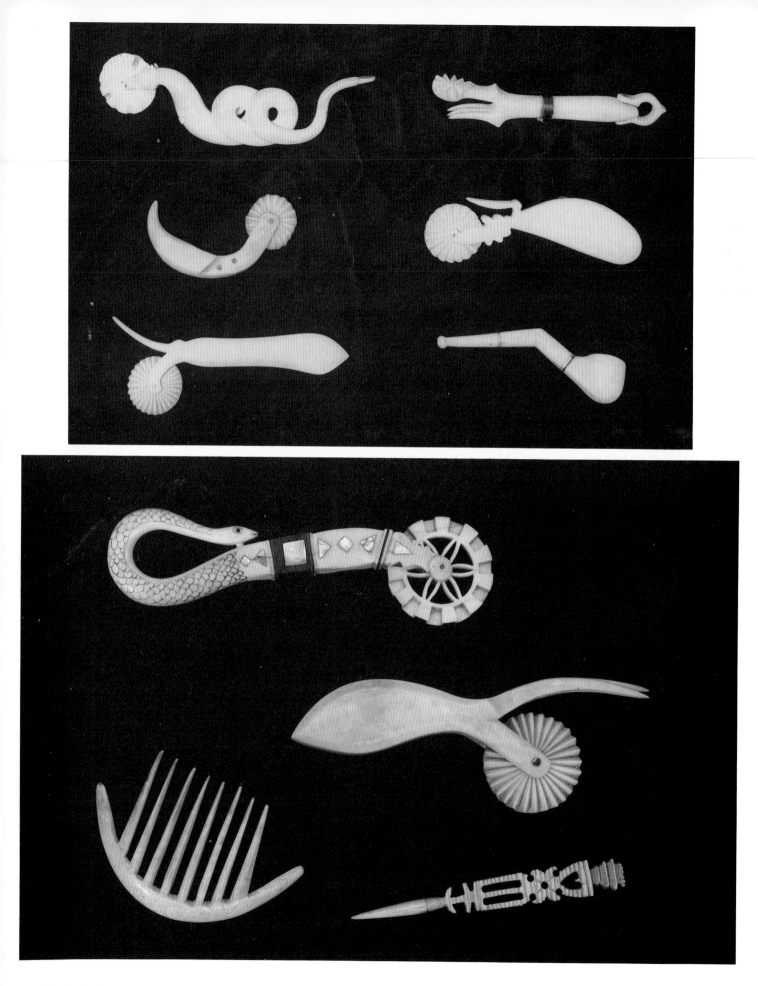

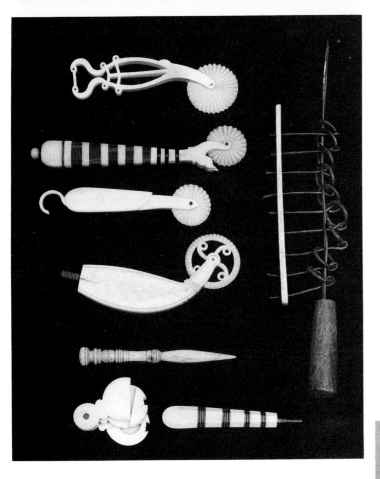

Top to bottom: **1.** Scrimshaw jagging wheel made of whale ivory. Ca. mid-Nineteenth century. Length 6". **2.** Scrimshaw jagging wheel made of whale ivory and exotic wood. Ca. 2nd quarter nineteenth century. Length 7.75". **3.** Scrimshaw jagging wheel with walrus ivory handle and whale ivory wheel. Handle carved from one piece with a hanging hook at the end. Ca. mid-nineteenth century. Length 6". **4.** Fine early jagging wheel made of whale ivory with vines engraved on either side of the handle. Done in colored inks and having an exceptional wheel with four scrolled spokes. Ca. early to mid-nineteenth century. Length 6.25". **5.** Whalebone bodkin nicely turned from one piece. Ca. early to mid-nineteenth century. Length 5.38". **6.** Rare scrimshaw puzzle made entirely from whale ivory in the form of a jeweler's loupe. It was probably made to hold several coins of small denomination. Ca. mid-nineteenth century. Length 2.50". **7.** Scrimshaw handle made of whale ivory sections alternating with metal rings. Ca. mid-nineteenth century. Length 4.75". *Right:* A metal, wood and whalebone Japanese puzzle, probably a copy made by an American. Ca. nineteenth century. Length 12.25".

Opposite page, top:

Top left: Unusual and quite unique scrimshaw jagging wheel in the shape of a Sea Horse which resembles a combination of sea serpent and horse with a whale-like tail and two tiny forelegs. Ca. mid-nineteenth century or earlier. Length 7.88". *Top right:* A scrimshaw pastry tool made of whale ivory with three-tined fork, fixed crimper and pinned hanger. Ca. early nineteenth century. Length 6.75". *Center left:* Unusual comma-shaped jagging wheel made of whale ivory. Ca. early to mid-nineteenth century. Length 4.13". *Center right:* Fine early jagging wheel with broad handle, unusual three-tined fork and wheel holder. Ca. mid-nineteenth century. Length 6". *Bottom left:* Scrimshaw jagging wheel with three-tined fork and exceptionally fine wheel. The handle and fork are made from one very large whale's tooth. Ca. mid-nineteenth century. Length 6.50". *Bottom right:* Rare scrimshaw pipe; a working pipe with elbow shape made of whale ivory with silver and baleen rings separating the sections. Ca. 3rd quarter nineteenth century. Length 5.13".

Opposite page, bottom

Top: Very important scrimshaw jagging wheel with ivory handle in the form of a serpent with engraved scales, lignum vitae separator, mother-of-pearl inlays and an exceptionally fine wheel. Ca. 2nd quarter nineteenth century. Length 7.25". *Center:* Sturdy whale ivory jagging wheel with three-tined fork. The handle, wheel holder and fork all made from a single piece of whale ivory that must have been removed from a very large tooth, since this part of the wheel alone measures 6.75" in length. The fork has a heart carved near the base, and the wheel is of very fine quality. Ca. early to mid-nineteenth century. Length 6.75". *Bottom left:* Rare ivory hair comb made from a single piece of ivory. Ca. early to mid-nineteenth century. Height 3.13", width 4". *Bottom right:* Elaborately carved whale ivory bodkin. Ca. early to mid-nineteenth century. Length 5.13".

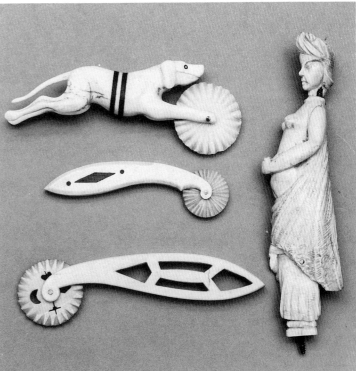

Top left: Extremely rare and unusual scrimshaw jagging wheel with handle fully carved in the form of a running dog with outstretched front legs holding the wheel. Made entirely of whale ivory with two coconut wood rings in the center of the dog's body. Ca. 1840-1860. Length 6.63". *Center left:* Petite scrimshaw jagging wheel with ebony inlaid whale ivory handle. Ca. mid-nineteenth century. Length 5.25". *Bottom left:* Fine jagging wheel with open-carved whale ivory handle and unusual open-carved wheel. Ca. mid-nineteenth century. Length 7". *Right:* Exceptional early scrimshaw cane handle of a semi-nude pregnant woman. Ca. 2nd quarter nineteenth century. Length 8.13".

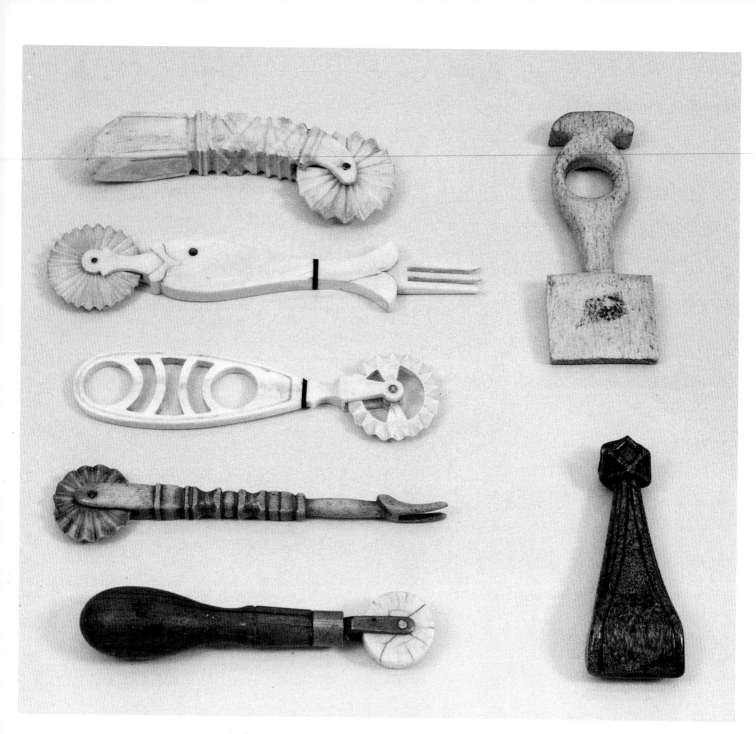

Left, top to bottom: **1.** Very rare heavy scrimshaw jagging wheel made of whale ivory. This is an exceptionally heavy example with geometrically arranged carvings with hearts, triangles and diamonds worked into the design. Ca. mid-nineteenth century. Length 6.13". **2.** Unusual whale ivory scrimshaw jagging wheel with handle carved as a fish with inlaid baleen eyes, a ring at the tail, and a fork coming out of the tail and the wheel out of the mouth. Ca. mid-nineteenth century. Length 8.25". **3.** Early jagging wheel with open carved walrus ivory handle and whale ivory wheel. Ca. mid-nineteenth century. Length 6.88". **4.** Very early Nantucket-type jagging wheel of whalebone with whale ivory wheel. Ca. late eighteenth century or possibly early nineteenth century. Length 7.13". **5.** Interesting device for creasing seams, consisting of a brass mounted whale ivory roller with turned wooden handle. Ca. mid-nineteenth century. Length 6.13". *Top right:* Whalebone seam rubber, ca. mid-nineteenth century. Length 5.25". *Bottom right:* Seam rubber.

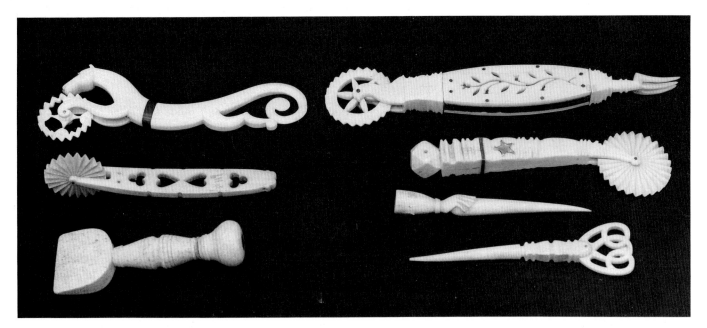

Top left: Very rare scrimshaw Unicorn jagging wheel made of whale ivory and ebony, ca. first half nineteenth century. Length 7.38". *Center left:* Fine scrimshaw jagging wheel made entirely of walrus ivory. Handle is open cut with hearts and clubs, and is further engraved with leaves and berries down one side. Ca. first half nineteenth century. Length 6". *Bottom left:* Early whalebone seam rubber with a turned whale ivory knob with baleen inlay. Ca. first half nineteenth century. Length 4.75". *Top right:* Unusual scrimshaw jagging wheel of whale ivory and baleen. The unusual features include bird's head supports for the wheel, three piece handle with open carved whale ivory sides with baleen insets on the outer edges and fabric within, as well as a

three-tined fork on the end opposite the wheel. American, ca. mid-nineteenth century. Length 10". *Center right:* Scrimshaw jagging wheel made entirely of whale ivory with three coin silver inlays of stars and a diamond, as well as two mother-of-pearl inlays of a diamond and a heart. Engraved rosettes on either side of the handle. American, ca. 2nd quarter nineteenth century. Length 7". *Center right:* Small whale ivory fid in the form of a forearm and hand holding the pointing fid. American, ca. mid-nineteenth century. Length 5.25". *Bottom right:* Small scrimshaw fid made of whale ivory with reticulated heart-shaped handle. Ca. mid-nineteenth century. Length 5.75".

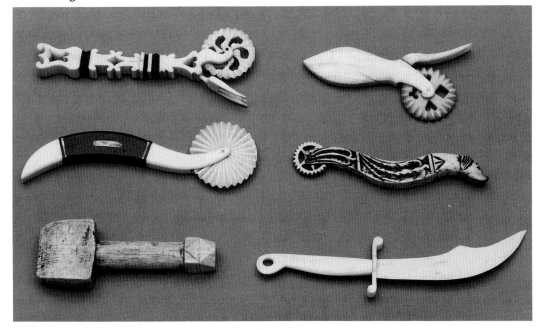

Top left: Scrimshaw jagging wheel with reticulated whale ivory handle separated by three thick pieces of baleen; three-tined fork under wheel. Ca. First half nineteenth century. Length 6.75". *Center left:* Simple, graceful scrimshaw whale ivory jagging wheel with whale ivory and island wood handle with silver bands and inlay. Ca. 3rd quarter nineteenth century. Length 7". *Bottom left:* Whalebone seam rubber, ca. mid-nineteenth century. Length 5.25". *Top right:* Small whale ivory jagging wheel

with a heart, diamond, club and spade carved in the wheel; also with a three-tined fork. Ca. 2nd quarter nineteenth century. Length 5.38". *Center right:* Interesting primitive jagging wheel with serpentine handle, a dog's head at one end and a wheel opposite. Ca. 2nd quarter nineteenth century. Length 6". *Bottom right:* Lovely scimitar-shaped scrimshaw letter opener. Ca. mid-nineteenth century. Length 8".

Swifts

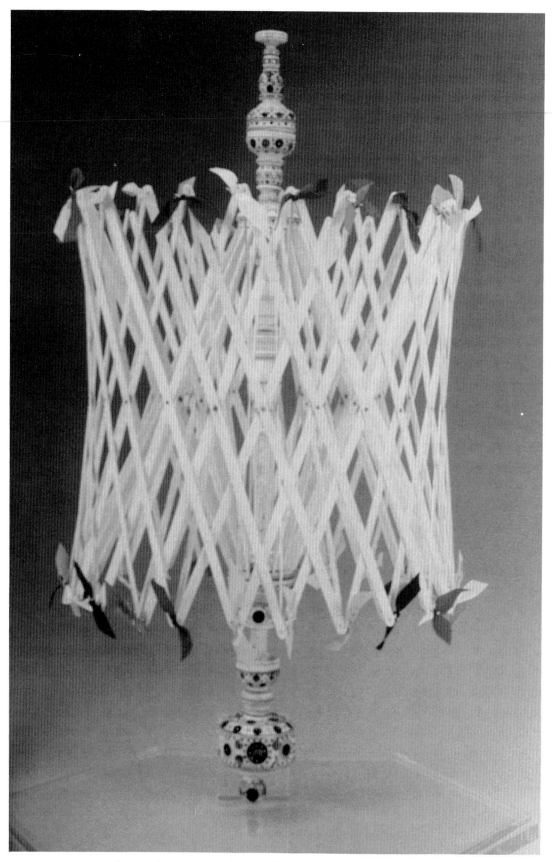

Extremely rare scrimshaw swift, made from whale ivory and whalebone, with turned center post and exceptional diminutive inlays of shell, silver and abalone. Ca. mid-nineteenth century. Height 23".

Extremely rare scrimshaw swift with silver inlays, complete with its original scrimshaw box which also has whalebone inlays, and a small center plaque in color. Information from the Duke's County Historical Society indicates that the piece was made by Capt. Henry Daggett (1811-1873) for his wife, Mary Ann Daggett, of Fairhaven, Mass. (1815-1886). The swift is inlaid with small coin silver inlays with engraving and also a small plaque with Mrs. Daggett's initials. Ca. mid-nineteenth century. Overall length of the case is 27".

Left: Fine large scrimshaw swift made entirely of whalebone with a hand-forged thumbscrew. Ca. mid-nineteenth century. Height 24". *Center:* Exquisite small scrimshaw swift made of whale ivory and mounted on a custom metal base. Ca. mid-nineteenth century. Height 16". *Right:* Lovely old scrimshaw swift with Sag Harbor-style engraving. Swift has a barrel-shaped clamp and displays an engraved whale on the shaft. Each of the outer arms of the swift is done in several engraved designs of ropes and vines. Ca. early nineteenth century. Height 20.75".

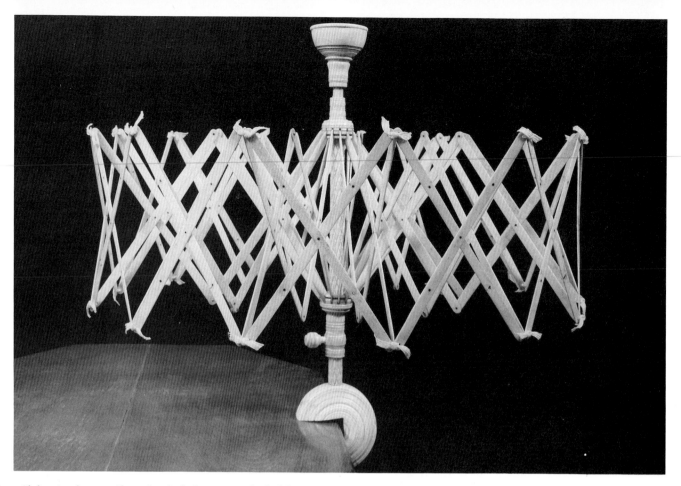

Beautiful scrimshaw swift made of whale ivory and whalebone; a double swift with unusual carved center support. Ca. mid-nineteenth century. Height 15.50".

Fine scrimshaw swift made of whale ivory and whalebone. Double swift with unusual carved center support. Ca. mid-nineteenth century. Height 15.50".

Corset Busks

Top: Exceptional scrimshawed rectangular piece of panbone engraved on one side with a whaleship; on the opposite a superb whaling scene. Mounted on a rosewood base. Ca. 2nd quarter nineteenth century. Length 9.13"; height 6.75". *Bottom:* Lovely, exceptionally large scrimshaw corset busk, with equally unusual engraving. On one side from top to bottom are a pair of intertwined hearts, a patriotic female figure with anchor and American flag, a portrait of a man on a pedestal (presumably Washington with a trophy of American flags and a Masonic square and compass over him); beneath this figure is a compass rose followed by a sunburst with a face; sawtooth design engraving around the sides and bottom. On the opposite are a row of three large American sailing ships with foliage and intertwining hearts at the top. Mounted on a wrought iron base. Ca. 2nd quarter nineteenth century. Length 15".

The opposite view of the above pieces.

Left to right: **1.** Scrimshaw corset busk beautifully engraved with geometric designs and plants. Ca. early to mid-nineteenth century. Length 13.88". **2.** Fine scrimshaw corset busk with four engravings and some use of color. Engravings are of a plant, two ships and a peacock. Ca. 2nd. quarter nineteenth century. Length 12.25". **3.** Engraved scrimshaw corset busk with a panoramic marine scene depicting a seaport, with a rose at one end and a tulip at the opposite. Ca. mid-nineteenth century. Length 13.13". **4.** Scrimshaw corset busk engraved with a trophy of American flags, a flag shield, banners, stars and flowers. Ca. mid-nineteenth century. Length 13.50". **5.** Early scrimshaw corset busk engraved with plants, geometric designs, a tree, a house and a heart. Ca. 2nd quarter nineteenth century.

Typical scrimshawed whale ivory corset busk from the author's family. This piece was done by one of the many ancestors who took to the life of whaling, and has been in the family for generations. Engraved in black and green inks, the eagle with tro-phy of arrows, the shrubs and willow tree, as well as the geometric designs all are typical of the original primitive nature of this art. Ca. early to mid-nineteenth century. Length 15".

Top to bottom: **1.** Unique corset busk, elaborately carved with designs, including a sailor with an American flag at the bottom, above which is a flower and grape enhanced vine with a bird perched on it. This busk once held a backing secured by brass rivets; the backing is gone, but the rivets remain. Ca. early to mid-nineteenth century. Length 13". **2.** A fine scrimshaw corset busk with engraving and coloring on both sides. On one side is Neptune in a nautilus shell drawn by a pair of sea horses with three ships in the background. This scene is flanked with a nesting bird to the left, and a landscape with house, tower, and boat on the right. On the reverse is a humorous primitive engraving of a leopard flanked by flowers. Ca. mid-nineteenth century. Length 13.13". **3.** Rare old scrimshaw corset busk engraved with a panoramic scene of a ship launching; the scene is of Thomaston Harbor, Maine. Ca. early to mid-Nineteenth century. Length 13.50" **4.** Another rare scrimshaw corset busk, engraved and colored with a whaling scene in the center, a storm tossed ship to the right, and a plant to the left. Ca. mid-nineteenth century. Length 14".

Left to right: **1.** Scrimshaw corset busk engraved from top to bottom with a heraldic eagle, and a woman holding a cornucopia filled with flowers, beneath which are a number of geometric and foliate designs; on the side, the crudely worked initials "FDW." Ca. 1st quarter nineteenth century. Length 13.50". **2.** Early scrimshaw corset busk engraved with numerous rosettes and hearts and a full-figure female portrait at the bottom. The reverse features another portrait of a lady. Ca. first third nineteenth century. Length 12.94". **3.** Scrimshaw corset busk with finely detailed engraving of a building and numerous geometric designs. Ca. first third nineteenth century. Length 12.63". **4.** Exceptional scrimshaw corset busk finely engraved with colored eagles, ship, American flags, anchors, stars, a large flowering plant and an elaborately worked border of leaves. Ca. early nineteenth century. Length 13.25". **5.** Fine scrimshaw corset busk with four engravings with some color, including two ships and a peacock. Ca. 2nd quarter nineteenth century. Length 12.25".

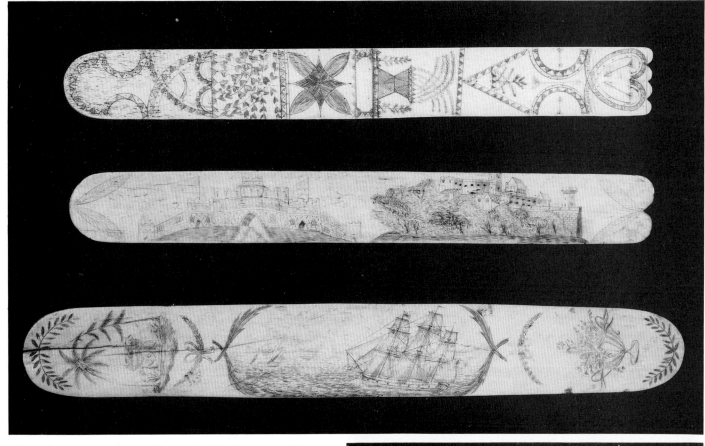

Top to bottom: **1.** Fine scrimshaw corset busk engraved in green and blue with hearts, arrows, plants and geometric designs; beautifully and symmetrically arranged. Ca. 2nd quarter nineteenth century. Length 13.50". **2.** Scrimshaw corset busk engraved on the left half with a castle, and on the right half of the same side, a walled town; foliate leaves at each end. Ca. 2nd quarter nineteenth century. Length 13.25". **3.** Very fine scrimshaw corset busk engraved on one side with a marine scene showing a large ship approaching a smaller ship. At one end, a large urn is filled with fruit and is flanked on the left with a palm tree and a spruce tree on the right; at the other end is a detailed basket of flowers. Ca. 2nd quarter nineteenth century. Length 15".

Top to bottom: **1.** Antique scrimshaw corset busk engraved on one side with flowers, birds and a butterfly; on the opposite, a ship among icebergs. The floral side is done in colored inks. Ca. mid-nineteenth century. Length 13". **2.** Outstanding antique scrimshaw corset busk engraved in color with six scenes, the first a portrait of Washington framed within a trophy of cornucopia, flags, and horns, all topped by an eagle; a portrait of a woman surrounded by flowers; a colorful basket of fruit; a fullfigure portrait of a man and woman linked arm-in-arm; a church with a person standing in front; lastly, two red flowers. Ca. early to mid-nineteenth century. Length 14". **3.** Rare scrimshaw corset busk engraved in color with five separate scenes: a group of flowers; a full-rigged ship under sail; an active marine scene with early paddle-wheel ship, five men rowing a small boat and the upper works of the ship viewed beyond a point of land on which there is a marine signal telegraph; a pair of hearts surrounded by leaves and flowers; a flowering tree; lastly, a heraldic eagle clutching flag, shield and arrows, a banner in its bill. Ca. mid-nineteenth century. Length 12.63". **4.** Early scrimshaw corset busk engraved in black ink with six separate scenes: a monument; flowers in a vase; bowl of fruit; ship with furled sails; a star or compass rose; and lastly, a ship under sail. Ca. mid-nineteenth century. Length 11.75".

Canes

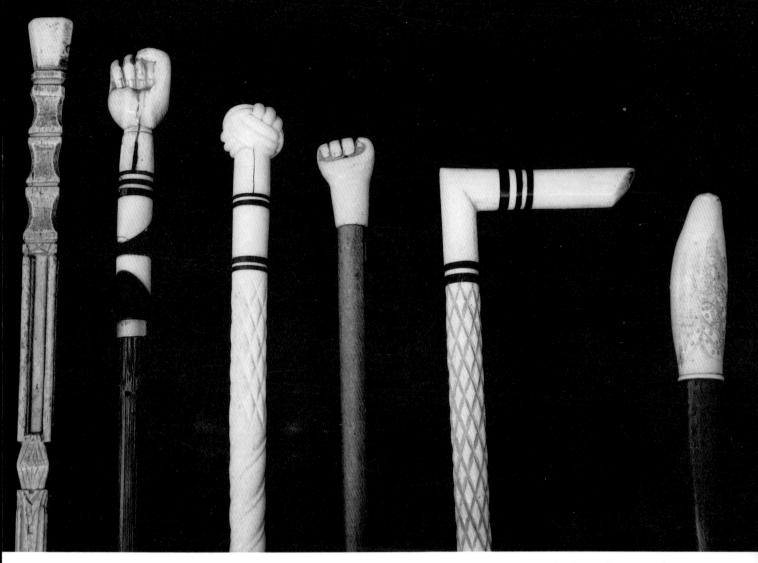

Left to right: **1.** Exceptional scrimshaw cane made entirely of whalebone with unusual carving. Ca. 2nd quarter nineteenth century. Length 33.50". **2.** Scrimshaw cane with coconut wood shaft and an elaborate multi-section upper shaft of wood and whale ivory parts topped by a carved whale ivory clenched hand. Ca. mid-nineteenth century. Length 34". **3.** Scrimshaw cane with rope and diamond carved whalebone shaft topped with whale ivory and wood separators terminating in a whale ivory turk's head knot. Ca. mid-nineteenth century. Length 35". **4.** Scrimshaw cane with tapered wooden shaft and fine whale ivory carved clenched hand as a knob. Ca. mid-nineteenth century. Length 33.50". **5.** Scrimshaw cane with rope and diamond point carved whalebone shaft, with an L-shaped whale ivory handle with five wood separators. Ca. mid-nineteenth century. Length 33". **6.** Fine scrimshaw cane with exotic wood shaft tipped with whale ivory and topped with a whale's tooth engraved in color on both sides with portraits of elaborately dressed personages. Ca. 3rd quarter nineteenth century. Length 36".

Opposite page:
Left: Beautiful old scrimshaw cane with spiral carved whalebone shaft, parquetry inlay of whale ivory and island wood at the top, and a herringbone carved whale ivory knob with mahogany circular inlay. Ca. 2nd quarter nineteenth century. Length 34.75". *Center:* Very fine whale ivory and whalebone walking stick, with delicate whalebone shaft and handle carved in the form of an arching snake with nude lady on the back side. Nantucket, ca. 3rd quarter nineteenth century. Length 34.38". *Right:* Heavy primitive walking stick, made from a section of narwhal tusk. Fitted with a mahogany tip and large turned mahogany head. Ca. mid-nineteenth century. Length 32".

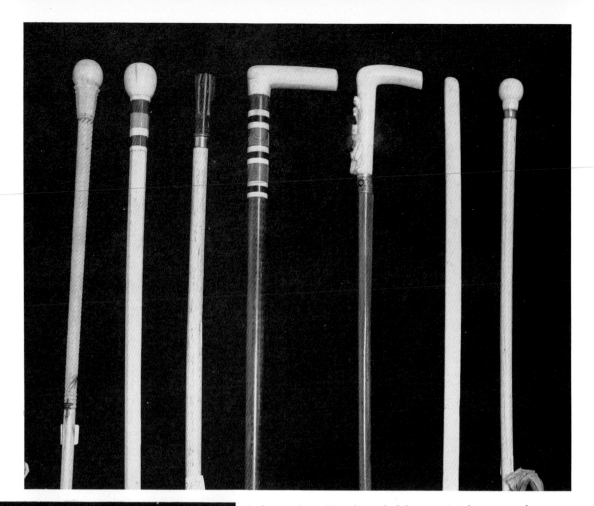

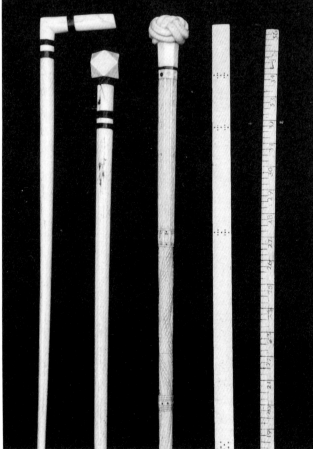

Left to right: **1.** Very fine whalebone scrimshaw cane, the upper shaft finely rope carved and the lower half paneled. Excellent turned whale ivory knob. Ca. early to mid-nineteenth century. Length 34.88". **2.** Scrimshaw cane. with 8-sided whalebone shaft, three wooden and three whale ivory rings connecting to a simple whale ivory knob. Ca. mid-nineteenth century. Length 38.25". **3.** Scrimshaw cane with whalebone shaft and fluted island wood knob. Ca. mid-nineteenth century. Length 33". **4.** Scrimshaw cane with select wood shaft, alternating whale ivory, ebony and wood rings below the L-shaped walrus ivory handle. Ca. mid-nineteenth century. Length 35.75". **5.** Antique cane with wooden shaft, carved animal bone handle with lion over its kill and two dogs above. Ca. mid-nineteenth century. Length 35.75". **6.** Scrimshaw yardstick made of whalebone. Ca. early to mid-nineteenth century. Length 35.88". **7.** Scrimshaw cane with partially paneled whalebone shaft and simple gold knob with gold connector. Ca. mid-nineteenth century. Length 34.25".

Left to right: **1.** Scrimshaw cane with whalebone shaft, L-shaped whale ivory handle with three wooden ring separators. Ca. mid-nineteenth century. Length 33.50". **2.** Scrimshaw cane with whalebone shaft, whale ivory faceted knob, three wooden and two whale ivory ring separators. Ca. mid-nineteenth century. Length 35". **3.** Outstanding scrimshaw cane with elaborately carved whalebone shaft and whale ivory turk's head knob. Small inlays of tortoiseshell and abalone in shaft. Ca. 2nd quarter nineteenth century. Length 35". **4.** Rare whalebone yardstick with inlaid tortoiseshell divisions. Ca. mid-nineteenth century. Length 36". **5.** Rare scrimshaw yardstick made of whalebone and engraved with numerals and division lines. Three small geometric engravings on the opposite side. Ca. mid-nineteenth century. Length 36".

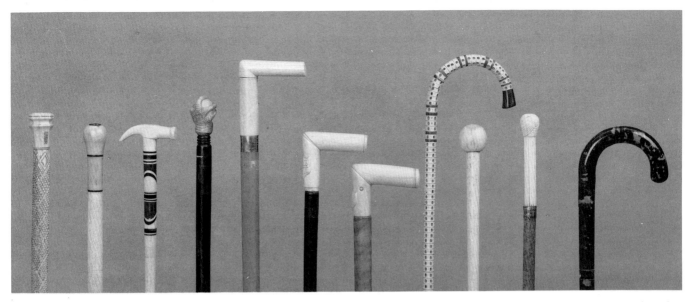

Left to right: **1.** Early scrimshaw cane with elaborately carved whalebone shaft and octagonal whale ivory head. Ca. 2nd quarter nineteenth century. Length 33.50". **2.** Fine early scrimshaw cane with rope, spiral and crosshatch carved whalebone shaft and turned whale ivory knob with silver medallion set in the top. Ca. 2nd quarter nineteenth century. Length 33.25". **3.** Scrimshaw cane with tapered whalebone shaft and whale ivory handle in the form of a claw hammer. The handle is separated from the shaft with various sections of island wood and whale ivory. Ca. mid-nineteenth century. Length 33.25". **4.** Scrimshaw cane with wooden shaft and ivory knob in the form of a talon clutching a ball. Ca. early to mid-nineteenth century. Length 34.75". **5.** Antique cane with wooden shaft and ivory L-shaped handle carved with a single rose against leaves and several buds, fitted with a gold presentation band dated 1865. Length 35".

6. Scrimshaw cane with ebony-colored wooden shaft and L-shaped bone handle carved with the American flag shield. Ca. mid-nineteenth century. Length 34.75". **7.** Scrimshaw cane with tiger maple shaft and L-shaped bone handle carved with a shield. Ca. mid-nineteenth century. Length 33". **8.** Scrimshaw cane made of shark vertebrae with baleen at each end. Ca. mid-nineteenth century. Length 35.25". **9.** Scrimshaw cane with whalebone shaft and simple turned whale ivory knob. Ca. nineteenth century. Length 33.75". **10.** Scrimshaw cane with bird's-eye maple shaft and unusual whale ivory upper shaft and knob delicately fluted and terminating in a Turk's head knot. Silver presentation band between the shaft and knob dated July 4, 1863. Length 37.50". **11.** Extremely rare cane completely covered in tortoiseshell. Ca. last half nineteenth century. Length 37".

Left to right: **1.** Fine scrimshaw cane with delicately tapered whalebone shaft and carved whale ivory clenched hand, complete with cuff. Ca. mid-nineteenth century. Length 35". **2.** Lovely scrimshaw cane featuring a tapered island wood shaft connected by two sections of whale ivory with baleen and brass separators and knob in the form of a clenched hand. Ca. mid-nineteenth century. Length 33.50". **3.** Very fine lady's scrimshaw cane with tapered rope-carved whalebone shaft and rope-carved whale ivory handle with turk's head knot at the top. Ca. early to mid-nineteenth century. Length 34".

4. Exceptional scrimshaw cane made of rings of shark's vertebrae and exotic woods. Ca. 3rd quarter nineteenth century. Length 35.50". **5.** Early scrimshaw cane made of an octagonal-shaped piece of whalebone with attached leather thong and brass tip. Ca. nineteenth century. Length 35". **6.** Scrimshaw cane made of shark vertebrae with a horn handle. Ca. 3rd quarter nineteenth century. Length 36.75". **7.** Swordfish bill mounted as a sword with mahogany handle rope carved with guard and star inlay. Ca. late nineteenth century. Length 34.25".

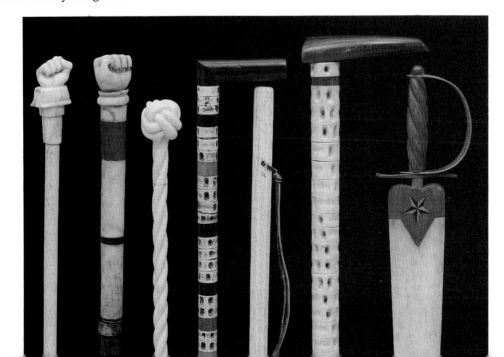

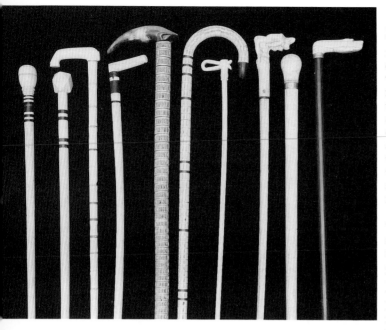

Left to right: **1.** Scrimshaw cane, whalebone shaft with turned whale ivory knob and 11 assorted rings of wood, shell, and whale ivory separating the knob and the shaft. Ca. mid-nineteenth century. Length 36.50". **2.** Scrimshaw cane, the whalebone shaft with faceted whale ivory knob separated from the shaft by four rings of horn and three of whale ivory. Ca. mid-nineteenth century. Length 36.25". **3.** Ivory cane made in the form of bamboo and handle shaped like a horse's foreleg. Ca. last half nineteenth century. Length 36.50". **4.** Scrimshaw cane with whalebone shaft and L-shaped whale ivory handle separated from the shaft by three rings of wood and two rings of whale ivory. Ca. mid-nineteenth century. Length 34.50". **5.** Scrimshaw cane made of graduated whale vertebrae, fitted with a horn handle and tip. Ca. mid-nineteenth century. Length 35.25".

6. Scrimshaw cane made of shark vertebrae; C-shaped handle with horn tip, and 3 wood rings in a regular pattern down the shaft. Ca. mid-nineteenth century. Length 34.75". **7.** Delicate scrimshaw lady's riding crop or pointer, with whalebone shaft and carved whale ivory handle. Ca. mid-nineteenth century. Length 35.50". **8.** Exceptional scrimshaw cane with square topped whalebone shaft and elaborately carved elephant ivory handle in the form of a female reclining nude. Ca. 3rd quarter nineteenth century. Length 32.75". **9.** Scrimshaw cane with heavy whalebone shaft, simple turned whale ivory knob separated by a metal ring engraved "H. McG." Ca. early to mid-nineteenth century. Length 34.50". **10.** Fine old cane with wooden shaft and L-shaped handle in the form of a dog's head that has inset paperweight eyes. Handle is separated from the shaft by a metal ring engraved with "Shubael White." Ca. early to mid-nineteenth century. Length 32.50".

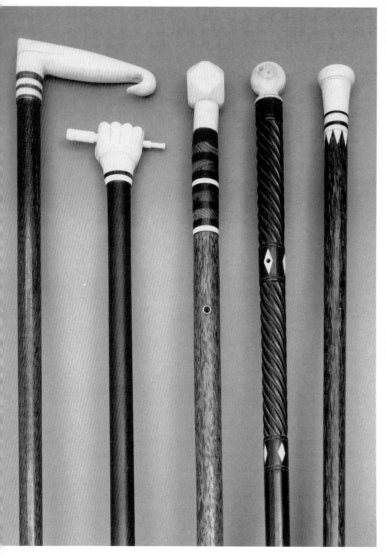

Left to right: **1.** This unusual scrimshaw cane has an L-shaped handle with a hood on the end that resembles the emblem of royalty worn by Hawaiian island natives. Exotic wood shaft with separators of brass and what appears to be red lacquer or red wax. Ca. 3rd quarter nineteenth century. Length 37". **2.** Scrimshaw cane with ebony shaft and carved walrus ivory clenched hand holding a telescope. Ca. 3rd quarter nineteenth century. Length 36.50". **3.** Scrimshaw cane with coconut wood shaft and faceted whale ivory knob separated from the shaft with rings of whale ivory, ebony, and possibly rosewood. Ca. mid-nineteenth Century. Length 35.25". **4.** Fine scrimshaw cane with dark hardwood shaft, possibly mahogany with whale ivory inlays in the shape of diamonds, rope carved at the top. Has a simple turned whale ivory knob. Ca. 2nd quarter nineteenth century. Length 32.25". **5.** Scrimshaw cane with coconut wood shaft, saw tooth whale ivory inlays at the top, and turned whale ivory knob with tortoiseshell inlay and rings. Ca. mid-nineteenth century. Length 35.50".

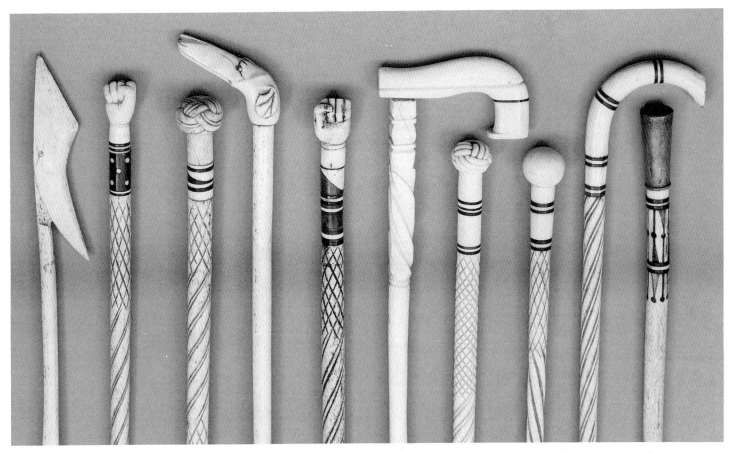

Left to right: **1.** Rare and unique scrimshaw model of a toggle harpoon made entirely of whalebone. Ca. mid-nineteenth century. Length 35.50". **2.** Early scrimshaw cane with rope carved whalebone shaft, diamond quilting at the top, inlaid wood bands and carved whale ivory knob in the form of a clenched fist. Ca. 2nd quarter nineteenth century. Length 30.50". **3.** Fine scrimshaw cane with whalebone shaft, rope and diamond quilt carving, inlaid baleen rings, and whale ivory knob in the form of a Turk's head knot. Ca. 2nd quarter nineteenth century. Length 35.75". **4.** Rare scrimshaw cane; plain whalebone shaft with dog's head handle made of whale ivory and set with opalescent colored eyes. Ca. mid-nineteenth century. Length 35.75". **5.** Early scrimshaw cane, rope and diamond quilted carved whalebone shaft, baleen and wood rings at top with carved whale ivory clenched hand for a knob. Ca. 2nd quarter nineteenth century. Length 35".

6. Unusual elephant ivory, sailor-made cane with shaft in four sections, surmounted by a square rope carved section, and fitted with a two-piece J-shaped handle, with two baleen rings. Ca. mid-nineteenth century. Length 35.75". **7.** Very fine scrimshaw cane, rope and diamond quilt carved whalebone shaft, five coconut wood rings separating two small whale ivory sections and terminating in a whale ivory Turk's head knob. Ca. 2nd quarter nineteenth century. Length 34.50". **8.** Early scrimshaw cane with deep rope carving and shallow diamond quilting on the whalebone shaft; four rings of coconut wood and two of whale ivory with a plain whale ivory knob. Ca. 2nd quarter nineteenth century. Length 32.50". **9.** Early scrimshaw cane with rope carved whalebone shaft, C-shaped whale ivory handle; made in four sections with eight rings of coconut wood and four rings of whale ivory. Ca. 2nd quarter nineteenth century. Length 35.50". **10.** Old scrimshaw cane with plain whalebone shaft decorated with unusual wood and whale ivory inlays, and sporting a silver knob. Ca. 2nd quarter nineteenth century. Length 35".

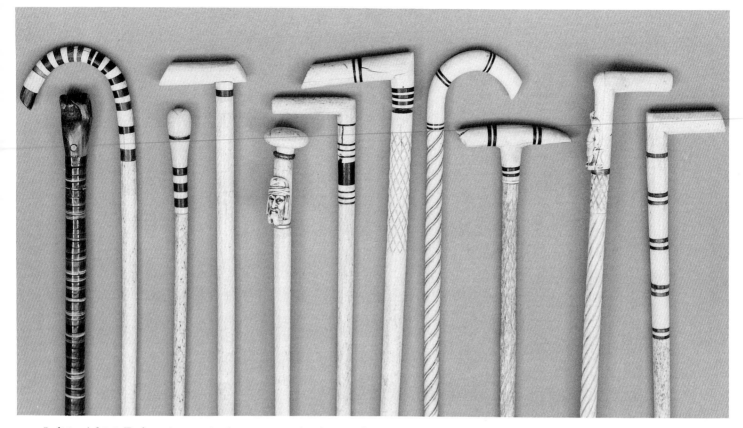

Left to right: **1.** Truly unique scrimshaw cane made of rings of tortoiseshell, with carved tortoiseshell clenched hand as the handle. Ca. mid-nineteenth century. Length 34". **2.** Scrimshaw cane, whalebone shaft with C-shaped handle made of alternating rings of whale ivory, baleen and ebony. Ca. 2nd quarter nineteenth century. Length 34.50". **3.** Scrimshaw cane with plain whalebone shaft with knob, made of four rings of coconut wood and five rings of whale ivory. Ca. 2nd quarter nineteenth century. Length 31". **4.** Simple scrimshaw cane with heavy whalebone shaft and a cylindrical piece of whale ivory mounted at right angles to form a handle. Ca. mid-nineteenth century. Length 32.75". **5.** Unusual scrimshaw cane with plain whalebone shaft, walrus ivory connector carved with an Arab's head and fitted with a flat circular whale ivory knob. Ca. 3rd quarter nineteenth century. Length 36.75". **6.** Simple scrimshaw cane with whalebone shaft, alternating rings of coconut wood and whale ivory with L-shaped whalebone handle. Ca. 2nd quarter nineteenth century. Length 33.75".

7. Early scrimshaw cane, whalebone shaft with diamond quilt-ing at the top and an L-shaped handle made of rings of coconut wood, whale ivory and whalebone. Ca. 2nd quarter nineteenth century. Length 31.50". **8.** Scrimshaw cane with spiral carved whalebone shaft; three-section C-shaped whale ivory handle separated by rings of coconut wood and whale ivory. Ca. 2nd quarter nineteenth century. Length 35". **9.** Early scrimshaw cane with spiral and diamond quilt carved whalebone shaft; three part T-shaped whale ivory handle with separating rings of coconut wood and whale ivory. Ca. 2nd quarter nineteenth century. Length 31.75". **10.** Scrimshaw cane, spiral carved whalebone shaft with carved diamond quilted section of whale ivory between the shaft and the handle. L-shaped whale ivory handle carved with a representation of cupid as a blacksmith. Handle appears to have been made from a very large whale's tooth. Ca. mid-nineteenth century. Length 34.25". **11.** Fine early scrimshaw cane with 3/4 length whalebone shaft, the last quarter consisting of three sections of whale ivory separated by coconut wood and whale ivory rings, ending in an L-shaped whale ivory handle. Ca. 2nd quarter nineteenth century. Length 33".

Opposite page, bottom:

Left to right: **1.** Rare scrimshaw cane with delicately tapered whalebone shaft and whale ivory handle carved in the form of a curled serpent with inlaid baleen eyes. Two dark wood rings separate the shaft from the handle. Ca. mid-nineteenth century. Length 37". **2.** Unusual scrimshaw cane with shaft made of 42 graduated bone sections that are fitted over an iron rod and mounted with a bone handle in the shape of a goose head. Ca. mid-nineteenth century. Length 38". **3.** Fine scrimshaw cane with rope carved whalebone shaft and walrus ivory and rubber at top and bottom. The construction is unusual in that the handle fits deeply into the shaft and is secured with two whale ivory pins. American, ca. mid-nineteenth century. Length 36". **4.** Fine scrimshaw cane with whalebone shaft and L-shaped handle separated by rings of teak and whale ivory from the shaft. Ca. mid-Nineteenth Century. Length 36.50". **5.** Scrimshaw cane with burl hardwood shaft and slender whale's tooth mounted as a handle. Ca. mid-nineteenth century. Length 32.50".

6. Scrimshaw cane with heavy wooden shaft, whalebone tip and octagonal whale ivory knob. Ca. 2nd quarter nineteenth century. Length 34". **7.** Scrimshaw cane with shaft made from 72 graduated shark vertebrae, with a cow's horn mounted as a handle. Ca. early to mid-nineteenth century. Length 35". **8.** Scrimshaw cane with shaft made from 61 graduated shark's vertebrae and fitted with a horn handle. Ca. mid-nineteenth century. Length 35". **9.** Small cane made entirely from rings of cattle horn, with an L-shaped handle. Ca. mid-nineteenth century. Length 33.50". **10.** Heavy mahogany cane with walrus ivory button-shaped end engraved with old English-style letter "B." Ca. 3rd quarter nineteenth century. Length 35.75".

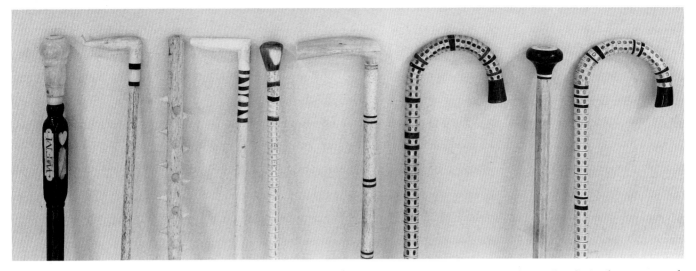

Left to right: **1.** Very rare scrimshaw cane with turned whale ivory knob, nicely shaped wooden shaft containing three mother-of-pearl inlays and whale ivory inlay with the initials "WFM" carved through the mother-of-pearl inlay beneath. Ca. 2nd quarter nineteenth century. Length 32.50". **2.** Small scrimshaw cane with whale ivory handle in the form of a female leg, with a tapered whalebone shaft. Ca. mid-nineteenth century. Length 33". **3.** Unusual scrimshaw cane with nicely turned whalebone shaft, fitted with 20 whalebone or ivory "teeth" for use in self defense. A highly unusual piece of scrimshaw. Ca. mid-nineteenth century. Length 36.88". **4.** Scrimshaw cane with L-shaped whale ivory handle engraved with the name "H.E. Frick" and with alternating wood and whale ivory inlays between the handle and the whalebone shaft. Ca. mid-nineteenth century. Length 34.50". **5.** Scrimshaw cane made from shark vertebrae featuring horn knob and rings. Ca. mid-nineteenth century. Length 35.38".

6. Scrimshaw cane with L-shaped walrus ivory handle and 6-piece whalebone shaft with baleen and bone ring separators. Ca. early to mid-nineteenth century. Length 33.25". **7.** Scrimshaw cane made of shark vertebrae and horn rings with curved handle terminating in a piece of horn. Ca. mid-nineteenth century. Length 36". **8.** Early scrimshaw cane with whalebone shaft, octagonal shaped at the top, turned wooden knob with whale ivory inlay and an 1857 dime set into the ivory. Ca. 3rd quarter nineteenth century. Length 32.50". **9.** Scrimshaw shark vertebrae cane with regularly spaced horn or baleen rings and curved handle with horn tip. Ca. mid-nineteenth century. Length 33.75".

A cased bone prisoner-of-war game set together with a polychromed bone panel of a female figure holding a trident, presumably representing Britannia. Ca. early nineteenth century. Length 12.50"; width 8.25"; height 9.13".

Opposite page
An extremely rare prisoner-of-war sculptured bone and wood guillotine. An elaborate and imaginative piece depicting a guillotine on wheels in the form of a two story structure mounted with 26 cannons and showing 27 uniformed figures, 26 of whom hold swords with the 27th operating the guillotine. A 28th figure lies prone on the top deck, and has a removable head. Ca. early nineteenth century. Height 31"; width 10.25"; length 22.50".

Left: Prisoner-of-war straw-work marquetry box featuring four corner compartments and two glass topped center pieces, with an open tray of colored geometric straw work design. Ca. early nineteenth century. Length 16"; width 10". *Right:* Prisoner-of-war straw-work game set with checkerboard top, and two hinged side compartments, each divided into two sections containing game pieces. Ca. early nineteenth century. Length 13.50"; width 9".

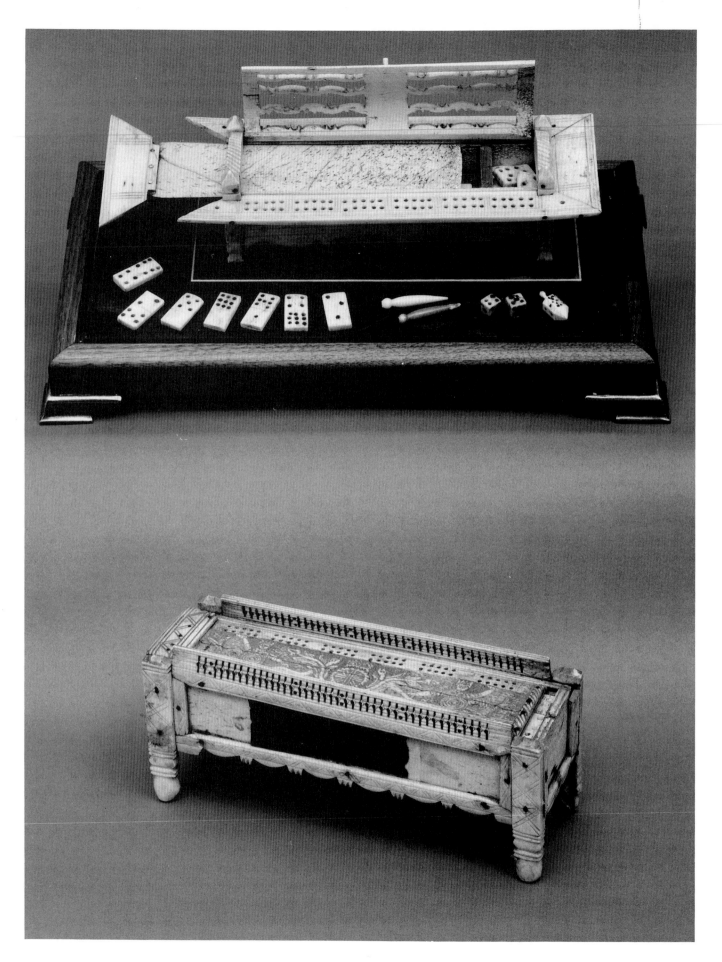

Rare prisoner-of-war miniature whalebone and whale ivory carved fort. French or British, ca. late eighteenth century. Width 12"; depth 9"; height 11.5".

Opposite page

Top: Cased prisoner-of-war bone game box with domed open-carved top, sliding lid and game pieces, including dominoes, cribbage, dice and a top. Ca. early nineteenth century. Length 13"; width 7"; height 5.50". ***Bottom:*** Prisoner-of-war game box filled with bone dominoes. Relief carved sliding lid replete with mermaids and sea serpents. A small engraving affixed to one side. Ca. early nineteenth century. Length 7.38".

Unusual prisoner-of-war crucifixion scene with Christ viewed on the cross and two polychromed mourning figures standing beneath the cross. Note the dice at the foot of the cross, the ladder and spear flanking the Christ figure, and the urns and tongs on top of the cross. All the figures are bone, while the glass-fronted case is straw-work. Ca. early nineteenth century. Width 8"; depth 4.88"; Height 10.38".

Top, left to right: **1.** Prisoner-of-war game casket, complete with dominoes and dice. Features paper panels colorfully painted with touches of gilt visible in the bone. Ca. early nineteenth century. Length 6". **2.** Rare prisoner-of-war bone loom lady mounted in a clear blown glass jar with top-mounted crank which activates the piece. Ca. early nineteenth century. Overall height 8". **3.** Small prisoner-of-war work figure of a loom lady. Ca. early nineteenth century. Height 3.75". **4.** Prisoner-of-war bone game box containing dominoes. Exterior is faced with bone carvings including a cribbage board, as well as ten glass covered watercolor renderings of people and buildings. Ca. early nineteenth century. Length 6".

Bottom, left to right: **1.** Very fine bone prisoner-of-war game box with a beautifully carved hunting scene on the cover and reticulated panels on all four sides. Ca. early nineteenth century. Length 8.13"; width 6.25"; height 2.13". **2.** Prisoner-of-war bone faced jewel box. Ca. early nineteenth century. Length 9"; width 6.25"; height 5". **3.** Prisoner-of-war bone needle case with inset decorated glass panels. Ca. early nineteenth century. Length 3.38". **4.** Prisoner-of-war bone set of serving tongs. Affixed to the tongs is a very old note revealing that the tongs were made by a French prisoner while imprisoned at Portchester Castle. Ca. early nineteenth century. Length 11.50".

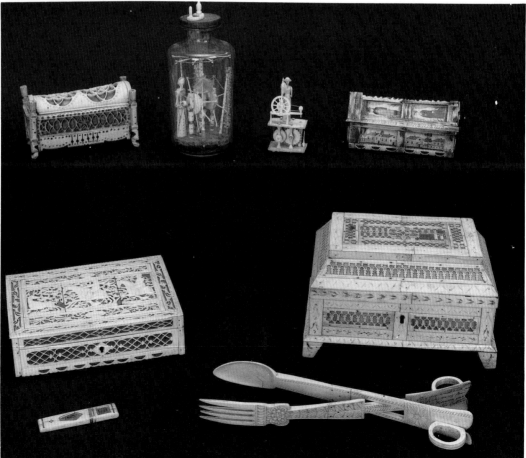

Below:

Top, left to right: A most unusual and beautiful prisoner-of-war bone sculpture of a church with glass windows and a figure of Christ on the cross mounted on a walnut base. Ca. very early nineteenth century. Length 7.13"; width 4.13"; height 4.88". **2.** Prisoner-of-war watch holder in the form of a secretary with a single drawer at the bottom. Ca. early nineteenth century. Height 10.50"; width 6.25"; depth 3.50". **3.** Scrimshaw toy in the form of a woman working at a loom. Ca. early nineteenth century. Height 5.50". **4.** Fully articulated prisoner-of-war bone sculpture of a nude woman mounted on a circular wooden base. Ca. early nineteenth century. Height 3.25".

Center: **1.** Decorative prisoner-of-war piece in the form of nine small watercolor paintings of figures and buildings mounted under glass on a triangular piece of wood with decorative bone overlay. Ca. early nineteenth century. Length 8.50". **2.** Prisoner-of-war bone cribbage board made in table form. Ca. early nineteenth century. Length 9.25".

Bottom: **1.** Decorative box carved in the form of a vessel with hinged compartments; figures of armored knights on one lid, and a bow ornament in the form of a bearded king with crown on the other lid. Continental, ca. early nineteenth century. Length 5.50". **2.** Small wooden box in the form of a clenched hand; thumb forms a hinged lid. Continental, probably English, ca. late Eighteenth or early nineteenth century. Length 3.75".

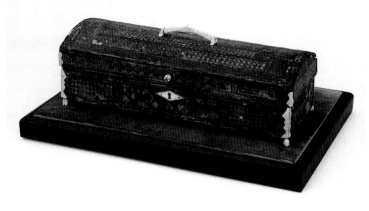

French prisoner-of-war domed straw work box with bone handles and knobs, a bone escutcheon, and a mirrored interior. Ca. early nineteenth century. Length 20"; width 13"; height 13".

Miscellaneous

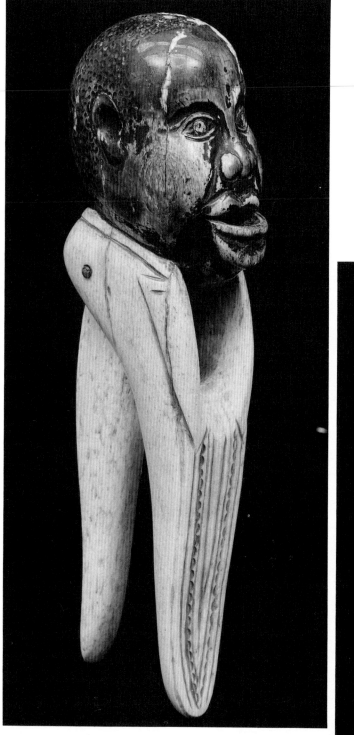

Very rare and unusual scrimshaw nutcracker in the form of a black man in a shirt and jacket. Jaw opens to hold and crack a nut. American, 3rd quarter nineteenth century. Length 6.75".

Miniature scrimshaw ladder-back rocking chair with arms. An eighteenth century style chair made entirely of whalebone with seat carved to represent a rush seat. Ca. early twentieth century. Height 7.50".

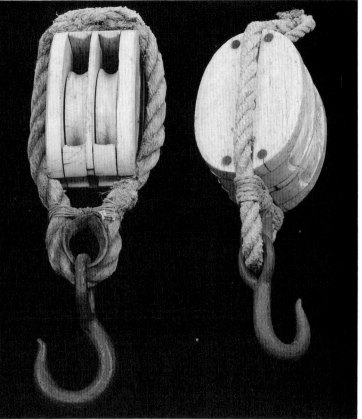

Pair of very rare large whalebone working ship's double blocks, rope mounted and fitted with iron hooks. Ca. early to mid-nineteenth century. Length, blocks only, 6".

Extremely rare scrimshaw toy made of whale ivory and wood, with polychromed decoration representing a minstrel man doing a balancing act. Ca. mid-nineteenth century. Height 7.75".

Pair of rare working whalebone double blocks, with the original ropes and iron mountings. Ca. early to mid-nineteenth century. Height, block only, 3.25".

Left: Whalebone spatula, early to mid-nineteenth century. Length 13.50". *Center:* Whalebone belaying pin, finely turned and scribed with three lines on the handle. Ca. mid-nineteenth century. Length 14.50". *Right:* Whalebone measure, ca. nineteenth century. Length 10.88".

Top left: Coffin shaped log book stamp , engraved "BARK/ELLA/1841." Made of whale ivory in the form of a whale's tail with coffin stamp. Faintly engraved with a sperm whale on the reverse. Length 2". *Bottom left:* Straight razor with engraved bone or ivory handle; a fine example of erotic scrimshaw. Engraved on one side of the handle is an elaborately gowned Victorian lady with the date 1850 above her and the name "Joshua" beneath her. On the opposite side, is a reverse view of the lady wearing only her boots, corset and bonnet, with the word "Liberty" divided into syllables above and below her. Length 6 .13". *Top center:* Rare carved whale ivory ring made in the form of a nude lady with back arched to form the ring; her feet are fitted into a shield inlaid with red wax. Ca. nineteenth century. *Center:* Scrimshaw ring carved from whale ivory with a sperm whale on top. Ca. nineteenth century. *Bottom center:* Carved whale ivory spelling game, globular with 25 facets, each incised and red wax inlaid with a letter of the alphabet. The letter "J" is absent. Ca. mid-nineteenth century. Diameter 1.50". *Right:* Pair of scrimshaw twisters, with two whalebone handles connected by a finely made stout line. These were used as handcuffs to control a prisoner. Ca. 3rd quarter nineteenth century. Length 11.25".

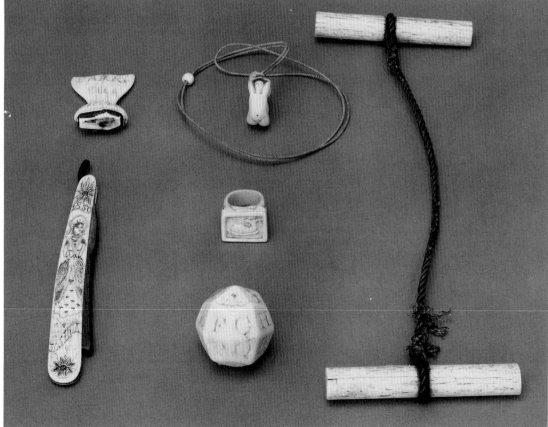

Very rare painting on panbone, depicting a whaling scene, and identified as "Whale's jawbone flattened out and painted by Capt. Peck on His Sea Voyage." The picture has a painted border of scrolled green leaves and red and yellow flowers. Ca. early to mid-nineteenth century. Height 11"; length 19.75".

Fine scrimshaw panel made of panbone; shaped at the sides and the top, and engraved with a large whaling scene. Signed at the top "W.B.L./November/1851." Also engraved with foliage, cornucopia, and at the upper corners with female angels. Ca. mid-nineteenth century. Height 7.50"; Length 12".

Extremely rare sculptured walrus ivory badge of rank, known to the Hawaiians as "Lei Niho Palaoa," and second in rarity only to feathered cloaks and capes. This piece is made in the form of a hook and is mounted on a heavy necklace of braided human hair. Such pieces were only worn by royalty, and the fact that this example is made of walrus ivory indicates a direct connection with whalers. Ca. nineteenth century.

Top: Rare scrimshaw needle case in the form of a rolling pin with turned and hollowed wood case for sailmaker's needles, with turned whalebone handles. Ca. 3rd quarter nineteenth century. Length 10". *Center:* Scrimshaw rolling pin with dark wood roller and nicely turned whale ivory ends. Ca. mid-nineteenth century. Length 16". *Bottom:* A similar scrimshaw rolling pin with dark wood roller and well turned whale ivory ends. Ca. mid-nineteenth century. Length 14.88".

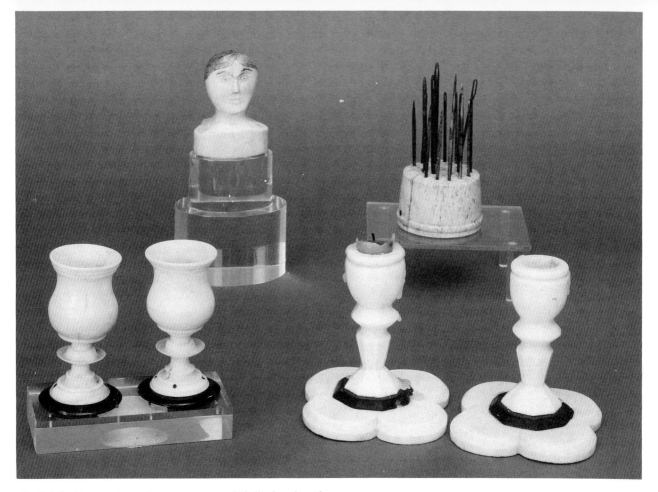

Back left: Rare early walrus ivory carved doll's head with engraved hair, eyebrows and eyes, carved facial features. American, ca. early to mid-nineteenth century. Height (head only) 2.75". *Back right:* Scrimshaw sail maker's whalebone needle holder, shown with original needles. Ca. mid-to late nineteenth century. Height 1.50". *Bottom left:* Pair of turned whale ivory salt cellars mounted on tortoiseshell bases. Unusual and delicate turnings. Ca. mid-nineteenth century. Height (cellars only) 3.25". *Bottom right:* Pair of whalebone and ebony candlesticks, lily pad bases. Height 3.88".

Ivory inlaid lift-top chest, with late engraving indicating that the box contained "The Mortal Remains of Capt. T. Wortham." Presentation seaman's arms and two gulls on the cover, a whaling scene on the front panel, and another whaling scene on the back panel. Whaler's arms are on one end panel, while a compass rose is on the other. Overall length 21.25".

Exceptional scrimshaw sewing chest made of select mahogany
with elaborate and detailed inlays of horn, baleen, whale ivory,
whalebone, tropical woods, silver and abalone; truly a labor of
love and one of the most elaborate pieces of its kind. The chest
is fitted with a mirror inside the cover, five drawers on the exterior and six drawers and a hidden compartment on the interior.
Ca. 3rd quarter nineteenth century or earlier. Width 14.25"; depth
11"; overall height 13.25".

Rare scrimshaw coat rack with a large piece of panbone mounted on pine and fitted with three sperm whale teeth that serve as hangers. Ca. early to mid-nineteenth century. Length 23.88".

Top: Very unusual scrimshaw coat rack made of four sperm whale teeth mounted in panbone inset into a walnut mounting. Ca. mid-nineteenth century. Length 35.50". ***Bottom:*** Another beautifully done scrimshaw coat rack similar to the one above, but with only three teeth; the whalebone hangers provide an interesting additional feature. Ca. mid-nineteenth century. Length 29.50".

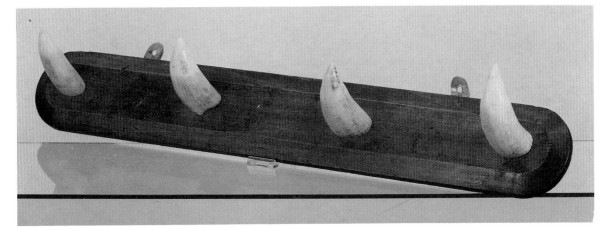

Scrimshaw coat rack with four large sperm whale teeth mounted on a long piece of nicely molded hardwood. Ca. early to mid-nineteenth century. Length 31.75".

Extremely rare heavy panbone holder for log book stamps. Ca. mid-nineteenth century. Height 6".

Fine scrimshaw tiered sewing stand, with provision for 12 spools of thread on revolving tiers; includes the original pincushion. Ca. early to mid-nineteenth century. Height 8.50".

Exceptional scrimshaw powder horn engraved in a band around the bottom with an American ship and two Mediterranean-type vessels encircling the horn. At the bottom, the following: "James Waterhouse of Bath 1805." A very early piece of scrimshaw that predates the Susan's teeth by over 20 years. Length 13".

Top, left to right: **1.** Delicate scrimshaw jagging wheel with turned handle and three-tined fork. Ca. mid-nineteenth century. Length 7.63". **2.** Small early scrimshaw jagging wheel, possibly Nantucket. Ca. first half nineteenth century. Length 6.38". **3.** Early scrimshaw jagging wheel made entirely of whale ivory. Three-tined fork with bird-shaped wheel arms with small hearts on either side. Ca. first half nineteenth century. Length 6.25".

Upper center, top to bottom: **1. & 2.** Two unusual scrimshaw spoons, each with a flattened diamond point carving on handle and a coconut shell bowl. One spoon is oval, the other round; both handles are made from several pieces of whale ivory. Ca. early nineteenth century. Lengths 8.75" and 10". **3.** Fine whalebone fid. Ca. early nineteenth century. Length 12.38". **4.** Early bodkin or small fid with three rings of dark wood separating the end from the point. The broad end is carved in the form of a clenched hand complete with cuff and buttons. Ca. early nineteenth century. Length 4.50".

Lower center, left to right: **1.** Lovely heavy facet cut whalebone seam rubber. Ca. early to mid-nineteenth century. Length 6". **2.** Simple whalebone seam rubber. Ca. early to mid-nineteenth century. Length 6". **3.** Small whalebone seam rubber, carved in an unusual style. Ca. mid-nineteenth century. Length 4.50". **4.** Small primitive whalebone seam rubber. Ca. early nineteenth century. Length 4.13". **5.** Sturdy whalebone seam rubber. Ca. early to mid-nineteenth century. Length 3.25". **6. & 7.** Two whalebone clothespins. Ca. mid-nineteenth century. Lengths 5.50" and 5.38".

Bottom: Two pieces of bone flatware. A non-matching fork and spoon with incised design on each. Ca. nineteenth century. Lengths (fork) 5.75", (spoon) 5".

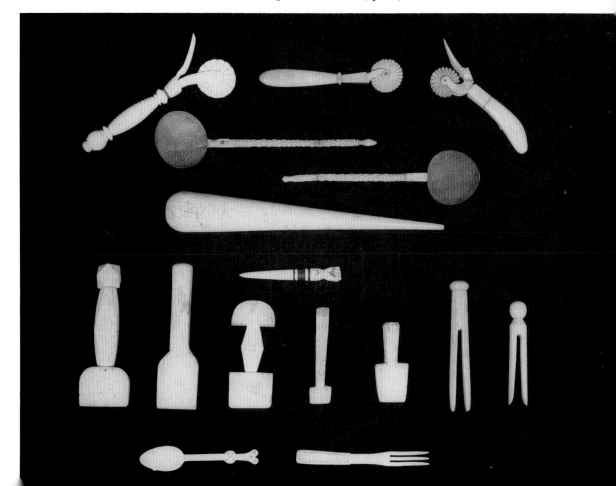

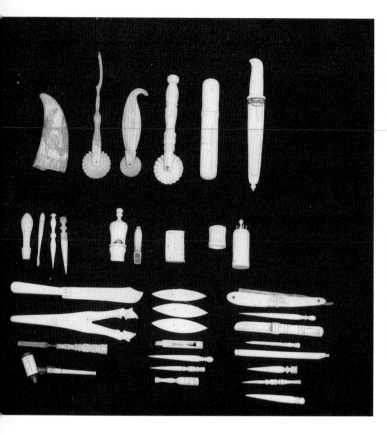

Top, left to right: **1.** Small scrimshaw whale's tooth engraved on one side with a seventeenth century dancing couple, and on the opposite side a pair of lovers with an exotic bird above them. Ca. 2nd quarter nineteenth century. Length 4.75".
2. Of simple design, an early scrimshaw jagging wheel with a graceful two-tined fork; possibly Nantucket origin. Ca. very early nineteenth century. Length 7". **3.** Small whale ivory jagging wheel terminating in a hook, probably for hanging. Ca. early nineteenth century. Length 5". **4.** Nantucket type jagging wheel with turned handle. Ca. early nineteenth century. Length 6.13". **5.** Animal bone needle case with scrimshaw engraving of a whaling scene, two whales, a harpoon, a spade, and an anchor. case has a screw top. Ca. nineteenth century. Length 5.63".
6. Small walrus ivory dagger with matching sheath. Ca. last half nineteenth century. Length 7.50".
Center, left to right: **1.-4.** Lot of two scrimshaw bodkins together with an unfinished handle and a snuff spoon. Ca. mid-nineteenth century. **5.-6.** Two animal bone turned whistles. Ca. nineteenth century. **7.-9.** Tiny whalebone box in the form of a book. With it is a bone dentist's kit, with removable handle and four metal picks in a bone screw top holder. Ca. nineteenth century.

Bottom: An array of 19 assorted bone and ivory items including glove tongs, letter opener, bodkins, scoop, razor, needle case, sewing knife and numerous other miscellaneous related items. All ca. nineteenth century.

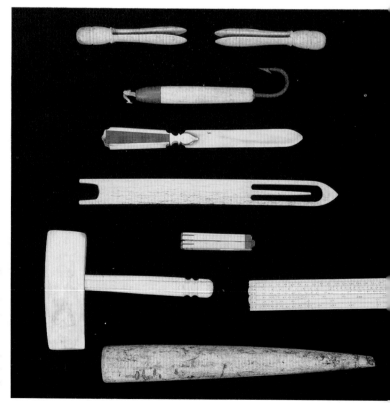

Top to bottom: **1.** A pair of turned whalebone clothespins. Ca. early to mid-nineteenth century. **2.** Rare fishing lure made of whalebone and lead. Ca. last half nineteenth century. Length 7". **3.** Scrimshaw letter opener made of whale ivory with inset wood handle. Ca. mid-nineteenth century. Length 9". **4.** Shuttle made from whalebone. Ca. mid-nineteenth century. Length 11". **5.** Small folding ivory 12" ruler. Ca. nineteenth century. **6.** Scrimshaw mallet made entirely of walrus ivory. Ca. late nineteenth century. Length 7.13". **7.** Ivory navigator's rule. Ca. nineteenth century. Length 6". **8.** Heavy whalebone fid. Ca. mid-nineteenth century. Length 11.50".

Top: Whalebone ditty box, wood bottom, tortoiseshell lid with whalebone sides. Ca. early to mid-nineteenth century. Length 8.88"; width 6.50"; height 3". *Bottom:* Bone Prisoner-of-War jewel box fashioned at the Norman Cross Depot for Napoleonic prisoners of war, ca. 1807. This box was made by Jean De La Rez, who was captured from a French Battleship of the line in 1806. On the cover is a finely carved hunting scene. Length 8.38"; width 7"; height 2.75".

Quite rare small whalebone ditty box from Nantucket. Carved on the top of the lid with a large, three story house with circular drive and trees, and on the sides with another house, ship, eagle with flag, heart and trees. Intricate demi-lune border designs.

The box features seven delicate fingers and the lid three delicate fingers. Ca. 2nd quarter nineteenth century. Length 4.25"; height 1.88".

Unique scrimshaw dinner gong consisting of a gong mounted on a brace supported by a pair of scrimshaw whale's teeth. The whale's teeth are mounted in silver on an ebonized wooden stand complete with striker and holder for the gong. The teeth are engraved with dividers and an octant with ship portraits and record events relating to the American whaleships the

"Horatio," the "Lancer," and the "James Arnold." Apparently all three ships arrived at Taloahuano on March 19, 1885. One tooth is marked "Engraved by G. Brown Ship James Arnold." On the reverse of this tooth is a monument, while the other shows an urn of flowers. Ca. 1885. Length of teeth approximately 6".

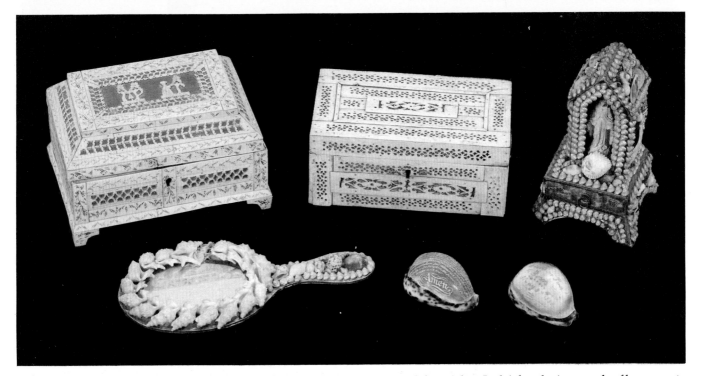

Back, left to right: **1.** Prisoner-of-war bone jewelry box with elaborate cut-out panels, many of which are backed by foil. Ca. early nineteenth century. Length 8.75". **2.** Bone prisoner-of-war card box with hinged lid and three compartments. Ca. early nineteenth century. Length 8.38". **3.** Small pasteboard shrine decorated with seashells. a chalk figure of the Virgin Mary is contained within. Ca. nineteenth century. Height 6.75".

Front, left to right **1.** Lady's hand mirror made of heavy pasteboard covered with pink foil and faced with sea shells. Ca. nineteenth century. Length 10.50". **2.-3.** Two sculptured cowrie shells, one carved with the Lord's Prayer, and the other reads "Gleason Pease Born May 8th 1880," with sculptured signature "BFM." Ca. nineteenth century.

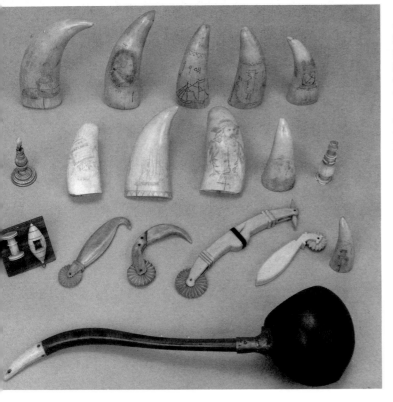

Top row, left to right: **1.** Large scrimshaw whale's tooth engraved with a pirate holding a cutlass and standing on a large rock. Ca. mid-nineteenth century. Length 6.75". **2.** Scrimshaw whale's tooth engraved with a portrait of George Washington. Ca. 3rd quarter nineteenth century. Length 5.75". **3.** Pair of scrimshaw whale's teeth engraved in pinpoint work with a schooner, building, initials, ghost, a man and the date "1904." Length 5". **4.** Very fine small scrimshaw whale's tooth engraved in color with a monument, anchor, flags, flowers, and a ship on one side; the opposite side features a grouping of various weapons and a ship. Ca. mid-nineteenth century. Length 4".

Second row, left to right: **1.** Early scrimshaw pickwick. Ca. early to mid-nineteenth century. Length 3.25". **2.** Scrimshaw whale's tooth engraved with "The Holy Bible" surrounded by light rays. Ca. 3rd quarter nineteenth century. Length 4.25". **3.** Scrimshaw whale's tooth engraved with a ship under sail. Ca. mid-nineteenth century. Length 5". **4.** Scrimshaw whale's tooth engraved with a half figure portrait of a bearded man entitled "California Joe." Ca. mid-nineteenth century. Length 5". **5.** Scrimshaw whale's tooth engraved with the portrait of a woman wearing a hat. Ca. last quarter nineteenth century. Length 4". **6.** Ivory perfume bottle. Ca. last half nineteenth century. Height 3".

Third row, left to right: **1.** Rare matching whale ivory shuttle and spool mounted on Anton block. Ca. mid-nineteenth century. **2.** Scrimshaw jagging wheel made entirely of whale ivory. Ca. early to mid-nineteenth century. Length 5". **3.** Scrimshaw jagging wheel made entirely of whale ivory. Ca. early to mid-nineteenth century. Length 4.25". **4.** Large scrimshaw jagging wheel made of whale ivory with one wood band. Ca. mid-nineteenth century. Length 8.25". **5.** Small scrimshaw jagging wheel made entirely of walrus ivory. Ca. mid-nineteenth century. Length 4.88". **6.** Small scrimshaw whale's tooth engraved with a man on one side and a rose on the opposite. Ca. mid-nineteenth century. Length 3".

Bottom: Scrimshaw dipper; a coconut shell bowl with curved wooden handle terminating in a small whale's tooth, with a pewter connector to the bowl. Ca. mid-nineteenth century. Length 17".

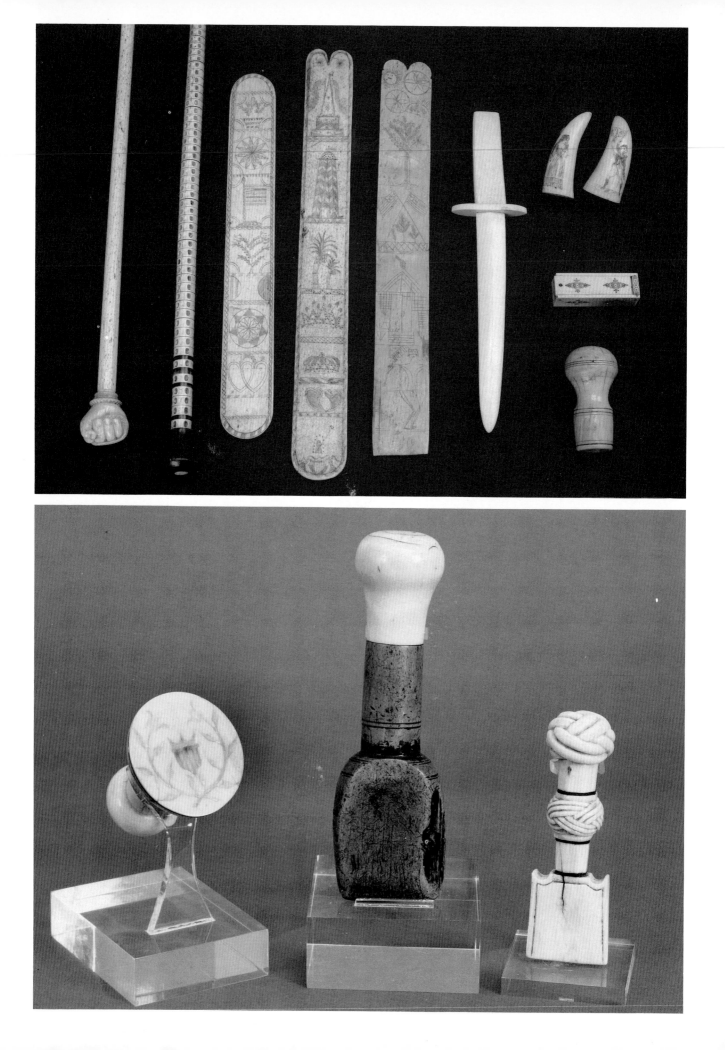

Top left: Rare, possibly unique pie crimper made of whale ivory and wood. The piece consists of a sturdy three-tined fork below which is a fixed half wheel-shaped crimper. Ca. early to mid-nineteenth century. Length 6.13". *Top center:* Pair of fine scrimshaw whale's teeth, one side engraved with the figure of a ballerina, while the other shows the full-figure of a seated Liberty. Both are done in color. Ca. mid-nineteenth century. Length 3.88". *Top right:* Fine large scrimshaw whale's tooth engraved with a horse and rider being attacked by a lion. Ca. 2nd quarter nineteenth century. Length 6.88". *Bottom:* Extremely rare scrimshaw jagging wheel in the form of a unicorn. Ca. mid-nineteenth century. Length 8.25".

Opposite page, top:
Left to right: **1.** Scrimshaw cane with whalebone shaft and carved whale ivory knob in the form of a hand clutching a serpent. Ca. mid-nineteenth century. Length 23.50". **2.** Scrimshaw cane made of shark vertebrae and horn, with a wooden knob. Ca. mid-nineteenth century. Length 32.50". **3.** Scrimshaw corset busk. 12.50". **4.** Scrimshaw corset busk engraved with monuments, American flags, palm trees, crowns, and Liberty with the Liberty cap. Ca. mid-nineteenth century. Length 14.50". **5.** Scrimshaw corset busk engraved with American flags, a house, human figure, palm tree, sunbursts and rosettes. Ca. early to mid-nineteenth century. Length 13.25". **6.** Scrimshaw dagger made entirely from walrus ivory. Ca. last quarter nineteenth century. Length 10.75". **7.** Pair of small scrimshaw whale's teeth engraved with figures of two patriots of the French Revolution. Ca. mid-nineteenth century. Length 2.75". **8.** Bone domino set with complete set of miniature dominoes in a box scrimshawed in color with interlocking circles on all sides except the bottom. Ca. nineteenth century. Length 1.38". **9.** Scrimshaw cane head turned from a large whale's tooth. Ca. mid-nineteenth century. Height 3.13".

Opposite page, bottom:
Left: Very unique cookie or butter mold, with incised designs of the American flag shield within a wreath. Turned from two pieces of whale ivory. American c. 1860. *Center:* Large early seam rubber, made of hardwood, probably maple with turned whale ivory knob. American, ca. early to mid-nineteenth century. Length 7". *Right:* Rare scrimshaw seam rubber, with carved ropework decoration; made of whale ivory with three baleen separators. Ca. mid-nineteenth century. Length 4.88".

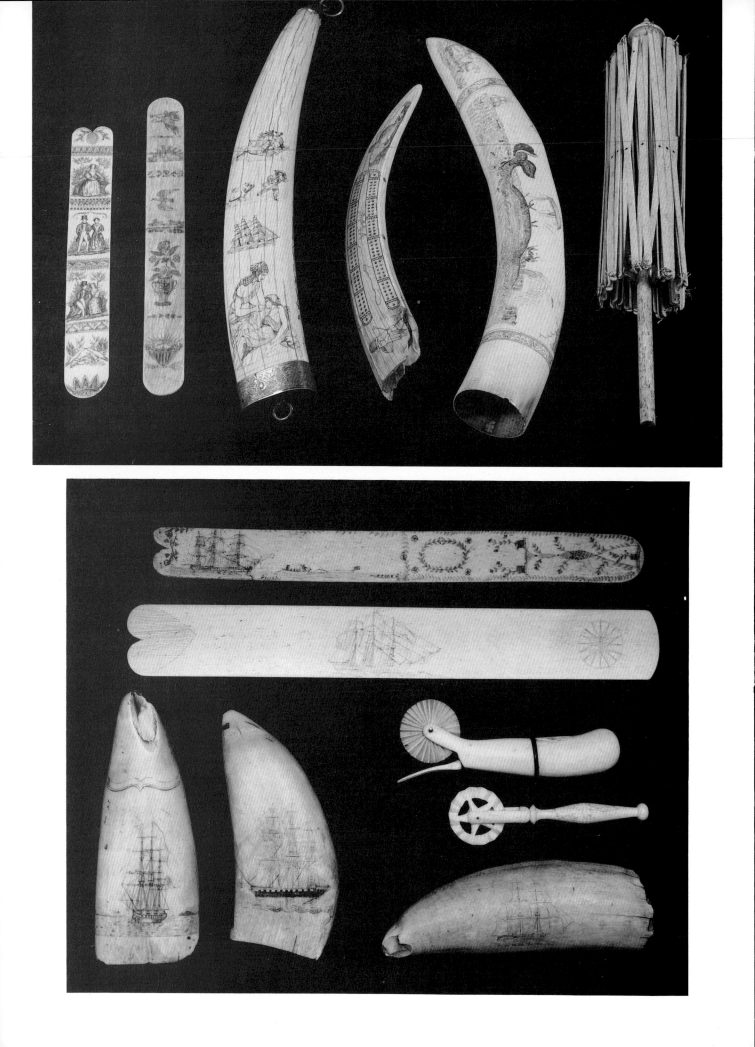

Opposite page, top:

Left to right: **1.** An exceptional scrimshaw corset busk engraved with panel portraits of various people, including, from top to bottom, an attractive young woman in a garden; a young couple in full figure; another youthful couple seated in a garden, and a pair of lovebirds. Ca. 2nd quarter nineteenth century. Length 12.50". **2.** A very lovely scrimshaw corset busk engraved in color with, from top to bottom; the angel Gabriel, a sunset, a pigeon carrying a message, an urn of flowers, and the U.S. emblem flanked by two cornucopia. Ca. 2nd quarter nineteenth century. Length 14". **3.** Outstanding scrimshaw walrus tusk, mounted with engraved silver at the base and the tip. Engraved on one side, from top to bottom, with a panther chasing a stag, boy running from a pig, an American sailing ship, and a woman offering water to a reclining figure. On the opposite side, from top to bottom, are a cherub with wine, a semi-nude figure with grapes, a large figure of a nude lady, and a woman sheltering a child. On the narrow portion of one side is an engraving of different flowers and two Dickens-like characters; on the opposite narrow portion is a man smoking a pipe, and a floral branch. Ca. 1860. Length 20.50". **4.** Eskimo scrimshaw walrus tusk cribbage board, engraved on both sides with hunting scenes. Ca. late nineteenth century. **5.** Elephant tusk with late engraving of a whaling scene, ships, verses, and other small engravings, with some use of color. Ca. twentieth century engraving on a very old tusk. Length 19". **6.** Scrimshaw swift, Ca. mid-nineteenth century. Length 19.50".

Above:
Very rare scrimshaw "Poor Box" made of island wood and faced with whalebone and baleen in the form of a church. Fitted with a sliding cover. Ca. 2nd quarter nineteenth century. Length 6.75"; height 7"; width 3.13".

Opposite page, bottom:

Top: Lovely old scrimshaw corset busk made of panbone and engraved with a well executed whaling scene. Ca. 2nd quarter nineteenth century. Length 13.50". *Center:* Fine scrimshaw corset busk made of panbone and engraved on both sides with hearts and compass roses, and in the center of one side with an American ship. Ca. mid-nineteenth century. Length 14.50".

Bottom, left to right: **1.** Very fine scrimshaw whale's tooth engraved with a British ship at anchor. Ca. 2nd quarter nineteenth century. Length 7". **2.** Excellent scrimshaw whale's tooth engraved on one side with an American ship under sail. Ca. 2nd quarter nineteenth century. Length 6". **3.** Scrimshaw jagging wheel with 2-tined fork made entirely of whale ivory with one baleen divider. Ca. early nineteenth century. Length 6.25". **4.** Simple Nantucket-style jagging wheel made of whalebone. Ca. 3rd quarter nineteenth century. Length 5.75". **5.** Scrimshaw whale's tooth engraved on one side with a whaleship under sail. Ca. mid-nineteenth century. Length 7.38".

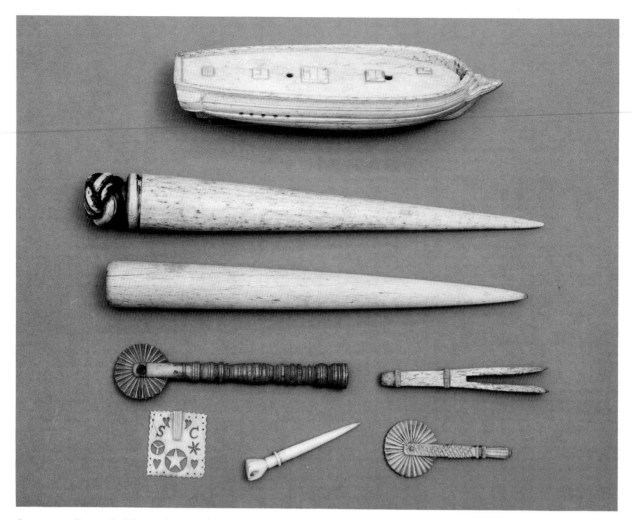

Top to bottom: **1.** Rare whalebone ship model with removable deck and provision for two masts. Ca. mid-nineteenth century. Length 9.38". **2.** Rare scrimshaw fid made from one piece of whalebone with carved and polychromed Turk's head knot. Ca. early nineteenth century. Length 13.50". **3.** Plain whalebone fid, weathered from much exposure. Ca. early nineteenth century. Length 12". **4.** Early turned Nantucket scrimshaw jagging wheel. Ca. late eighteenth or early nineteenth century. Length 6.50". **5.** Nicely carved and very weathered whalebone clothespin. Ca. mid-nineteenth century. Length 4.75". **6.** Delicate whale ivory open carved needle holder, decorated with hearts, stars, rosettes, and the initials "SC." Ca. early to mid-nineteenth century. Height 1.75"; width 1.50". **7.** Rare whale ivory bodkin carved with a hand holding a baton. Ca. mid-nineteenth century. Length 3.50". **8.** Early Nantucket scrimshaw whalebone jagging wheel, missing half of the handle. Late Eighteenth Century. Length 3.63".

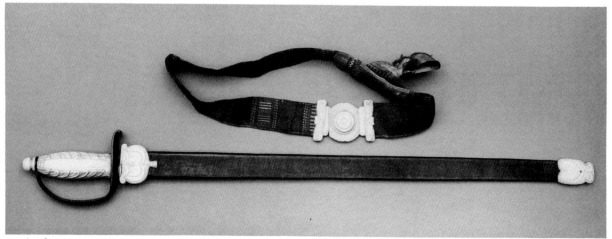

Unique scrimshaw sword fitted with whale ivory hilt with raised leaf patterns carved from a large bull whale's tooth, and equipped with a heavy copper guard. The original leather scabbard is fitted with throat and tip mounts of single pieces of whale ivory carved with raised patterns and secured to the leather with a single copper pin for each mount. Complete with the original belt made of hand-stitched native cloth, with a two-piece relief carved whale ivory belt buckle. This style of buckle was very popular with the military from the 1830s through the 1870s. Ca. early to mid-nineteenth century. Overall length 36".

Exceptional large piece of scrimshawed baleen with a panoramic engraving of what is believed to be Long Island Sound. Scene shows land on both sides of the Sound with many details of towns lining the shores, and thirteen American flag vessels in view. The narrow end of the piece, which represents the New York end of the Sound, terminates in a whale's tail followed by a large three-story structure and an engraving of a sperm whale. Superb quality engraving dating ca. 1840-1860. Length 71.50"; width 9" at broadest point.

Continued view of above.

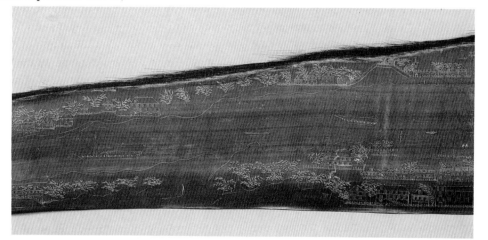

Continued view of above

End view of above.

Top to bottom, left to right **1.** Very unusual dipper featuring a coconut shell bowl with pewter inlay of an eagle perched on a globe and the following: "Remember the Giver May 14, 1850." An inlaid pewter heart connects to the rope carved mahogany handle, which in turn terminates in a carved whale ivory clenched fist holding a ring of whale ivory to be used as a hanger. Ca. mid-nineteenth century. Length 15". **2.** Very large working double block made entirely of whalebone fastened with five heavy copper rivets. Ca. early nineteenth century. Length 4.50". **3.** Rare scrimshaw block plane consisting of whalebone except for the blade. Ca. early to mid-nineteenth century. Length 5". **4.**

Very early Nantucket-style jagging wheel with single mother-of-pearl diamond-shaped inlay. Ca. first quarter nineteenth century. Length 5.63". **5.** Simple jagging wheel with whalebone handle and whale ivory wheel. Ca. mid-nineteenth century. Length 6". **6.** Elaborate whalebone seam rubber engraved with the initials "SS." Ca. 2nd quarter nineteenth century. Length 5.25". **7.** Early scrimshaw whalebone carpenter's square with the initials "JF." Ca. early to mid-nineteenth century. Length 4.75". **8.** Large scrimshaw panel with engraving of a whaleship; made as a decorative hanging. Ca. 2nd quarter nineteenth century. Width 13.25"; Height 5.50".

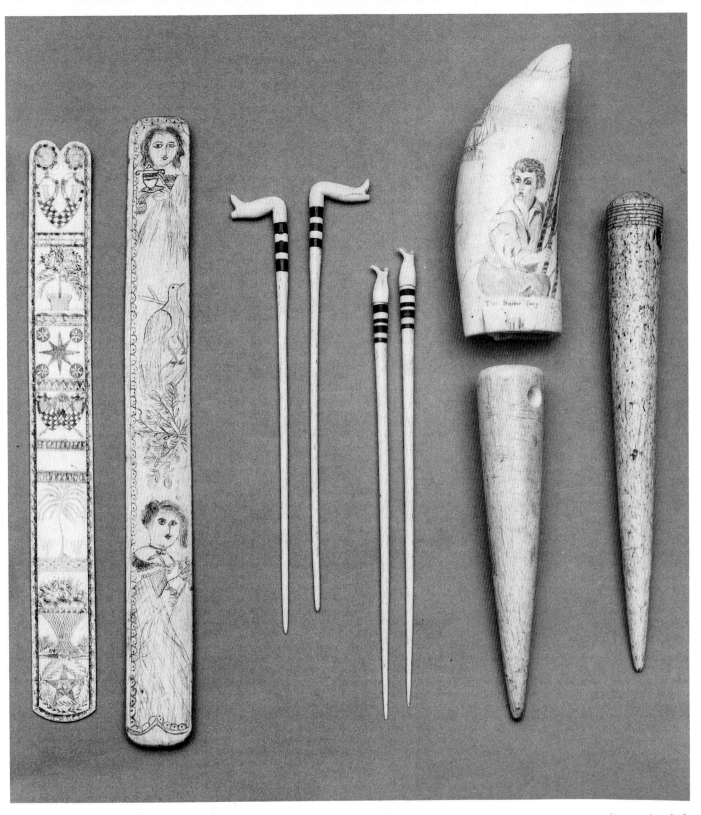

Left to right: **1.** Fine scrimshaw corset busk engraved in exceptional detail with a star, heart, palm tree, potted plants and geometric designs. Ca. 2nd quarter nineteenth century. Length 13.38". **2.** Very early scrimshaw corset busk engraved with wonderful primitive portraits of two women and a bird perched in a tree; on the back, in script, the initials "M. McB." Ca. 2nd quarter nineteenth century. Length 14.50". **3.** Pair of rare scrimshaw whalebone knitting needles with whale ivory booted legs at the tip, separated from the needles by three inlays of wood and two inlays of whale ivory. Ca. mid-nineteenth century. Length 10.25".

4. Pair of scrimshaw whalebone knitting needles with whale ivory feet at the ends, separated from the needles by four rings of shell and three rings of whale ivory. Ca. mid-nineteenth century. Length 10.50". **5.** Fine scrimshaw whale's tooth engraved on one side with a portrait of "The Sailor Boy," on one edge with a ship and on the back side with a larger representation of a ship. Ca. mid-nineteenth century. Length 6.50". **6.** Whalebone fid, a simple heavy functional piece. Ca. mid-nineteenth century. Length 8". **7.** Very fine whalebone fid nicely scribed with seven lines around the top. Ca. mid-nineteenth century.

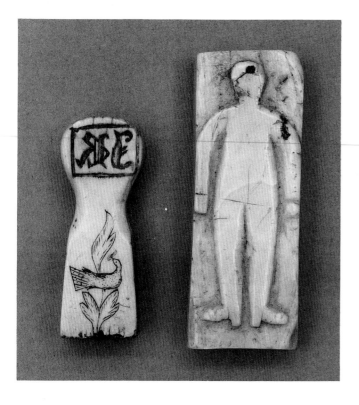

Left: Very rare whale ivory log book stamp, carved with English-style initials at the top and engraved on all sides with a ship, King Neptune, an anchor and a bird. Such stamps in a log book signify a gam. Ca. mid-nineteenth century. Length 1.75".
Right: Whale ivory carving with a raised full-bodied figure of a man. Purpose unknown, possibly intended as a stamp, but never used. Ca. mid-nineteenth Century. Length 2.50".

Top left: Fine scrimshaw thread holder for 6 or 9 spools of thread. Made of a turned wood center post joining a circular top and base and supported by three turned whalebone posts with three whalebone pins for holding the spools. Three egg-shaped feet. Ca. mid-nineteenth century. Height 5". *Top center:* Hourglass-style timer with three twist-carved whalebone supports, and finely turned wood base and top. Ca. early nineteenth century. Height 3.25". *Top right:* Scrimshaw cup with coconut shell bowl and lignum vitae lid and foot, joined by a turned whale ivory stem with walrus ivory finial. Ca. mid-nineteenth century. Length 6.38"; diameter 3.50".

Bottom left: Fine early coconut shell dipper with the name "John J. McLaren" in script. Finely carved leaves circle the lower edge, while around the top are a superb American coat of arms, eagle, banner, flags, shield, stars, etc. Ca. mid-nineteenth century. Length 5". *Bottom center:* Pair of unusual scrimshaw figures of a man and a woman. Carved bodies with whale ivory heads, arms, and the lady's legs. Ca. early nineteenth century. Height 6" and 5.50". *Bottom right:* Coconut shell with marine scene of three vessels and a fortification named "Pendennis castle." The ships are identified as the "Rose," "Alfred," and "Kite." A superb example of the sailor's skill in coconut shell art work. British, ca. 1825. Height 4".

Top, left to right: **1.** Fine scrimshaw whale ivory watch fob in the form of a book engraved and colored with Masonic symbols. Ca. early nineteenth century. **2.** Pair of scrimshaw napkin rings made of whale ivory; nicely turned with inlaid bands of red wax. Ca. mid-nineteenth century. **3.** Eskimo walrus ivory carving of a seal. Ca. nineteenth century. Length 5.50".

Bottom, left to right: **1.** Old walrus ivory scrimshaw pipe. Ca. nineteenth century. Length 4". **2.** Rare scrimshaw butter mold; a circular rosette-carved wooden mold with a large whale ivory handle. Ca. early to mid-nineteenth century. Height 5.13". **3.** Eskimo harpoon with steel tip and whale ivory head. Ca. nineteenth century.

Top ends: Pair of extremely rare scrimshaw pickwicks in the shape of miniature candlesticks, complete with candles. Picks were never mounted. The pieces are made of turned whale ivory with inlaid scribe lines of red, blue, yellow and green. Ca. mid-nineteenth century. Height 4.50". *Top center:* Very rare whale and walrus ivory jagging wheel with folding pinned fork. The four column open carved handle and the fork are made from walrus ivory, while the carved wheel held by a silver pin is of whale ivory. Ca. mid-nineteenth century. Length 9.88". *Bottom:* Extremely unusual whale ivory ladle. A very rare form in scrimshaw which had to involve the use of very large whale's teeth, particularly in forming the bowl of the ladle. The piece is made of three separate sections of whale ivory, with the handle fashioned in two parts and the bowl with its connecting arm made from a single piece of whale ivory. Superb workmanship! Ca. mid-nineteenth century. Length 12".

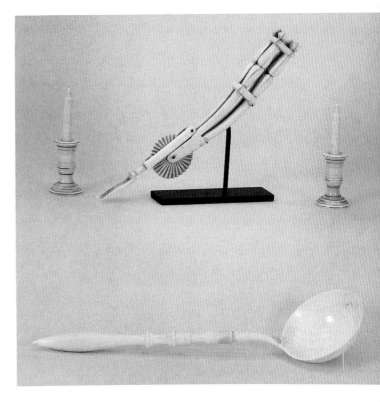

Top left: Superb scrimshaw mahogany rolling pin on stand; diamond inlays of whale ivory and baleen, turned whale ivory handles, and a cleverly constructed revolving roller. Ca. mid-nineteenth century. Length 22". *Top right:* Humorous scrimshaw scene of a chess game between a tortoise and a snail, each perched upon a toadstool. Mahogany base with inlaid and banded border, mounted on whale ivory feet, the players and toadstools also made of whale ivory. The elephant ivory chess table features rosewood and abalone squares with chess pieces of ivory and ebony. Ca. 3rd quarter Nineteenth century. Length 8.25".

Bottom left: Fine scrimshaw sewing box with simple whalebone finials, ivory knobs and inlays of whale ivory and abalone. Ca. mid-nineteenth century. Height 9". *Bottom right:* Unusual walnut scrimshaw watch holder in the form of a doorway with ivory foot scraper, door knob and knocker, and three ivory-tipped wooden finials. Ca. mid-nineteenth century. Height 14".

Top: Fine scrimshaw powder horn engraved with six different American sailing vessels. Ca. 3rd quarter nineteenth century. Length 14". *Center:* Early scrimshaw powder horn engraved with the initials "W.W.R." and over most of its surface with a horse, swan, deer feeding from a fruit tree, an Indian catching a large fish, an eagle and various other designs including the date of August 10th 1854. Ca. mid-nineteenth century. Length 12". *Bottom:* Very early scrimshaw powder horn with primitive engravings of various animals, abstract designs and the name "Peter Miller." Ca. late eighteenth century. Length 13".

Rare old scrimshaw bodkin stand of whale ivory engraved with a presentation on the bottom that reads "Presented to/Miss E.L. Brownell/By A Friend." The engraving includes two ships in a marine scene. Ca. mid-nineteenth century. Height 5.75".

Left: Early scrimshaw whale ivory jagging wheel with comma-shaped handle with baleen ring and heart inlays. American, ca. 2nd quarter nineteenth century. Length 5". *Center:* Early engraved scrimshaw whale's tooth. On one side the full-figure portrait of a young couple wearing highly detailed clothing; on the opposite, a full-rigged ship and rayed sun with a face above. Ca. 2nd quarter nineteenth century. *Right:* Early whalebone seam rubber, ca. early to mid-nineteenth century. Length 5.38".

Top left: Unique whalebone and whale ivory blotter holder with rounded bottom. Ca. 3rd quarter nineteenth century. Length 5.75". **Top right:** Lovely small lidded whalebone box. Ca. mid-nineteenth century. Length 3.88"; width 2.38"; height 2".

Bottom left: Rare example of a scrimshaw whale's tooth featuring deep relief carving of a reclining female figure with book. This pose is quite daring for the period, with most of the female's legs, shoulders and arms exposed. Ca. 3rd quarter nineteenth century. Length 6.50". **Bottom center:** Exceptional carved scrimshaw whale's tooth with a head and shoulders portrait of a woman done in a wonderful folksy-style. On the back are the words "Maitro Memo." This piece was discovered in Valpariso, Chile, and is most likely the work of a whaleman who landed there. Ca. mid-nineteenth century. Length 5". **Bottom right:** Fine carved scrimshaw whale's tooth with the deep relief carving of a nude. Ca. 3rd quarter nineteenth century. Length 4.50".

Very large, heavy conch-like shell with wide vertical section polished and engraved with a Dickens-like character of a man in top hat and tails walking by a fence while searching in his pocket. Diameter at widest point 8.50".

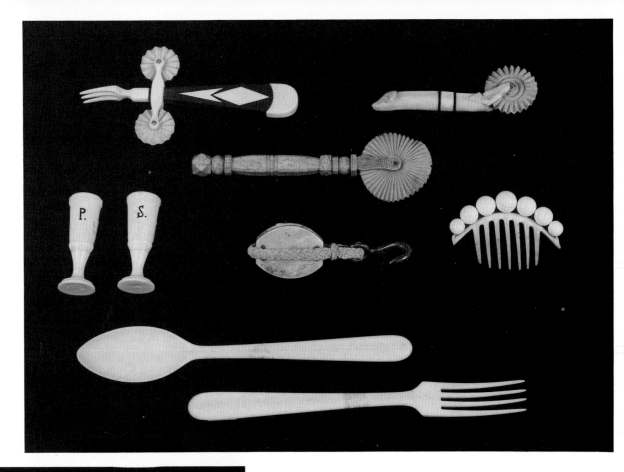

Top left: Rare and choice double scrimshaw whalebone jagging wheel with three-tined fork. The handle is made of exotic wood, with whale ivory inlays. Ca. mid-nineteenth century. Length 7.50". *Top right:* Early scrimshaw whale ivory jagging wheel with two baleen rings. Sturdy and unusual carved wheel, with the handle ending in a dog's head. Ca. 2nd quarter nineteenth century. Length 6". *Top center:* Extremely rare, large eighteenth century Nantucket-type jagging wheel with an unusually large 2.50" diameter wheel mounted on a typical Nantucket-style handle. Length 8.38".

Center, left to right: **1.** Rare and very unusual pair of scrimshaw whale ivory salt and pepper shakers. Made in two pieces that unscrew at the bottom for filling. Painted with a black "S" and "P." Ca. mid-nineteenth century. Height 3.19". **2.** Very fine small whale ivory working ship's block with single shiv, mounted in fine sailor's ropework, and fitted with a silver hook. Ca. 2nd quarter nineteenth century. Overall length 5.50". **3.** Interesting ivory hair comb, fitted with seven graduated balls. Ca. mid-nineteenth century. Width 3.88"; height 3.25". **4.** Rare elephant ivory serving fork and spoon, each made from a single piece of ivory. Ca. mid-nineteenth century. Length 11".

Top: Beautiful chambered nautilus shell with highly detailed, rococo-style carving. Length 6.75". *Bottom:* Chambered Nautilus shell in its natural state. Length 5.38".

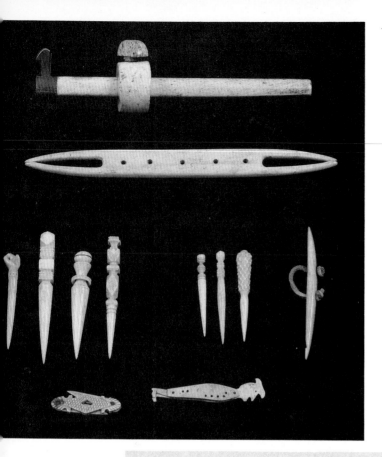

Top: Early scrimshaw whalebone scribe. American, ca. 2nd quarter nineteenth century. Length 9". ***Below top:*** Ivory loom shuttle made from some form of tusk. Ca. mid-nineteenth century. Length 10.19".

Center row, left to right: **1.** Scrimshaw bodkin with clenched fist and multi-sided cuff with tiny abalone inlays at one end. Ca. early to mid-nineteenth century. Length 3". **2.** Walrus ivory scrimshaw bodkin nicely carved and turned. Ca. mid-nineteenth century. Length 4.13". **3.** Fine scrimshaw whalebone bodkin with ring around the area between the handle and the point. Ca. mid-nineteenth century. Length 3.38". **4.** Elaborately carved scrimshaw bodkin with crosshatched stamp at the upper end for sealing a letter with wax. Ca. early to mid-nineteenth century. Length 3.88". **5.** Lot of three tiny bodkins, ca. mid-nineteenth century. **6.** Sailmaker's needle of bone fitted with a rawhide thumbpiece. Possibly Eskimo. Length 4.75".

Bottom: Two scrimshaw bone lady's sewing knives, one in the form of a walking sailor. Ca. nineteenth century.

Top: **1.** Elaborate scrimshaw corset busk engraved on one side with two ships and an eagle. American, ca. 2nd quarter nineteenth century. Length 13.50". **2.** Small scrimshaw whale ivory jagging wheel with an open carved handle in the shape of three hearts. Ca. 2nd quarter nineteenth century. Length 5.25". ***Bottom left:*** Prisoner-of-war casket shaped bone game box filled with dominoes. Ca. early nineteenth century. Length 6". ***Bottom right:*** Rare scrimshaw octagonal pincushion mounted on a walnut, ebony, whalebone and mother-of-pearl inlay base. Ca. mid-nineteenth century. Diameter 6.75" across the flats.

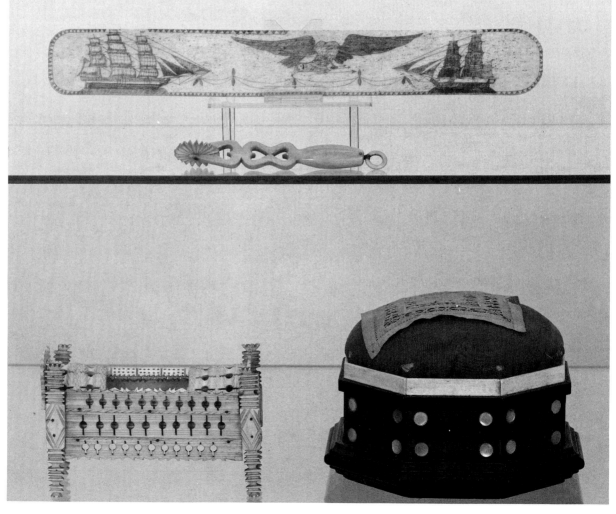

Top: Wonderful old oval scrimshaw basket of reticulated whale-bone with wood bottom and whalebone swing handle. Held together with hand-made coin silver rivets. Ca. early to mid-nineteenth century. Length 8.13". *Bottom:* Rare oval whalebone scrimshaw ditty box with mahogany bottom. The sides of the box are engraved in fine detail all around with a panoramic American port scene, a large urn containing an ivy plant, a large colonial house with four figures carrying a sedan chair, plus another house. The heavy whalebone cover is engraved with an elaborate street scene featuring a church and municipal buildings. Ca. mid-nineteenth century. Length 6.88".

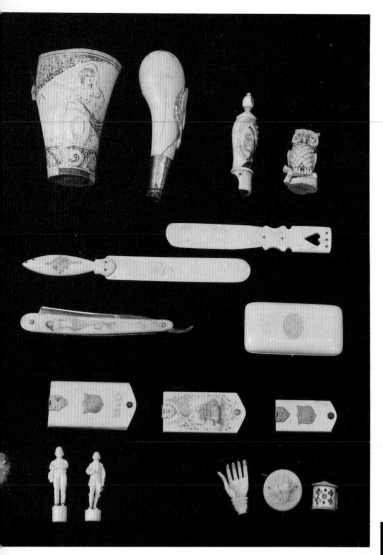

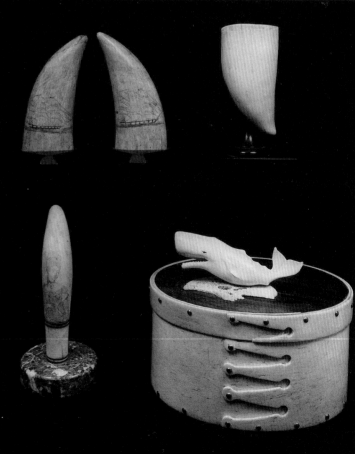

Top left: Pair of fine scrimshaw whale's teeth mounted on wooden bases, each engraved on all sides with different sailing ships. Ca. nineteenth century. Height 5.50". *Top right:* Very unique scrimshaw vase, made by mounting a large sperm whale tooth in an inverted position on a turned wooden stem with a rectangular wooden base. Ca. mid-nineteenth century. Length 6.50".

Bottom left: Slender scrimshaw whale's tooth mounted on a marble base. Tooth is engraved on one side with the portrait of an eighteenth century lady of high fashion. Lower part of the tooth is cut into sections and separated by baleen rings. Ca. early to mid-nineteenth century. Length 5.50". *Bottom right:* Late scrimshaw day box made of pan bone, with the top and bottom made of rosewood. On the top is a beautifully carved whalebone sperm whale. Length 7.25"; width 6"; height 5.50" overall.

Top row, left to right: **1.** Scrimshaw bone cup made from an animal's leg bone and engraved with a semi-nude female figure in an outdoor landscape. European, ca. early nineteenth century. Height 4.63". **2.** Heavy silver mounted ivory cane handle engraved in silver with the name "S.R. Harter/Union(?)/Iowa." The ivory knob is carved with foliate carving and a shield. Ca. nineteenth century. Length 5.50". **3.** Large whistle carved from animal bone; carved and colored American Indian head on the front. Ca. mid-nineteenth century. Length 3.88". **4.** Carved bone figure of an owl. Ca. nineteenth century. Height 2.50".

Second row: Two letter openers, one made of animal bone with an open heart carved handle; the other, in table knife form, is made of ivory and engraved and colored with flowers and flourishes. Both ca. nineteenth century. Length 8.38".

Third row: **1.** Razor with scrimshaw animal bone handle engraved with a mermaid on one side and the initials "ELD" on the opposite. Ca. nineteenth century. Length 6.25". **2.** Ivory sewing kit case with elaborate carved initials in the lid. Ca. nineteenth century. Length 3.50".

Fourth row: Three ivory weekly calendars, each marked with the days of the week. One has an engraving of a ship and eagle on the front. All pieces are ca. nineteenth century.

Bottom row, left to right: **1.** Pair of carved ivory figurines, one of a farmer, the other of William Shakespeare. Ca. nineteenth century. Height 2.50". **2.** Three odd carvings, including a bone carved hand from a back scratcher, a small circular floral carved bone brooch and a prisoner-of-war bone tape measured. All pieces are early to mid-nineteenth century.

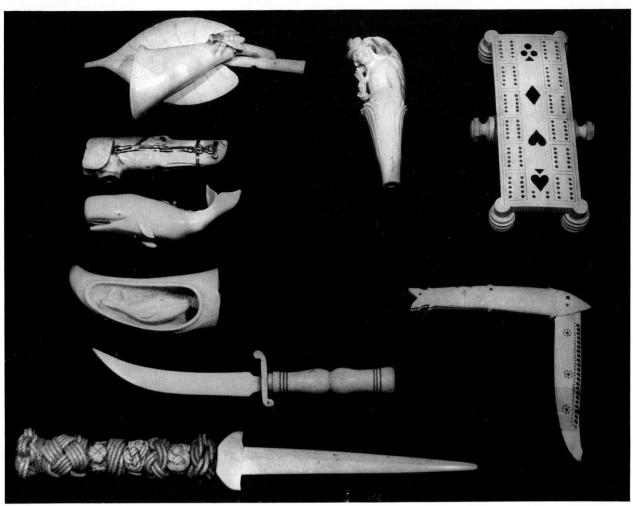

Left, top to bottom: **1.** Fine carved bone and whale ivory calla lily, with a carved bee resting on the petal. Ca. mid-nineteenth century. Length 7.50". **2.** Whippet's head whalebone cane handle, mounted with a silver muzzle. Ca. nineteenth century. Length 4.50". **3.** Late carved whalebone figure of a sperm whale. Length 4.75". **4.** Open-carved sperm whale tooth showing hump-back whale. Length 4.75". **5.** Dagger-shaped whalebone scrimshaw letter opener. Ca. nineteenth century. Length 8.75". **6.** Outstanding scrimshaw dagger with bone blade and elaborate sailor knot-work handle. Length 12.50".

Top center: Superb sculptured ivory cane handle in the shape of a Victorian woman enclosed in a flower. Length 5.25". *Top right:* Fine scrimshaw cribbage board, unusual design, inlaid with tortoiseshell heart, club, spade and diamond, with unique cylinder-like container to hold the pegs. Length 7". *Bottom right:* Sailor-made model of a jack knife, carved from ivory and bone in the shape of a fish. Length 5.50".

Extremely rare scrimshaw dipper; serpentine-shaped exotic wood handle with whale ivory connector and finial; beautifully carved coconut shell bowl with an eagle, shield and trophy of arrows, as well as American flags. Such dippers with carving are extremely rare. Ca. third quarter nineteenth century. Length 15".

Left, top to bottom: **1.** Sailor-made fine scrimshaw dipper with a coconut shell bowl, pewter connector and turned handle made from whale ivory, ebony and exotic wood. Ca. mid-nineteenth century. Length 16". **2.** Scrimshaw dipper with coconut shell bowl, whalebone connector and turned ebony handle. Ca. mid-nineteenth century. Length 16.50". **3.** Scrimshaw dipper with coconut shell bowl that has a pewter rim and connector with whalebone, whale ivory and a teak or rosewood handle. Ca. mid-nineteenth century. Length 15". **4.** Scrimshaw dipper with coconut shell bowl, whalebone connector, and nicely carved mahogany handle. Ca. mid-nineteenth century. Length 16.50". **5.** Unusual ornamental or stage dagger with a brass blade and a scrimshawed whale's tooth for a handle. Engraved with an eagle

with emblem and flags on one side, and a portrait of a Victorian lady on the opposite side. Ca. mid-nineteenth century. Length 15".

Right, top to bottom: **1.** Unusual dipper with coconut shell bowl and short twist-carved wooden handle ornamented with bone. The bowl is engraved overall with foliage and "Jamaica." Ca. 3rd quarter nineteenth century. Length 8.50". **2.** Scrimshaw dipper with coconut shell bowl with a small whale's tooth for a handle. Ca. 3rd quarter nineteenth century. Length 5". **3.** Boxed set of bone and ebony dominoes in a simple mortised box fitted with a bone carving of a whale on the lid. Ca. late nineteenth century. Length 7.50".

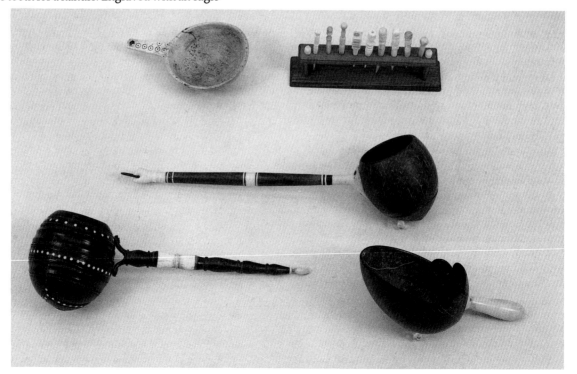

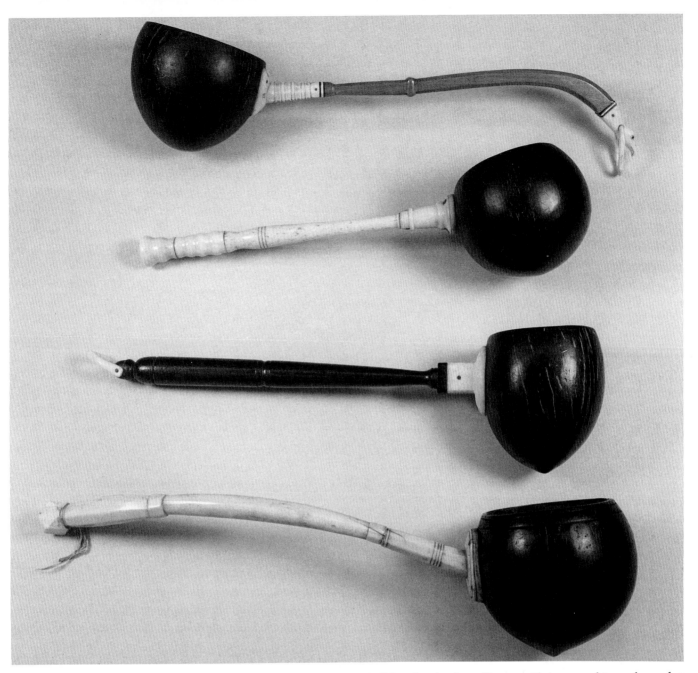

Top to bottom: **1.** Outstanding scrimshaw dipper with coconut shell bowl and ivory and wood handle. There is a carved shield on the bowl and an eagle's head at the end of the handle with a hanging ring. Ca. nineteenth century. Length 18.50". **2.** Choice scrimshaw dipper with coconut shell bowl and turned bone and ivory handle. Ca. nineteenth century. Length 14.75". **3.** Coconut shell bowl scrimshaw dipper, with ivory and turned wooden handle, as well as an ivory ring hanging from the handle. Ca. nineteenth century. Length 17". **4.** Fine scrimshaw coconut shell bowl dipper with nicely turned ivory and bone handle. Ca. nineteenth century. Length 18".

Opposite page, bottom:
Top: **1.** Carved ivory ladle or dipper from one piece of elephant ivory with small circular designs on the short handle. Probably African, ca. early nineteenth century. Length 7.13". **2.** Collection of scrimshaw bodkins in a custom made holder, all ca. mid-nineteenth century.

Middle: Very early coconut shell dipper, the bowl has a whale ivory connector to the two-part mahogany handle with whale ivory and baleen rings. Tip of handle is finished with a whale ivory hand clutching a brass ring. Ca. early to mid-nineteenth century. Length 15.13".

Bottom: **1.** Fine early dipper of horn, beef or ham bone, with beautifully turned coconut shell bowl ornamented with small points of bone. Ca. mid-nineteenth century. Length 13.25". **2.** Rare scrimshaw coconut shell scoop; whale ivory handle. Ca. mid-nineteenth century.

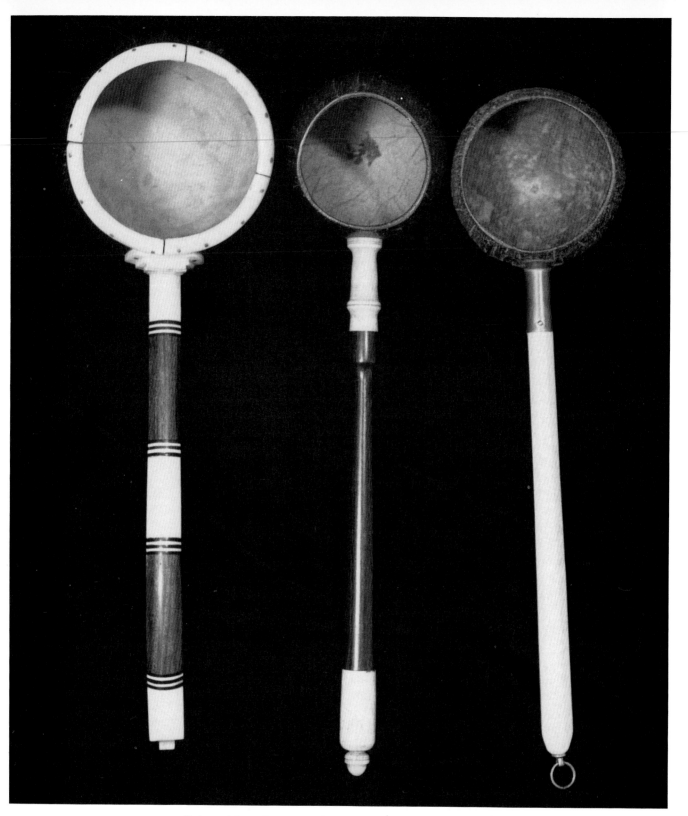

Left to right: **1.** Fine scrimshaw dipper with coconut shell bowl lined with paper. It has a whalebone rim and connector that is fitted to a mahogany and whale ivory handle consisting of five sections with baleen and whale ivory rings between each. Ca. mid-nineteenth century. Length 15.50". **2.** Lovely scrimshaw dipper with coconut shell bowl and a wood and whalebone handle. Ca. mid-nineteenth century. Length 15". **3.** Scrimshaw dipper with coconut shell bowl, brass and copper connector attached to an octagonal whalebone handle with brass hanging ring. Ca. mid-nineteenth century. Length 14.50".

SAILOR-MADE SHIP MODELS

In the days of long voyages under sail, sailors had many hours of off-work time. They turned to crafts to fill the time, either below decks or, during fair weather, on deck. Naturally, the most traditional of the crafts practiced was ship model making. These were fashioned in several different styles, including three-dimensional models and framed half-block models. Many three-dimensional models were done inside bottles, further challenging the skill of the craftsman. Due to the cramped space aboard ship, models were limited in size to approximately three feet or under. Secured to a form, the model was lashed down when not being worked on, in order that no harm would come to the work-in-progress from the action of the ship in a heavy sea.

Since the sailor was most often copying the ship on which he was sailing, these models were exceptionally accurate. The builder's tools were reduced to the bare essentials, mainly a sharpened knife with which to carve the hull, different size punches to create the holes, a miniature file or two, and various grades of sandpaper. Materials were begged or borrowed from the ship's stores, utilizing wood, lead, twine, paints and varnishes, all normally a part of supplies aboard ship. Large models were mounted in individual cradles during construction, while the smaller models, by a special technique, were mounted on a special jig that was attached to the bottom of the model, stayed with cord to tacks at different points of the hull, the whole then being wedged into the deck caulking to give support. In this way, the whole work-piece was transportable and remained in the rig until completed.

The framed half-block models were also very popular with sailors, as they could indulge their love of detail in this primitive art form. Made of thin pine boards where possible, the frame was slightly slanted inward, thereby creating the illusion of perspective. Half round, the hull was attached to the back of the diorama, with a plaster-of-paris rolling sea formed around the hull. The masts, spars and rigging were nailed and glued to the ship, as was all deck equipment. Blue skies, white clouds and whitecaps completed the background, with ship's colors, pennants and flags then added to produce a scene dear to the heart of the seaman.

Ships in bottles require the patience of a saint, but many a sailor was determined to take all the time required to make a putty sea in a bottle, paint it, construct and paint the waterline model ship with all masts and rigging intact and lying on the deck, insert and secure the hull, use wire hooks to raise and step the masts and brace the yards square--using glue as necessary--and then add sails when appropriate, working from the stern forward in all cases. The end result was a lovely diorama within a bottle, corked and sealed.

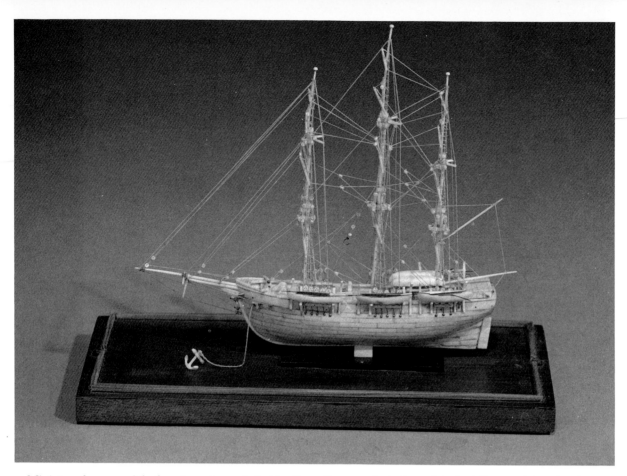

Miniature bone model of an American whaleship. Exceptionally well made and completely rigged with whaling equipment. Ship measures 11" long by 10" in height.

Sailor's model of a full-rigged ship finished in natural wood. A fine nineteenth century primitive model. Overall length 26", height 25.50".

Rare near-scale plank on frame model of a power lifeboat, complete with oars, mast and other gear. Length 41".

A very fine prisoner-of-war bone model of a Ship of the Line mounted on a straw work stand, shown in its case. Note the immaculate planking and rigging! Ca. early nineteenth century. Length 21"; height 19.50".

Fine small cased Dieppe bone model of a British frigate. Ca.
early nineteenth century. Height 13"; length 16.50".

Fine planked bone ship model of the U.S. Frigate "New York,"
1799-1814, scale 1/150. Ca. early nineteenth century. Length 23";
height 18".

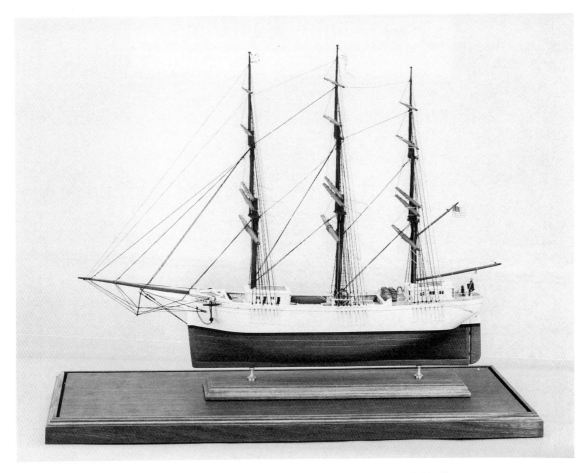

Antique sailor-made ship model of the "Ocean Rover." Solid hull construction. Ca. late nineteenth century. Length 35"; height 28".

Very fine large antique model of a whaleboat, in its davits with complete gear. A fully constructed plank-on-frame model of exceptional quality and workmanship. Ca. nineteenth century. Length (boat) 53"; overall length 61".

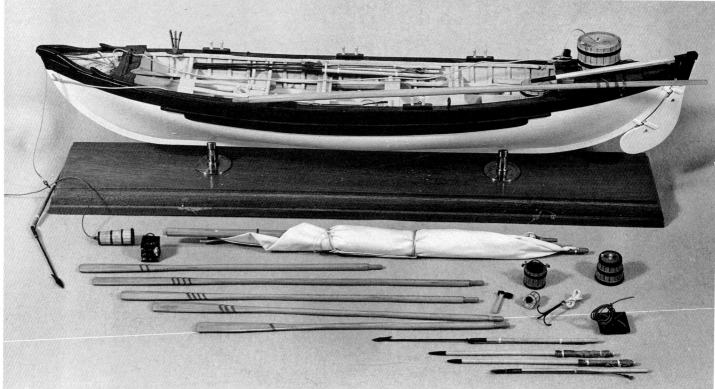

Extremely well-made near-scale model of the whale ship
"Charles W. Morgan"' now berthed in Mystic, Connecticut. The
detail is superb, with cutting stages rigged, whale boats hanging in their davits, and all equipment visible in the whale boats
and on deck, including dippers, sharpening wheels, mincing
knives, deck spades, complete try works, extra boats, with the
pump visible forward. Ca. twentieth century. Length 34"; height
26".

Opposite page, top:
Extremely fine sailor's model of the Gloucester fishing schooner "Gertrude L," complete with full canvas; excellent deck detail including two stacks of dories on deck. Length 65"; height
55".

Opposite page, bottom:
Superb near-scale model of a whaleboat, complete to the last
detail. By Peter Ness. Length 24".

Near-scale model of the Clipper Ship "Flying Cloud" by Peter Ness. Superbly detailed and rigged.

Superb scale model of the Topsail Schooner "Eagle," made to approximate scale, hollow carved and planked with outstanding detail.

Large full model of the Clipper Ship "Liberty" of New York; an excellent sailor-built model made to near scale. Ship is green-hulled, figurehead and side rails are gilded. Length 6'6"; height 4'1".

Rare period model of an East Indiaman, ca. 1815. Beautifully made with individual planking. Length 60"; height 46.50".

Sailor's primitive model of a whale ship named "The Sullivan,"
New Bedford. Length 64"; height 50".

Exceptionally fine scale model of the armed Brig "Swift." Built .25" scale by Harry Eckstein, New York City, 1935. Outstanding presentation! Length 30"; height 23.50".

Large whaleboat model with a lapstrake over rib hull. Equipment on board includes oars, paddles, line tubs, harpoons, lances, etc. Ca. nineteenth century. Length 39".

Large nineteenth century model of the Clipper Ship "Dreadnaught" out of Newburyport, Massachusetts. Fully rigged and complete in all detail. Length 48"; height 35".

Rare hull model of the Brig "Argus" with superb deck detail; complete with two additional anchors and a long gun. Ca. nineteenth century. Length 26.75".

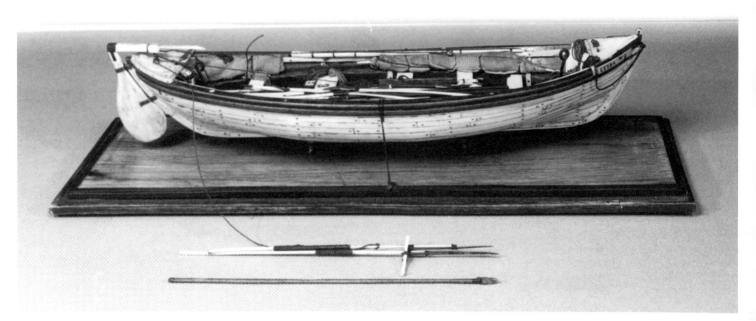

Whalebone planked model of a whaleboat with the name "Essex No.3." Boat is completely equipped with all necessary whaling implements. Ca. nineteenth century. Length 10.25".

Fine model of the Maine Schooner "Mexican." This vessel served as the Bangor-Boston Packet for many years and was known as the fastest top-sail schooner on Penobscot Bay. Length 42".

Scrimshaw whale boat model by A.S. Luz of the Azores, made of whalebone and complete with all implements, including oars, harpoons, kegs, lines etc. Length 14.75"; height 14".

Lovely, older Azorean model whale boat, complete with set sails and all implements. Ca. early Twentieth Century. Length 16".

Bone and baleen model of a two-deck ship-of-war, prisoner-of-war style. Length 16.50"; height 11.50".

Very fine cased bone prisoner-of-war model of an English three-masted frigate mounted on a tortoiseshell covered base, in its original handmade case. Length (ship) 15.50"; height 15".

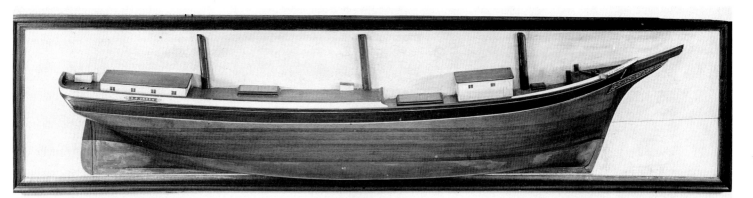

Outstanding large builder's half model of the Schooner "G.G. Green," built to scale and complete with deck details. This Schooner was engaged in intercoastal trade from 1879 until December of 1890, hauling coal, ice and general cargoes.

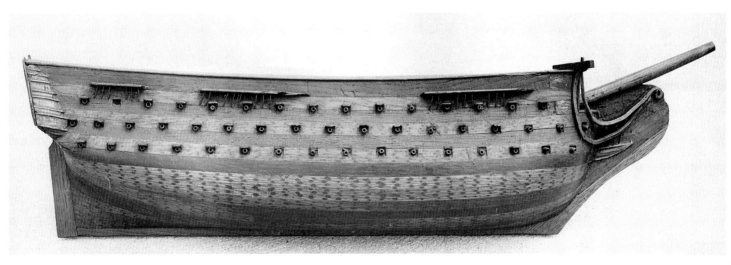

Antique half-model of a three-decked ship-of-war mounting 47 cannons. A superb individually planked half-model replete with detail, including the carved stern castle. Ca. late Eighteenth or early nineteenth century. Length 30.50".

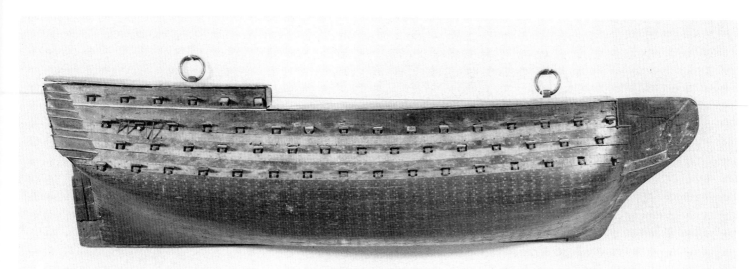

Unmounted early laminated half model of a three-deck warship with cannons. Beautifully made and fastened with brass rivets. Ca. late Eighteenth Century. Length 28.50".

Left: Fine old miniature ivory model of the Whaleship "Lagoda" of New Bedford. Made entirely of whale ivory. Ca. mid-nineteenth century. Length 6"; height 4.75". ***Right:*** Small ivory model of a warship, complete with cannon, etc. Ca. mid-nineteenth century. Length 6"; height 5".

Fine small model of the Clipper Ship "Waimea" of the New
Zealand Shipping Company, 871 tons. Shown under sail in simu-
lated water, all sails set on the starboard tack. Ca. nineteenth
century. Model is 8" long.

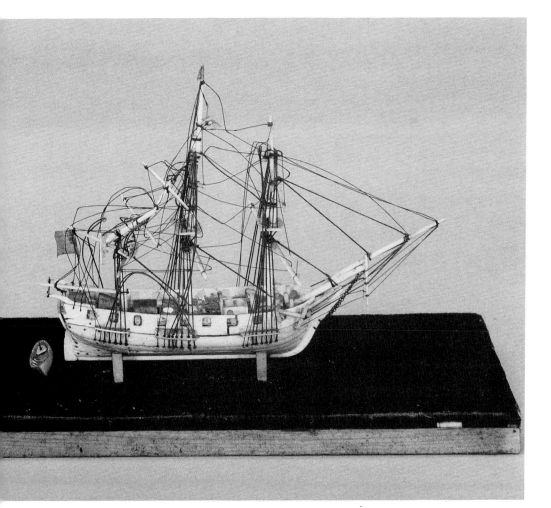

Top: Ship model in a bottle with lighthouse and tugboat. Mounted on a stand with decorative ropework around the neck. Ca. Twentieth Century. Length 12.50". *Bottom:* Model of a four-masted bark in a bottle with an approaching pilot boat. Fitted with stand and decorative ropework around the neck. Ca. Twentieth Century. Length 11.50".

A beautiful prisoner-of-war bone model of a British warship mounted in a prisoner-of-war straw box with mirrored back, folding glass front and doors. Ca. 1st quarter nineteenth century. Length 7"; depth 3.63"; height 7.13".

NAUTICAL INSTRUMENTS AND AIDS

When ancient man began to sail out of sight of land, he used dead reckoning to steer his craft. The direction sailed was noted, as well as the distance traveled. To return, it was then necessary to reverse direction and sail the same distance to, hopefully, arrive safely back at home port. Even with all the electronic navigational devices available, this is essentially the method undertaken by ships today when sailing between two points. The bearing is so accurately known and the course and speed so precisely followed, that the primitive method of dead reckoning is with us still!

Celestial navigation superseded dead reckoning. At first latitude could be determined by shooting the sun at noon with an astrolabe. Much later, with the invention of the chronometer, longitude was measured by a method using celestial sightings and this wonderful new instrument. Direction finding required the compass, which evolved over the centuries from a steel needle encased in straw and floating in a bowl of water to the gyro compass of today. In spite of the many technical advances made, magnetic compasses remain a vital instrument to be kept in reserve in the event of failure of some of the more complicated ones. The azimuth, or vertical compass is exceeding rare today.

Speed through the water has been determined by ships' logs, which, in the beginning, meant streaming a wooden log attached to a knotted line, the distance between knots set at 44' 6"; a half minute sandglass would be used to determine the distance elapsed when the sand ran out. This was done on every watch in order to average out the distances recorded. Over the years, improvements abounded, from the towed screw log, the counting of the revolutions of the ship's screw, the pitometer logs that work on the principle of the compression of air in a tube by the passage of the ship through the water, to the present day electronic logs that are operated by the forward movement of the ship through the water.

Plotting instruments, spheres and globes, planetary and armillary spheres, sand glasses and sand clocks, clocks, timepieces and chronometers, astronavigation--from the astrolabe to the sextant--hydrographic and oceanographic instruments, as well as numerous meteorological observation and forecasting instruments all harbor their own unique story in finding the pathways through the sea. Featured here are optical instruments of all types that were used aboard ship.

Rare brass universal ring dial, by J. Gilbert, London, whose name and address are engraved on the outer ring. A very complete double circle. Ca. early nineteenth Century. Diameter 6".

Left: An extremely rare and important backstaff made entirely of various woods including holly and mahogany wood, with an inlaid label that reads "Made By William Hart in Portsmouth N.E./for...1767." A truly outstanding eighteenth century navigational instrument which was distributed by a New England ship chandlery. *Right:* An large ebony quadrant with brass furniture and incised holly wood scale. Blank whale ivory nameplate.

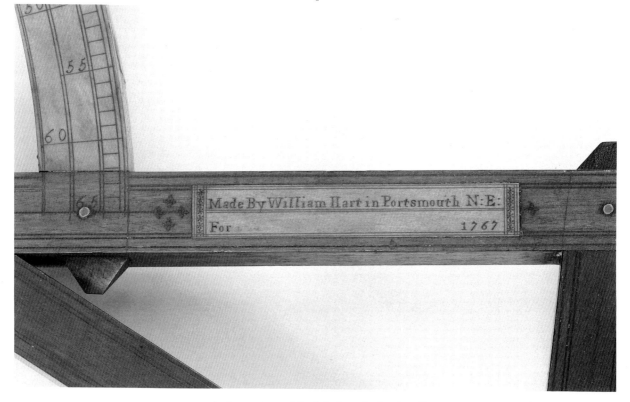

A closer view of the label on the backstaff.

Back, left to right: **1.** Silver desk ornament in the form of an anchor flanked by an anvil and a cast. The commemorative dates 1847 and 1872 are incised on the top of the anvil. The ornament is set into an oval base of black slate. Length 9"; height 6". **2.** Lacquered brass theodolite with silver scales by Stanley of London. Nineteenth century. **3.** Unusual large boxed sextant by J.Hicks, London. Made of brass with two silver inlaid scalers, two independent segment gear mechanisms with readouts, one to each side. Has a folding rosewood handle, rotating eyepiece and three different filters. Ca. last half nineteenth century.

Front left: Large brass level incised with the name "Stanley, Great Turnstyle Holborn, London." Late nineteenth century. *Right:* Lacquered brass graphometer, ball and socket connector with weighted brass base. French, ca. late nineteenth century. Diameter 7.50"; height 10".

Left: Very fine large ship's binnacle complete with original wooden base, lanterns and compass. Height 53". *Right:* Fine large ship's binnacle made by the Kelvin and Wilfred O. White Co. Complete with compensating balls and original compass. Mounted on original wooden base. Height 49".

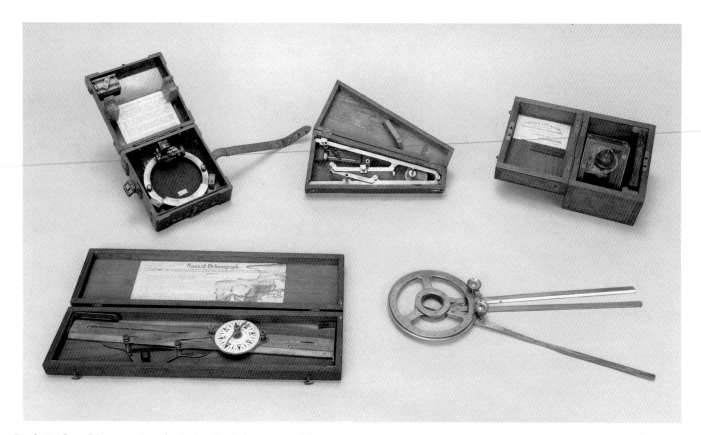

Back: **1.** Cased brass azimuth circle. English, patented 1880. Diameter 5.75". **2.** Brass pantograph stamped "A. Abraham, Bath." In original case with trade label. Ca. 2nd quarter nineteenth century. Length 11.50". **3.** Cased artificial horizon with paper label of George Lee & Son, Portsmouth, ca. mid-nineteenth century. *Front:* **1.** Cased nautical delineograph in its original mahogany case bearing the instruction label of Eugene M. Sherman, Seattle, Washington. Length 19.25". **2.** Brass station pointer stamped "E.R. Watts & Son, London." Ca. late nineteenth century. Length 18.25".

Back left: Rare brass theodolite marked "L. Casella Maker to the Admiralty & Ordnance London 3558." Ca. late nineteenth century. *Back right:* Cased polaris marked "D.M. McFregor & Co. Liverpool." Ca. 2nd quarter nineteenth century. *Front:* Cased circumferentor marked "A. Abraham Liverpool." Ca. 2nd quarter nineteenth century.

Rare brass navigational circle made by G. Dolland of London for the U.S. Navy. Contained in two mahogany cases each with the maker's label in the cover. There is a silver inlay in the scale, and the pieces are marked "U.S. Navy No. 13."

Back: **1.** Exceptionally fine chronometer in a brass bound case; made by Charles Frodsham, London. Clock is numbered 1774. Outer case 6.25" square. **2.** Excellent cased recording barometer by J. Lizars, Glasgow and Edinburgh, Scotland. Length 14.50"; width 9"; height 8.75". **3.** A rare cased artificial horizon, ca. nineteenth century.

Front: **1.** A fine brass ship's bell clock by Chelsea for William Wise & Son, New York. Diameter 5.50". **2.** A fine cased English brass and ebony chart roller; mahogany case. Length 19".

A rare small brass sextant by W. & L. Jones, London. Silver engraved scales with original case.

Left: Brass binnacle complete with compensating balls, compass and lanterns. Height 28". *Center:* Excellent large binnacle complete with wooden base, compensating balls and compass. Made by Lionel Corp., New York. Height 51". *Right:* English ship's telegraph by Chadburns, Liverpool and London. Height 42".

Steering station taken from a nineteenth century clipper ship, including its original oak stand. Wheel diameter 54".

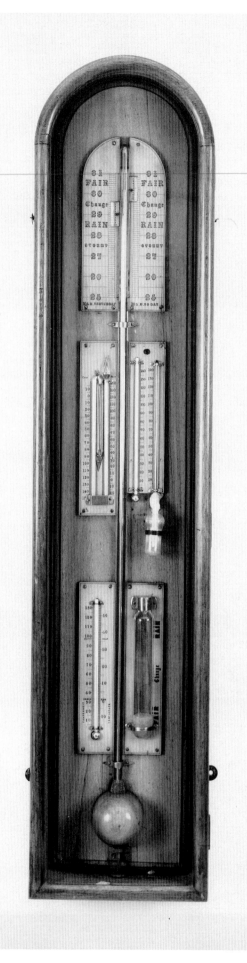

Rare Fitzroy barometer known for producing a large degree of information not only concerning the rise and fall of pressure, but the associated conditions of temperature and wind direction. It also includes a "Storm Glass" that can forecast weather changes. Ca. mid-nineteenth century. Height 40.75".

Top left: Very fine cased ebony quadrant with the engraved ivory label of Norie & Co., London. This quadrant was once the property of Capt. Nathaniel G. Herreshoff, who was given the quadrant by Dr. George DeMarini in 1867 when he was affiliated with the Mass. Institute of Technology. *Top right:* Fine cased brass sextant by E. Lorieux, Paris. *Bottom left:* Cased brass sextant with inlaid silver scale, maker unknown. *Bottom right:* Dutch iron and brass sextant marked "NV Observator Rotterdam."

Left: Early cased ebony quadrant bearing the ivory label of "G. Heath, London." The case has the label of F.W. Lincoln Jr. & Co., Boston. *Center:* Rare cased chronometer made by Joseph Sewell, Liverpool ("Makers to the Admiralty"). Brass bound coriander wood case with inset ivory maker's label. The chronometer is numbered #5844 and has a 50 hour movement. *Right:* Cased ebony quadrant with the engraved name of Spencer, Browning & Co., London. The oak case bears the label of A. Megary, New York.

Left: Extremely fine ship's wheel from the Vessel "M.S. Cape Hatteras." Complete with original brass stand and course indicator. Bears the label of "McKiernan-Terry Corp./Harrison N.J." Height 43.75"; wheel diameter 25". *Center:* Excellent ship's brass binnacle on original mahogany base, complete with original Kelvin White compass, together with original oil lamp and compensating balls. Height 51.50". *Right:* Brass ship's telegraph made by Mechans Ltd., Scotstoun, Glasgow. Height 47.50".

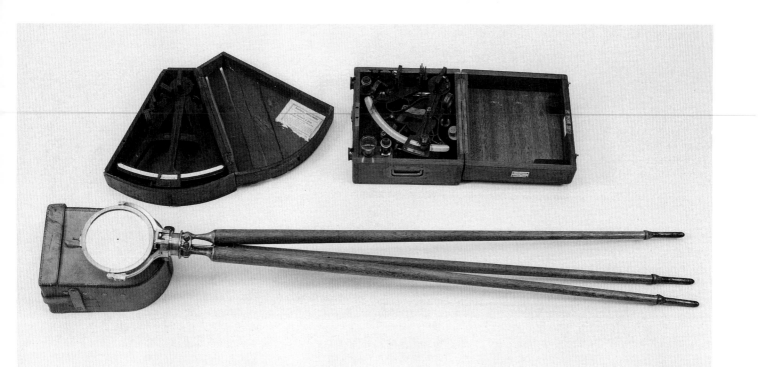

Top left: Fine old ebony-cased quadrant, with inlaid engraved ivory scales and brass fixtures. Sold by D. Eggert & Son, New York. *Top right:* Cased English brass sextant by Heath & Co. Ltd., London. Engraved on the end of the scale is "C.W.A. Baldwin, RN," the original owner. *Bottom:* Rare Mark V brass heliograph used by the military services of most countries as a signaling device.

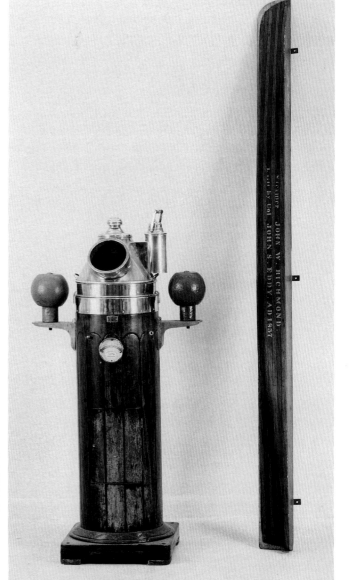

Left: Fine large ship's binnacle complete with wooden stand, compensating balls, compass and light. Ca. late nineteenth century. Height 55". *Right:* Very large shipbuilder's half model of the "Steamer John W. Richmond / Built by Col. John S. Eddy. AD 1837." Fine, sleek laminated hull of alternating dark and lighter colored wood. Length 98"; height 6.50".

Left: Fine large wooden ship's wheel, ca. nineteenth century.
Diameter 52". *Right:* Ship's bell marked Madaket, 1945.

Extremely rare early angle barometer by Charles Howorth,
Halifax. Ca. mid-nineteenth century. Length 37"; width 39.50".

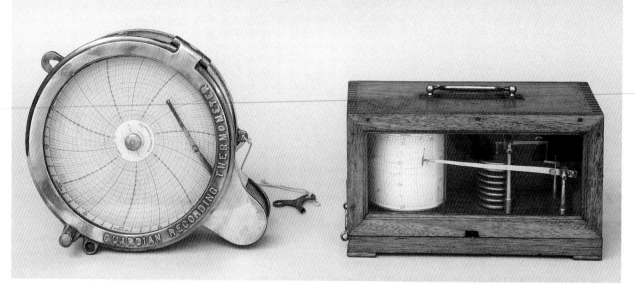

Left: Copper cased "Guardian Record Thermometer." Features key wind clockworks to turn the dial. Height 12"; diameter 9.75".
Right: Rare ship's recording barometer from the ship "Caroline." Ship's name is engraved on the handle plate. Length 11.38"; height 6.50"; width 5.25".

Ship's barometer by Stebbing and Wood, Southampton. Mahogany case with thermometer set in the center; both thermometer and barometer have engraved ivory dials. Instrument is complete with original brass gimbal. Ca. nineteenth Century. Height 37".

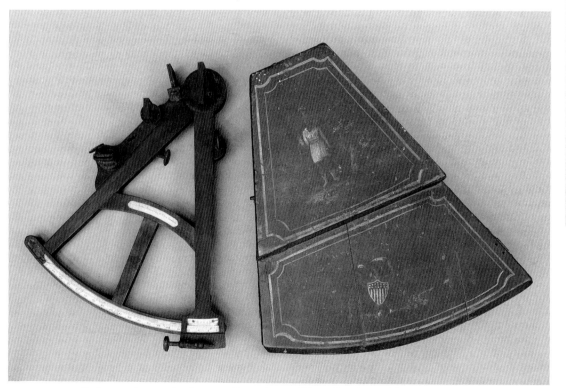

Early cased octant by Spencer, Browning and Rust, London, with the label of Samuel Emery of Salem. Case painted deep blue and decorated with eagle with flag shield and Indian on the cover.

Top: Rare "propeller log" ship's clock by Howard & Co., Boston, also bearing the name "George Walker, Boston, Mass., USA." Double wind movement with second bit, and two other functions. Diameter 12.50". *Bottom left:* Two Seth Thomas 8-day ship's bell clock. Diameter 5.25". *Bottom right:* Chelsea ship's navigation or engine room block. Diameter 5.25".

Top, left to right: **1.** Rare brass ship's bell clock with outside bell, by Seth Thomas. Diameter 6.25". **2.** Unusual cased chronometer by Ulysses Nardin. Diameter 4.75". **3.** Small yacht chronometer with frame holding gimbal, by Waltham Watch Co. Diameter 3". *Bottom, left to right:* **1.** Early boxed pocket compass with engraved sundial. Ca. late eighteenth century. Box is 3" square. **2.** Boxwood cased pocket compass with string sundial. English, ca. nineteenth century. Box is 2.13" by 21.31". **3.** Rare miniature boxed world globe in original cylindrical box with aquatint engraving of a navigator on the cover. Ca. early nineteenth century. Diameter 2.50".

Top left: Rare ship's brass Seth Thomas ship's bell clock, time and strike, with outside bell. Diameter 7". *Top right:* Nickel plated brass Seth Thomas ship's bell clock, time and strike with outside bell. Diameter 7". *Bottom:* Ship's bell clock and barometer set, with ship's bell clock by Seth Thomas and matching aneroid barometer by the Taylor Instrument Co. Diameters 7".

Pair of very fine large brass ship's anchor lights complete with original oil lamps. Ca. 3rd quarter nineteenth century. Height 21".

Top, left to right: **1.** Compensated measuring device that measures in meters. Made by Troughton & Simms, London. Ca. nineteenth century. Diameter 3.25". **2.** Nickel plated watch chronometer by F.B. Adams & Sons, London. Diameter 3.25". **3.** Surveyor's brass cased dry card compass complete with sighting device. Diameter 4".

Bottom: **1.** Small cased surveyor's compass complete with removable handle. Ca. nineteenth century. Box is 4.75" square; height 3.75". **2.** Case French portable inclinometer dated 1900. Made by H. Bellini of Nancy. Case: width 4.25"; Height 4.50"; diameter 1".

Top, left to right: **1.** Dutch copper ship's starboard lantern. Height 21.50". **2.** Dutch copper ship's port lantern. Height 21.50". **3.** Large Japanese copper ship's lantern, port and starboard type with the original Japanese label. Height 20".

Center: **1.** Steel Meteorite port lantern. Height 22". **2.** Copper ship's starboard lantern with a Birmingham, England label and screw top, complete with electric light fixture. Height 12.50". **3.** Fine old copper ship's lantern. Height 15".

Bottom: **1.** Lovely brass ship's lantern with original oil fixture and reflectors, beveled plate glass front and plain glass rides. Height 19.50". **2.** Early brass ship's port lantern incorporating some use of copper. Height 12.50". **3.** Brass ship's lantern. Height 17".

Top, left to right: **1.** Pair of large ship's port and starboard lanterns by I. Griffiths & Sons, Birmingham. Height 25". **2.** Handsome large nickel-plated brass lantern, complete with original oil fixture. Height 26.50".

Center: **1.** Ship's copper masthead lantern with original oil fixture. Height 21". **2.** Ship's copper masthead lantern identical to the preceding lantern. **3.** Small boat brass binnacle, complete with sidelight and compass. Height 8".

Bottom: **1.** Brass small boat port lantern with side blinder, complete with original oil fixture. **2.** Pair of copper signal lanterns with bull's-eye lenses, each with a red glass screen that may be used or stored on the side. Height 12".

Left: Fine copper ship's lantern bearing the name of the ship "Pacific Star"; contains original oil fixture. Ca. late nineteenth century. Height 15.75". *Center:* Late brass globular lantern with red onion-shaped globe. Ca. twentieth century. Height 14.50". *Right:* Copper ship's signal lantern from the ship "Pacific Star." Complete with original oil fixture.

Left: Pair of very large starboard lanterns from the ship "Pacific Star." Ca. late nineteenth century. Height 22.50". *Right:* Large copper ship's anchor light from the "Pacific Star." Ca. late nineteenth century. Height 20".

Top, left to right: **1.** A pair of ivory and brass field glasses, maker unknown. Ca. nineteenth century. **2.** Pair of early binoculars by Queen & Co., Philadelphia. Leather wrapped barrels, rack and pinion interpupillary adjustment. Ca. early twentieth century. **3.** Pair of early prism binoculars by Ross, London, ca. late nineteenth century. **5.** Pair of cased "Pocket Field Glasses," by Bardou & Son, Paris, ca. late nineteenth century.

1. Pair of brass binoculars engraved on one barrel "Cam- Lafontaine/Opticien," and on the other "24 Rue de la Paix/ Paris." Ca. late nineteenth century. **2.** Pair of polished brass binoculars by Verdi, Paris ca. late nineteenth century. **3.** Pair of polished brass binoculars with high power optics, marked "US Navy/R20176." Ca. late nineteenth century. **4.** Pair of prism binoculars by Barr & Stroud, Glasgow and London. Ca. early twentieth century.

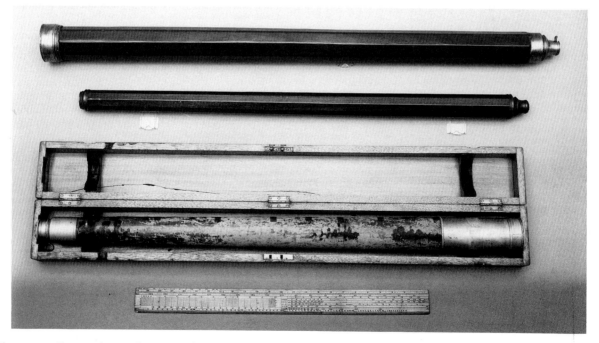

Top to bottom: **1.** Extremely rare large spyglass by T.& T. Galley, London, ca. eighteenth century. Brass scope housed in an octagonal tapered mahogany tube. Larger than usually encountered. Length closed 44". **2.** Rare eighteenth century single-draw spyglass housed in a ten-sided mahogany tube. Length closed 38". **3.** Very rare presentation spyglass by Troughton and Simms, London, complete with their signature. Leather wrapped silver-plated brass with the following inscription: "Presented by the British Government to / Captain Norton Master of the American Ship / "Graham's Polley" in acknowledgment of / his humanity and kindness to the Master / Crew and Passengers of the "Lilah" of / Montreal, whom he rescued from their / Waterlogged Vessel on the 21st March 1861." Length 40.25". **4.** Rare boxwood navigation scale by B. Dodd, ca. early nineteenth century. Length 24".

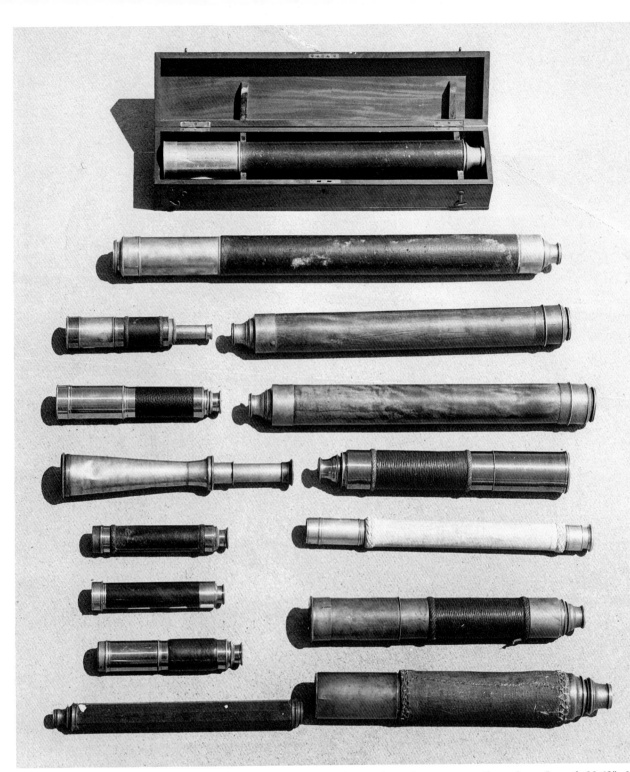

Top: Rare cased presentation telescope marked "Dolland, London," a day or night glass, partially made of German silver, complete with the original mahogany case. Dated 1871, the case bears an inscription from King Carl of Sweden to Capt. A.C. Hamkins "For Courage and Endurance." A one draw scope. Length 36.50".
Below top: Early spyglass by "J.P. Cutts, London, Day or Night," two-draw. Length 56.50".

Left, top to bottom: **1.** Brass telescope with partial leather covering, engraved to "H.R.Wing/Glens Falls N.Y./March 30th 1859," six-draw. Length 29". **2.** Brass telescope with partial leather covering, three-draw. Length 29". **3.** French brass telescope with interesting eye cover; marked "Le Vud, Paris/Brevete," two-draw. Length 20.50". **4.** Small three-draw partially leather-covered telescope. Length 23.50". **5.** Small brass telescope with se-lect grain mahogany case, three-draw. Length 22.63". **6.** Small brass telescope with partial leather covering, three-draw. **7.** Very early brass spyglass with octagonal wooden case, two-draw. Length 23".

Right, top to bottom: **1.** Early spyglass, mahogany and brass, one-draw. Length 37.50". **2.** Early spyglass, mahogany with brass scope fitted within, one-draw. Length 37.50". **3.** Fine brass telescope with leather and ropework grip, two-draw. Length 35.50". **4.** Canvas-covered silver-plated spyglass made by Gieve Matthews & Seagrove, Ltd., London, Portsmouth, and Devonshire, inscribed. Length 24.50". **5.** Early brass telescope with fine braided linen partial covering, two-draw. Length 33.50". **6.** Large brass telescope with canvas covering, two-draw. Length 36".

Top to bottom: **1.** Three-draw leather-wrapped telescope, ca. nineteenth century. **2.** Three-draw leather-wrapped telescope with double band of brass, ca. nineteenth century. **3.** Early two-draw leather-wrapped telescope made by Joseph Bothers, San Francisco; day or night glass. Ca. late nineteenth century. **4.** Early single-draw Captain's spyglass with wooden tube, made by R.L.Shaw, New York. Day or night glass. **5.** All brass single-draw telescope, missing the leather wrapping. Ca. nineteenth century.

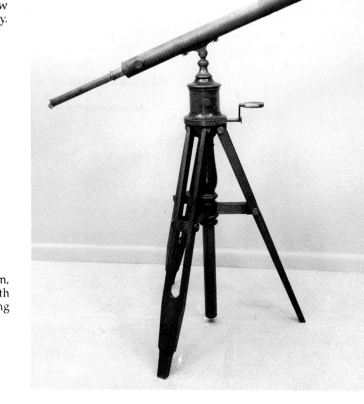

Superb French brass telescope manufactured by Bardou and Son, Paris, for Charles C. Hutchinson Co., Boston. Complete with exceptional adjustable mahogany tripod and case containing three extra scopes of differing powers.

NAUTICAL AND WHALING IMPLEMENTS

A cross section of those implements most often found aboard sailing ships are illustrated in this section. These include whaling tools used for rendering the oil of the whales captured, as well as the tools necessary for the countless repairs and upkeep necessary aboard a wooden sailing vessel, from the ship's carpenter's tools, to the often used caulking tool. While extensive, these items overlap with many other pieces of equipment to be found in other chapters of this book.

Top, left to right: **1.** Unusual wooden seam rubber with the initials "HW" on the sides and a clenched hand on the handle. Ca. early Nineteenth century. Length 5.75". **2.** Heavy wooden seam rubber with carved hearts and diamonds, rosettes, the initials "CS" on the handle and "WS" on the rubber. Ca. early nineteenth century. Length 5.38". **3.** Small wooden seam rubber with carved handle. Ca. early nineteenth century. Length 4.50". **4.** Carved wooden seam rubber with the letters "R" and "H" carved on the rubber. Ca. early nineteenth century. Length 6.50". **5.** Wooden sailmaker's needle case. Ca. nineteenth century. Length 7.38".

Bottom: Large wooden fid made of lignum vitae. Ca. nineteenth century. Length 14.13".

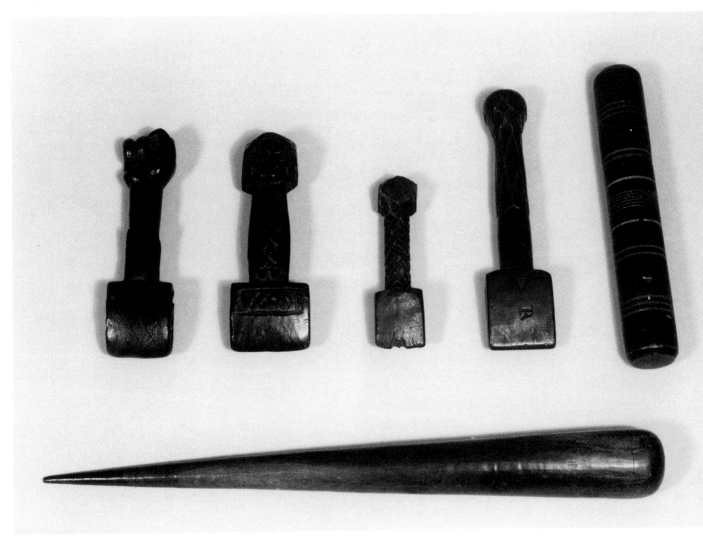

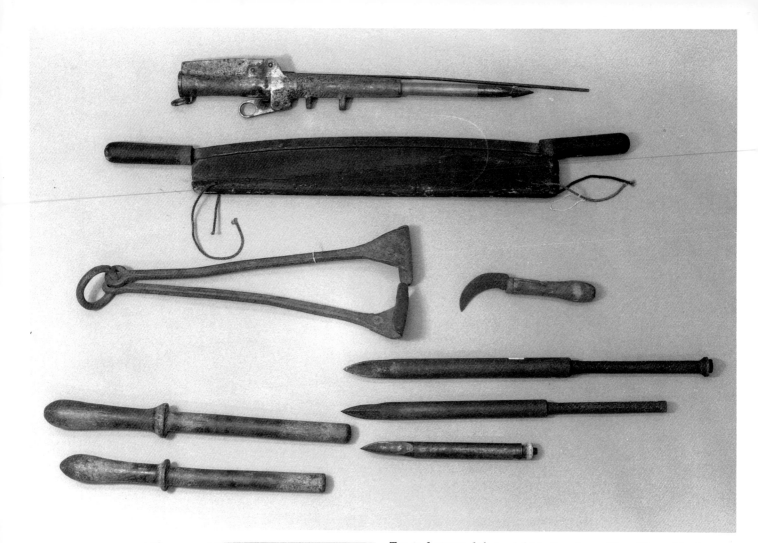

Top to bottom, left to right **1.** Rare brass Eben Pierce Darting Harpoon gun, complete with bomb. Stamped with an 1882 patent date. Overall length 28.75". **2.** Mincing knife complete with sheath. Overall length 36". **3.** Early iron cask lifter. Length 23". **4.** Small heavy curved mincing knife. Length 8.75". **5.** (bottom left) Two iron belaying pins. Lengths 16.75" and 19.50". **6.** (bottom right) Three different types of harpoon bombs, all from the last half of the nineteenth century.

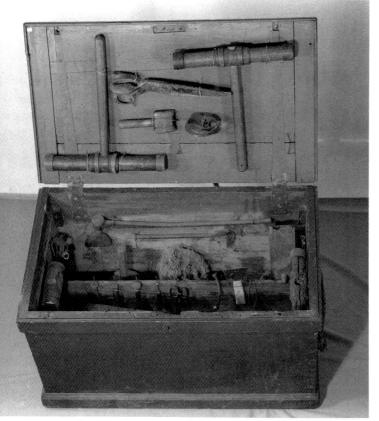

A very rare ship's work chest fitted with sail making, caulking and carpenter's tools. Set up as a display chest with pieces mounted inside the lid and the remainder in the chest. Ca. mid-nineteenth century. Length 37.38".

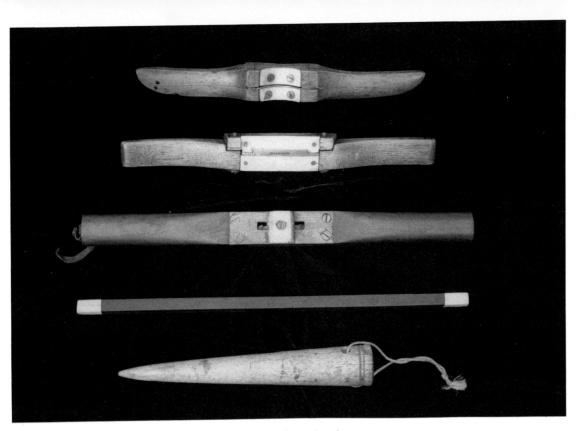

Top to bottom: **1.** Rare ship's carpenter's shave tool, made of hardwood with whale ivory. Ca. nineteenth century. Length 11.50". **2.** Ship's carpenter's wood shaving tool, marked on the blade "C.S. Osborne & Co." Made of walnut with the blade enclosed in flat pieces of whale ivory. Ca. nineteenth century. Length 12.50". **3.** Unusual ship's carpenter's gouging plane, made of cherry with double blades separated by a piece of whalebone. Ca. nineteenth century. Length 15". **4.** Straight edge made of ebony with whale ivory ends. Ca. mid-nineteenth century. Length 15.25". **5.** Whalebone fid, ca. mid-nineteenth century or earlier. Length 9.50".

Top left: Old lignum vitae block plane with signed blade. Ca. nineteenth century. *Top right:* Lignum vitae and walnut molding plane with the impressed signature of J.H. Hilton. Ca. nineteenth century. *Center left:* Unusual line serving mallet with attached reel. Partially made of lignum vitae. Ca. nineteenth century. *Center right:* Small brass mounted line server with reel. Ca. nineteenth century. *Center:* Ship's carpenter's race knife. ca. nineteenth century. *Bottom:* Sailmaker's belt with wax filled horn cup, knife, metal fid, each in its own sheath, and a snap hook. Ca. late nineteenth century.

Two rarely found pieces, the one sitting upon the other. *Top:* Caulker's rocker with tool box and tools. C. late nineteenth century. Height 12"; width 15"; depth 11". *Below:* Very old sailmaker's bench. Ca. nineteenth century. Length 72.50".

Top: Walrus ivory handled chisel with signed blade. Ca. mid-nineteenth century. Length 9.75". *Center:* Early chisel with walrus ivory handle and signed blade. Ca. mid-nineteenth century. Length 12.50". *Bottom:* Small chisel with wood and whalebone handle and signed blade. Ca. mid-nineteenth century. Length 8".

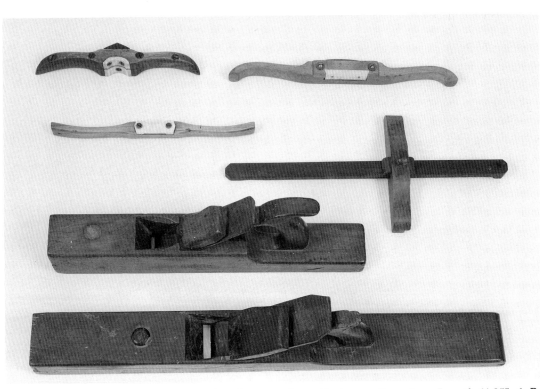

Top to bottom: **1.** A fine old scrimshaw semi-circular shave plane, with walrus ivory parts. Ca. mid-nineteenth century. Length 9.25". **2.** A rare scrimshaw flat shave plane with whalebone parts. Ca. mid-nineteenth century. Length 13.50". **3.** Another early scrimshaw flat shave plane with whale ivory parts. Ca. mid-nineteenth century. Length 11.25". **4.** Rosewood and mahogany adjustable scribe, ca. nineteenth century. Length 15.25". **5.** Two early ship carpenter's block planes, one made of lignum vitae, the other of walnut. Ca. nineteenth century. Lengths 16.25" and 24.50" respectively.

Top to bottom: **1.** Rare hand operated cutting block from the U.S. Navy Ropewalk. Ca. early nineteenth century. **2.** Two sailmakers' small tool bags, one with fancy ropework, together with a needle case, wax, needles and a sailor's palm. Ca. nineteenth century. **3.** Early copper dipper used for bailing out whale oil. Length 34". **4.** Old cutting stage chain, fastened to the corners of the cutting stage. Length 21". **5.** Early flensing spade, ca. Eighteenth Century. Length 12.75". **6.** Early nineteenth century iron blubber hook, used to raise the "blanket piece" from the whale when cutting in. Length 22".

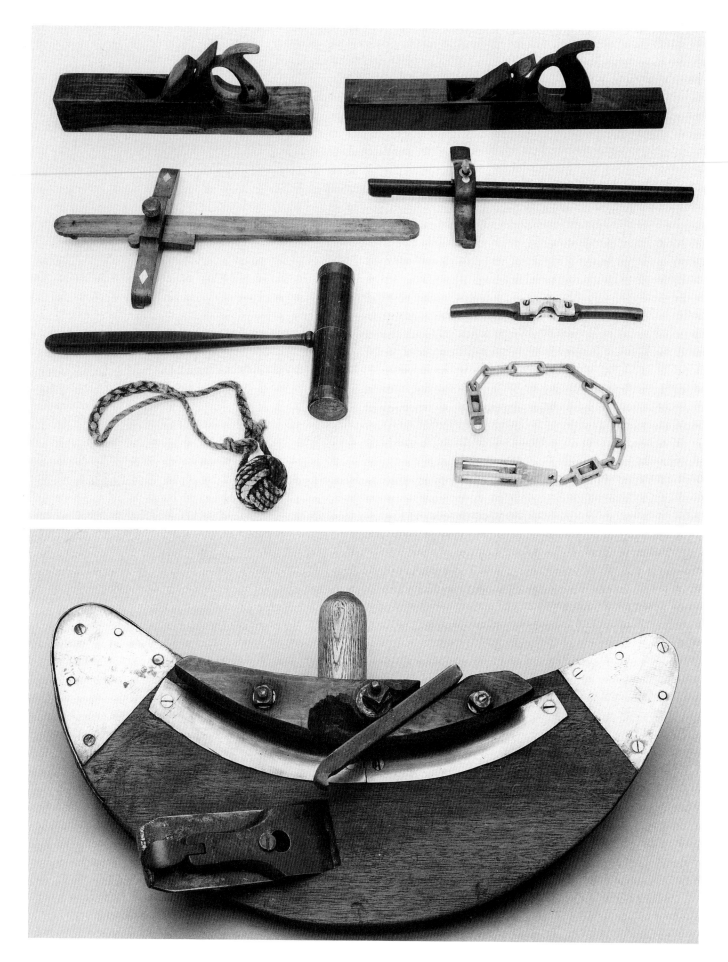

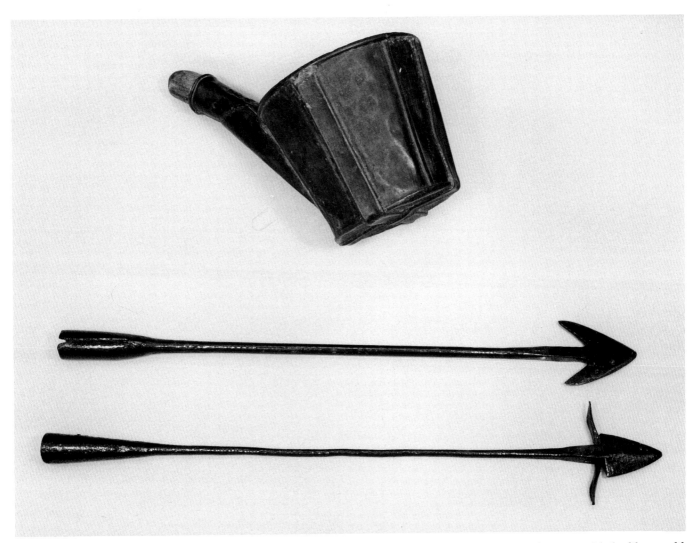

Top: Early brass dipper for removing oil. Ca. nineteenth century. Height 8.50". *Center:* Heavily constructed early arctic double-flue harpoon. Ca. late nineteenth century. Length 34".

Bottom: Early experimental-type harpoon with double movable flues, shown here in the open position. Ca. late nineteenth century. Length 34".

Opposite page, top:

Top to bottom, left to right **1.** Old ship's carpenter's plane, made of rosewood. Ca. late nineteenth century. Length 16.75". **2.** Lignum vitae ship's carpenter's plane with engraved handle. Ca. late nineteenth century. Length 22.25". **3.** Shipbuilder's cherrywood scribe with two diamond shaped mother-of-pearl inlays. Ca. mid-nineteenth century. Length 22". **4.** Rosewood ship's carpenter's scribe. Ca. mid-to late nineteenth century. Length 20.50". **5.** Heavy lignum vitae or teak ship's caulking mallet. Ca. last half nineteenth century. Length 17.50". **6.** Fine early mahogany shipbuilder's spoke shave, with whalebone parts. Ca. 3rd quarter nineteenth century. Length 11". **7.** Sailor's ropework line throwing ball, consisting of a piece of lead wrapped in a turk's head knot with line attached. Ca. last half nineteenth century. Ball diameter 2.75". **8.** Nineteenth century sailor's wooden carved puzzle chain. Ca. last half nineteenth century. Length 24.50".

Opposite page, bottom:

Rare cooper's plane used in making whale oil barrels, Made of walnut with oak handle; one attachment of maple with brass fittings. Length 16.50".

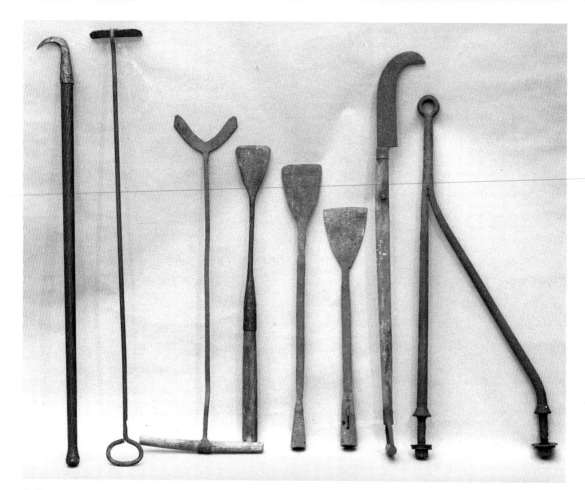

Left to right: **1.** Blubber pike on its original pole. Length 47.50".
2. Rare trypot rake used when boiling blubber. Length 47.75". **3.**
Wrought iron Y-shaped flensing iron with wooden handle. Used
to shave meat from large bones. Length 38". **4.** Short handled
deck spade made from an old bone spade when it became worn
down. Length 33.50". **5.** Heavy unmounted cutting spade.
Length 32". **6.** Heavy unmounted cutting spade. Length 27". **7.**
Long-handled flensing knife with curved blade. Used for cutting when the whale was tied up along the hull of the vessel.
Length 44.50". **8.** Iron whaleship davit brace. Length 40".

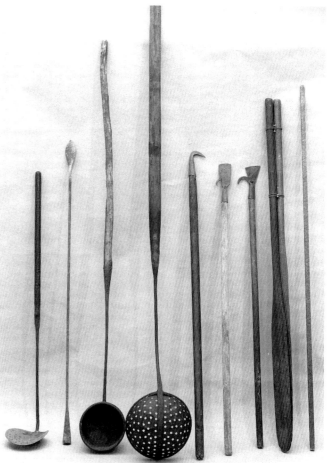

Left to right: **1.** A rare small copper skimmer mounted on an
iron shaft with original wooden pole. The piece is constructed
so that the skimmer is at a right angle to the pole, indicating
that it was made for a special purpose. Overall length 53". **2.**
Unmounted lance. Overall length 60". **3.** Copper dipper, original pole mounted with wrought iron. Length 80". **4.** Complete
skimmer mounted on its original pole. Length 99". **5.** Rare blubber pike used to pull pieces of blubber across the deck. Mounted
on its original pole. Length 60.75". **6.** Rare combination deck
spade with pike extension. Length 58". **7.** Combination deck
spade with pike extension mounted on a very old pole. Length
56.25". **8.** Pair of rare whaleboat paddles , each marked "SB" (Starboard Boat). Length 69". **9.** Quite rare measuring stick used on
whaling vessels to measure the amount of oil in a whale oil barrel. Overall length 6'.

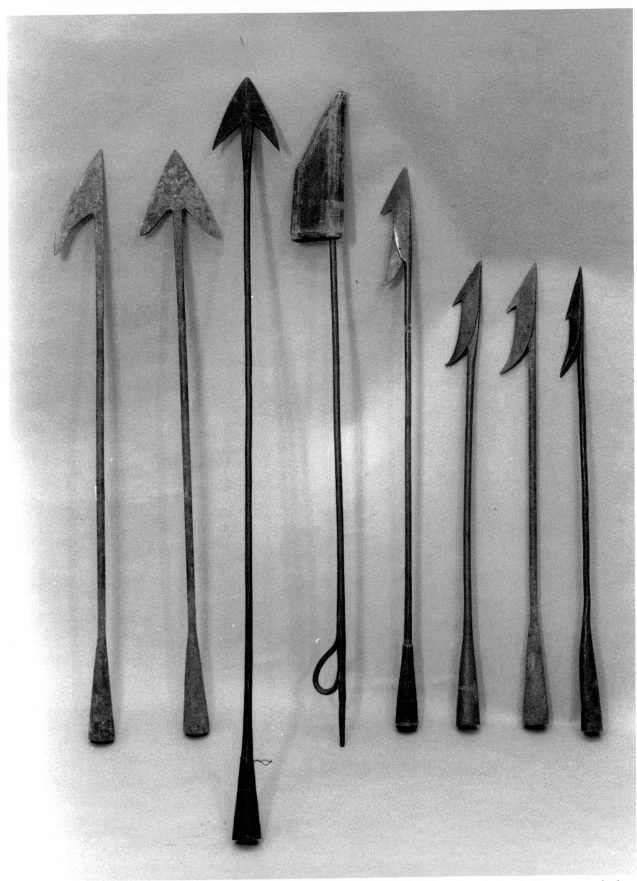

Left to right: **1.** Single flue arctic harpoon. Length 36". **2.** Double flue arctic harpoon. Length 35.50". **3.** Double flue arctic harpoon with long shaft, one side incised "WIS," and on the opposite side with a circle and four dots. Length 45". **4.** Rare toggle darting harpoon, complete with original wood and canvas sheath. Length 38.25". **5.** Rare temple toggle harpoon marked on one side with the initials "BSB", and on the opposite side with the numeral "3". Length 34.75". **6.** Toggle harpoon marked on one side "JDD." Length 29.75". **7.** Toggle harpoon. Length 29.25". **8.** Toggle harpoon. Length 29.25".

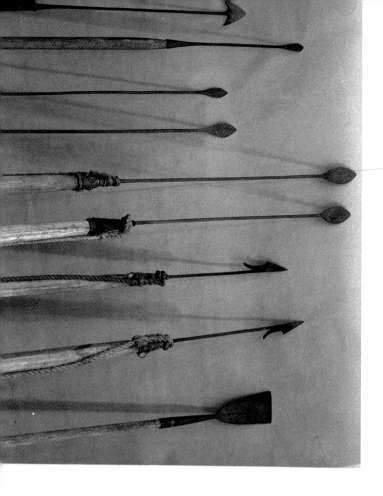

Top to bottom: **1.** Rare double fluted mounted arctic harpoon, with old pole and ropework. Length 87.50". **2.** Short lance mounted on a green stained pole. Length 99.63". **3.** Early long-shafted lance, unmounted. Length 55.25". **4.** Long-shafted lance, unmounted. Length 59.13" **5.** Long-shafted lance, mounted on a pole, possibly Azorean. Length 119.25". **6.** Long-shafted lance, mounted on a pole, possibly Azorean. Length 122.75". **7.** Mounted toggle harpoon, probably Azorean. Length 101.75". **8.** Mounted toggle harpoon, probably Azorean. Length 107.25". **9.** Mounted deck spade. Overall length 65".

Top to bottom: **1.** An early example of an arctic double flue harpoon. Length 32.25". **2.** Rare signed lance or killing iron, signed "J.Macy & Co./Cast Iron." Length 64.25". **3.** Early short lance or killing iron. Length 28.25". **4.** Early toggle harpoon. Length 33". **5.** Handwrought iron blubber hook for use on deck. Length 28". **6.** Rare deck spade; originally a head spade which has been altered for use as a deck spade. Length 62.50".

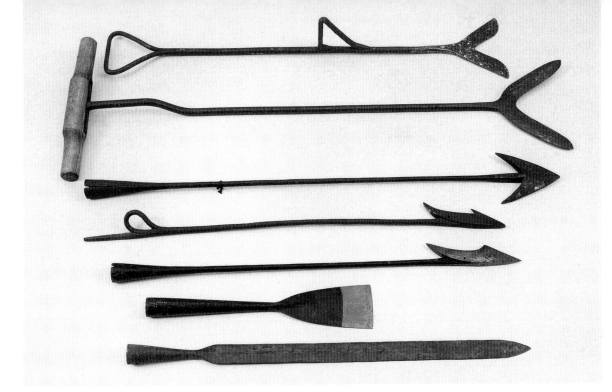

Top to bottom: **1.** Rare handwrought iron flensing knife with "Y" shaped double blade. Length 37". **2.** Rare handwrought iron flensing knife with "Y" shaped double blade and wooden handle. Length 44.50". **3.** Double flue arctic harpoon with the "JM" brand; this harpoon has a loan exhibit tag affixed stating that it was used by a Captain Hillman. Length 40". **4.** Toggle harpoon for a darting gun with crudely engraved lettering on both sides of the blade. Macy's "JM" brand legible. Length 34.50". **5.** Toggle harpoon bearing the maker's initials "C & EFG." Length 32.50". **6.** Very fine cutting-in spade, marked "Gifford / cast steel." Length 17.50". **7.** Rare long flensing knife used on a pole to sever the "blanket piece." Length 30.13".

Top: A very rare walnut stocked bomb harpoon gun by Grudchos & Eggers, New Bedford, Mass. An excellent percussion whaling instrument. *Center:* Another extremely rare walnut stocked bomb harpoon gun by Grudchos & Eggers, New Bedford, Mass. *Bottom:* Iron brand bomb harpoon gun; a percussion weapon with its original ramrod.

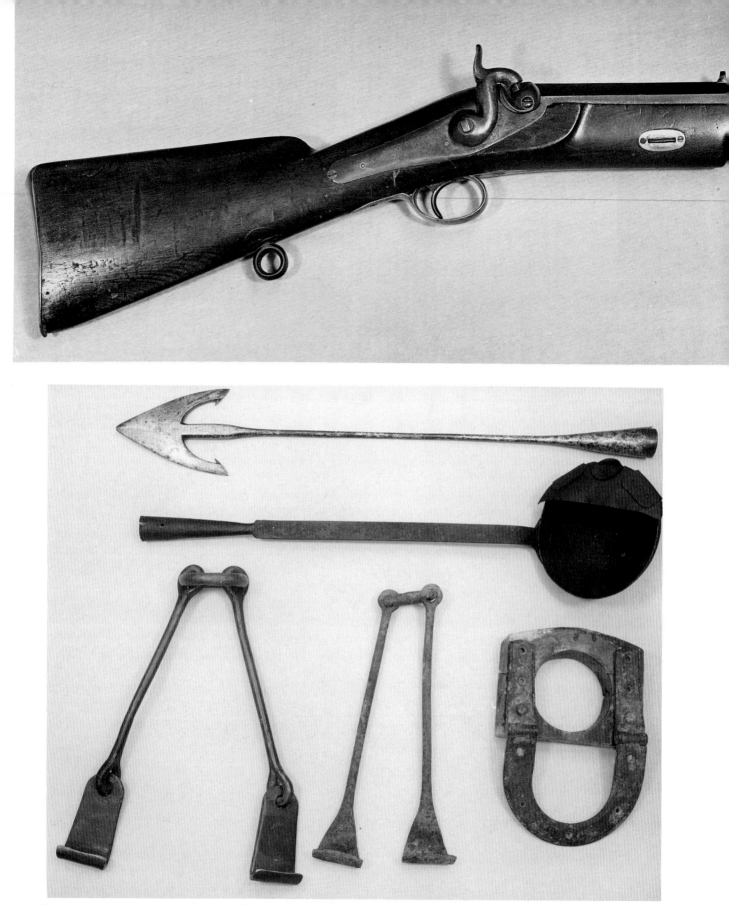

Top: Very large Greener-type hand thrown harpoon. ca. nineteenth century. Length 35.50". *Center:* Small wrought iron dipper for bailing fine whale oil. Length 33". ***Bottom, left to right:*** **1.** Rare old cask lifter, marked with the name of the maker, "H.H. Harris, Boston, Mass." in a circular mark. Ca. mid-nineteenth century. **2.** Early unmarked cask lifter. Ca. mid-nineteenth century. **3.** Old bronze hinged mast step for a whaleboat, mounted on the original piece of wood.

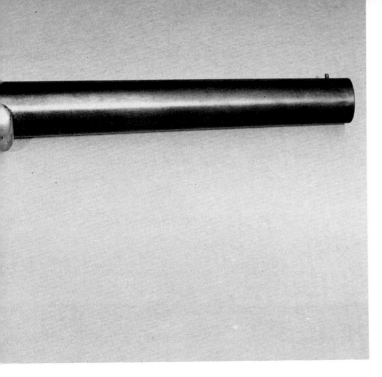

Rare percussion bomb harpoon gun by Grudchos & Eggers, New Bedford, Mass. Name and address engraved in the lock plate and on barrel, which is also identified as "Cast Steel." Walnut, stock, brass mountings, trigger guard and butt plate. Length of barrel 21.50".

Very rare brass device for testing whale oil in a cask; a unique device seldom found. Ca. mid-nineteenth century. Length 39".

Fine shipbuilder's tool chest originally belonging to Augustus Webber, who worked as a shipwright in Searsport, Maine, from 1840 until his death.

NAUTICAL FURNISHINGS
AND ACCESSORIES

All furnishings aboard an old-time sailing vessel were, of necessity, compact, made with the intention of accomplishing the most within the least space available. This applied to the officer's quarters, as well as those of any passengers. All furnishings were designed to be secured in the event of bad weather or permanently attached to the decks or bulkheads. Tables had rims and dividers to prevent crockery and utensils from flying off in the event of a heavy sea, while benches were permanently bolted to the deck. Cabinets were the epitome of the cabinetmaker's art, with all items stowed in such a manner as to be secure no matter what the weather. The ingenuity shown in utilizing extremely limited space must be seen to be believed. One outstanding example is found in the wall hung toilet cabinet, as shown in the following pages.

Here, too, are the sea chests, designed to hold all the earthly belongings the individual sailors brought aboard. These were made by the owner, and often lavishly decorated to show individuality. Today, these, and many other pieces are highly valued and collected.

Rare heavy oak table from a New Bedford whaleship and acquired by the Nye family. Ca. early to mid-nineteenth century. Length 60"; width 22.75"; height 27.25".

Top: Fine mahogany scrimshaw sewing box with beautifully inlaid garland of abalone shell on the top enclosing a dark wood inlaid quatrefoil. Four interior compartments with whale ivory knobs on the covers and tray. Ca. nineteenth century. Length 13.50". *Below:* Possibly unique sailor-made cherry wood scrimshaw table with tapered turned legs typical of the Sheraton period. Features 29 individual inlays of whale ivory, baleen and abalone. An original hand-written label on the bottom reads "This Table Was Made By/Moses Tennant/Great Grandfather Of/John & Blake Tennant." Ca. mid-nineteenth century. Top measures 17.75" x 18.25"; height 26".

Left: Victorian-style upholstered wooden frame armchair with metal base. From a nineteenth century steamer. *Right:* Elaborately carved mahogany swivel armchair with green velvet inset seat and iron base. From a nineteenth century steamer.

Top: Rare ship's hanging wash basin of mahogany with oval fluted china bowl, by Alfred B. Sands & Sons, Marine Plumbers, New York. The cabinet was intended to be mounted on the wall with the front containing the basin stowed vertically when not in use. To use, the front is unlatched and folds down to the horizontal position; the copper lined interior has a brass hand pump and spigot, as well as a copper soap dish. Ca. nineteenth century. Width 19"; height 19". *Bottom:* Exceptional brass-bound camphorwood travel desk with tambour cylinder top. English or Chinese, ca. nineteenth century. Width 20.50".

Fine travel desk bound in ivory with engraved garlands and ornamented with reticulated ivory carving. Ca. mid-nineteenth century. Length 12.25".

Fine antique scrimshaw hanging shelf with wood and whale ivory inlays. The single drawer is fitted with a turned whale ivory pull with mother of peal inlay. Height 30"; width 19.75"; depth 9.25".

Left: Fine sailor work box with inlaid eagle, trophy of flag shield, flags and arrows filling the cover. The box is laminated of various woods. Ca. last half of nineteenth century. Length 14.25"; width 10.50"; height 4.88". *Right:* Inlaid sailor made sewing box with decorative period paper lining and inlays of various woods including ebony. Ca. last half of nineteenth century. Length 11.50"; width 8.50"; height 6.50".

Left: A fine ship's apothecary chest featuring a mirrored door flanked by reverse painted panels. Ca. late nineteenth century. Height 31.50", Width 27", depth 6.75". *Right:* Very large German ship's lantern. Height 31.50".

This rare pine sea chest with fine detailed dovetailing has a slanted front elaborately carved on top and front panel. At the top is an American flag shield displayed on the breast of an eagle with banner. The front features a relief carving of a full-rigged ship passing a lighthouse. Ca. early nineteenth century. Length 47.50".

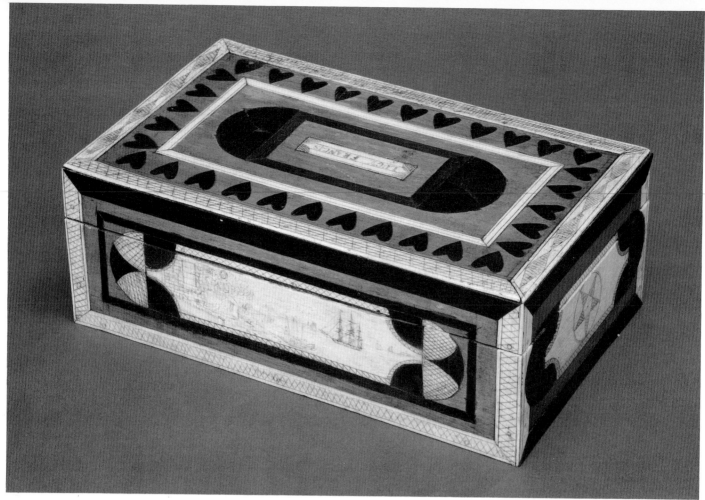

Very rare scrimshaw sewing box made of light mahogany with inlays of whalebone and various woods. Large pieces of whalebone are inlaid on all four sides with the use of colored inks. The front and side panels are done in geometric designs, while the back panel is engraved with a marine scene depicting the sailor's farewell. The top is engraved with the name "Lucy Francis." Ca. mid-nineteenth century. Length 10.25"; width 6.25"; height 3.50".

Another view of the "Lucy Francis" sewing box.

Left: Small early sea chest, slanted front and back, original green paint, bearing the name "H. Sherburne/1771" on the front. Length 26". *Right:* Small sailor's tool or personal effects box, in old green paint with metal binding. Decorated on the top with a five-pointed yellow and gold star. Ca. last half nineteenth century. Length 14", depth 10.50", height 8.50".

Back left: Excellent scrimshaw box beautifully inlaid in various woods with the American flag and eagle, an Indian head, large flowers and geometric designs on the cover. The name "Edna" with the initial "L" are also inlaid in the cover. The front, sides and back have geometric wood inlays. Ca. mid-nineteenth century. Length 14.50". *Back right:* Inlaid sewing box with large marine scene inlaid on the cover. English, ca. mid-nineteenth century. Length 12.63". *Front left:* Rare prisoner-of-war straw work jewel or sewing box. A truly exceptional example, with detailed exterior and interior including the four major covered compartments. Original mirror with drapery inside the cover. English, ca. early nineteenth century. Length 11". *Front center:* Prisoner-of-war straw-work tea chest. Colorful Oriental-style work. Ca. early nineteenth century. Length 8". *Front right:* Prisoner-of-war dome-top straw-work box with the initials "RT" on the front panel. Ca. early nineteenth century. Length 9.25".

Left: A fine brass-bound camphor wood travel desk with sliding tambour. Chinese, ca. nineteenth century. Height 8"; width 20.75"; depth 16.38". *Bottom right:* A fine large scrimshaw travel desk made of mahogany with whale ivory inlays. American or English, ca. mid-nineteenth century. Height 6.13"; width 20"; depth 12.50".

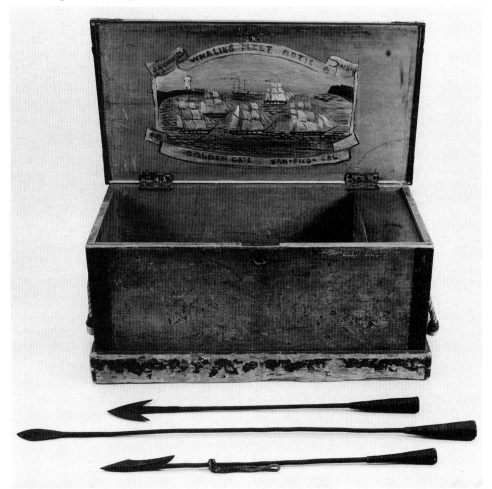

Rare pine sea chest, complete with period beckets and decorated on inside of cover with painting entitled "Whaling Fleet Arctic O." across the top, and below, "Golden Gate San Fico. Cal." Signed "J.N. Knowles-Ohio-1881." American, ca. last half nineteenth century. Length 37.50". *Below:* **1.** Early nineteenth century Double flue Arctic harpoon. Length 33.25". **2.** Rare "Peters" signed lance, or killing iron, with the letters "WB" indicating that this lance was used in the ship's waist boat. Length 47.50". **3.** Early toggle harpoon retaining a piece of the original rope and signed by "Macy." Length 33".

Top left: A fine small scrimshaw shaving stand with mirror and one tiny drawer; whalebone gallery and ornamentation. Ca. 3rd quarter nineteenth century. Width 9"; depth 3.75"; height 9". *Top right:* Exceptional scrimshaw sewing stand, consisting of a square base on turned whalebone feet containing one drawer with a whalebone knob. On a turned standard mounted in the center of this base is a square box with blue velvet pincushion top with provision for 16 to 32 spools of thread around the sides. Turned whalebone columns ornament each corner. The entire base and upper section are inlaid with various woods in geo-metric designs. Ca. 3rd quarter nineteenth century. Width 10.25"; depth 9.25"; height 11.50".

Bottom left: Early small circular Nantucket basket. Diameter 5.25". *Bottom right:* Unusual jewelry or sewing box, ornamented on all sides and lid with different types of shells. Ca. 3rd quarter nineteenth century. Length 12.50". *Bottom center:* Sailor-made ropework sapper, intricately woven with heavy cord and metal. Pieces such as this were used to control crowd uprisings, and this particular example is weighted with lead at each end. Ca. nineteenth century. Length 15.50".

Opposite page, top:

Top, left to right: **1.** Lovely scrimshaw knife box with whale ivory acorn finials at the ends of the carrying handle, and fitted with a drawer beneath with a whale ivory knob. Ca. mid-nineteenth century. Length 13". **2.** Scrimshaw sewing box made of walnut with hinged lid and single drawer. Mounted on four turned whale ivory feet, with whale ivory drawer knob and inlays of abalone. Lid is fitted with a mirror. Ca. 3rd quarter nineteenth century. Length 10". **3.** Small scrimshaw sewing box with dovetailed construction in the form of a sea chest with whale ivory handles and whale ivory corner inlays in the lid. The lid has been embellished by the addition of a nineteenth century Japanese ivory sculpture of a toad on a turtle's back. Ca. 3rd quarter nineteenth century. Length 8". *Bottom:* Very fine scrimshaw travel desk with elaborate inlays of abalone and baleen in foliate designs on the lid, front and sides. On the inside written in ink is the name "Mrs. Sarah S. Baldwin/Stockton/California." Ca. 3rd quarter nineteenth century. Length 20".

Opposite page, bottom:

Left: Oval baleen ditty box engraved with finely detailed buildings and trees. Coconut wood top and bottom. Ca. 2nd quarter nineteenth century. Length 7.50". *Top right:* Fine oval baleen ditty box beautifully engraved with ships and a port scene with finely detailed buildings. Pine top and bottom. Ca. 2nd quarter to mid-nineteenth century. Length 7.25". *Bottom right:* Oval baleen ditty box engraved with flowers, trees and large buildings. Walnut top and pine bottom. Ca. 2nd quarter nineteenth century. Length 8.50".

Above:

Top left: Simple rectangular scrimshaw sewing box with single drawer inside. Exterior is inlaid with wood and mother-of-pearl hearts, diamonds, stars, a small ceramic face, and a carved bone ornament. Name on the front reads "J B Collins Richmond Maine." Ca. late nineteenth century. Length 10.50". *Top right:* Scrimshaw tray with gallery, made of rosewood, coconut wood and other exotic woods, inlaid with bone ivory and other woods.. Ca. 3rd quarter nineteenth century. Length 13". *Bottom left:* Rare scrimshaw sewing stand with revolving thread holder, whalebone knobs, feet, finials and separators. A very unusual style with the head of a little girl wearing a bonnet sculptured from whale ivory atop the turntable. *Bottom right:* Lovely prisoner-of-war straw work sewing box with colorful interior. Ca. early nineteenth century. Length 10.50".

Top left: Exceptional inlaid tea chest, British, early nineteenth century. Made of many exotic woods, the box features two inlaid panels of scenes depicting ships with a coastline in the distance. The interior still retains its original paper lining with prints of hummingbirds; there is a foiled compartment for tea, a center compartment for a bowl, and two covers with inlaid rosettes. Length 13"; height 7"; width 7". *Top right:* Very fine inlaid sewing box, British, mid-nineteenth century, with an inlaid panel showing a large ship approaching a point with a lighthouse flanked by two colorful bands of inlay. Interior has a removable tray with pincushion, three covers inlaid with sailing yachts and British flags for its three compartments. Length 13"; width 10"; height 6". *Bottom:* Exceptional brass bound camphor wood cylinder top travel desk, English or Chinese, early nineteenth century. Width 18"; depth 14.75"; height 8.50".

Opposite page, top:

Top left: Outstanding sailor-made scrimshaw sewing basket with superb inlays of mother-of-pearl and various woods, mounted on four faceted whalebone feet. Interior has three lidded compartments. Ca. mid-nineteenth century. Length 14.50"; width 9.50"; height 5.50". *Top right:* Sailor-made inlaid sewing box with elaborate wood inlays. Ca. mid-nineteenth century. Length 11.25"; width 8.50"; height 8". *Bottom:* Very fine dovetailed oblong case with five drawers each having two scrimshaw knobs made of whale ivory. Ca. early nineteenth century. Length 31.38"; width 7.75"; height 6".

Opposite page, bottom:

Rare period sea chest with inside cover painted with a marine scene representing the Whaleship "Ohio." Complete with its beckets and in its original red paint. The chest probably belonged to the captain or the first mate judging by its sides and the fact that there is a sliding cover over a compartment intended to hold ten case bottles of liquor. Length 45.50".

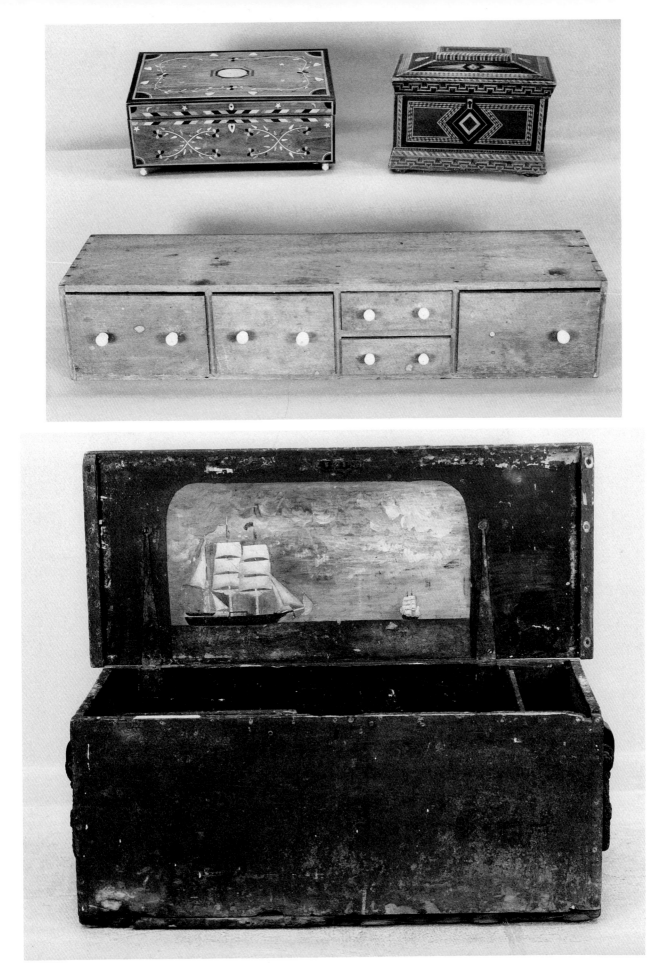

Left: Sailor-made carved wooden whale stamp showing a baleen whale. Ca. mid-nineteenth century. *Center:* Lovely scrimshaw sewing box sailor-made of island wood with geometric wood inlays and decorative inlays of compass rose, diamonds, and spandrels of whale ivory and abalone shell. Ca. mid-nineteenth century. Dimensions 8" square. *Right:* Carved fruitwood log book stamp with carving of a ship, and, above, a whale, Ca. mid-nineteenth century. *Front:* Pair of rare scrimshaw knitting needles made of coconut wood tipped with whale ivory with decorative finials of whale ivory and alternating rings of exotic woods and whale ivory. Ca. 2nd quarter nineteenth century. Length 14.50".

Top left: Fine Trinity House inlaid travel desk with colorful inlaid marine scene in the cover and with a blue velvet writing surface within. English, ca. nineteenth century. Length 14". *Top right:* Trinity House inlaid sewing box featuring a large ship passing a signal tower on the lid, with six covered compartments inside, each with inlaid crossed flags on the cover. English, nineteenth century. Length 13.13". *Bottom left:* Fine Trinity House sewing box inlaid with steam frigate flying commissioning flags on the cover. Still has the original lining paper. English, nineteenth century. Length 13.75". *Bottom right:* Hexagonal wooden box inlaid with geometric designs, stars and crescents around the sides and a flag shield in the cover. American, nineteenth century. Diameter 7.75".

Top left: Fine inlaid mahogany ship model, complete with ivory figurehead, masts and bowsprit. Ivory stand mounted on an inlaid wooden base. English, early nineteenth century. Length 12". *Top right:* Raised cased carved bone spelling game containing 6 each of the complete letters of the alphabet, together with 6 each of all the vowels and an extra 6 of the letter "Y." All compartments are marked for the appropriate letters, while one compartment is unmarked. Presumed to be prisoner-of-war made set. Ca. early nineteenth century. Case length 8". *Bottom left:* Fine scrimshaw sewing box of walnut and ebony, with American pine sub-wood, whale ivory handles, feet and the knob and star inlays. Ca. 2nd quarter nineteenth century. Length 12". *Bottom right:* Three tiered scrimshaw sewing box with two drawers, a sliding tray in the bottom and room for 8 spools of thread in the top compartment. Whale ivory pulls and ornamentation. Width 8.75".

Left: Scrimshaw portrait frame complete with portrait; frame is butternut with heavy facing of whale ivory inlaid with abalone hearts and diamonds, together with a small piece of tortoiseshell. Frame is banded with baleen around its outer edge. Ca. mid-nineteenth century. *Center:* Rare miniature in the form of a knife box, indicating that it was made in Sandwich, Mass., to hold the small spoons that accompany open salts. Made of mahogany with light wood inlays and two tiny whale ivory knobs on the covers. Ca. mid-nineteenth century. Length 6". *Right:* Early scrimshaw walnut picture frame with whale ivory, mother-of-pearl and ebony inlays. Ca. 2nd quarter nineteenth century. Height 6.75"; width 5.50".

Very rare carved oak table desk or bible box, Dutch, late seventeenth or early eighteenth century. The interesting carving on the front of the box includes, on the right, a whaling scene with whaleboat containing six men fast to a whale with icebergs surrounding them, while on the left is a hunter firing a flintlock weapon at a stag. The remainder of the box is carved with flowering plants and birds, while the upper and lower moldings are gadroon carved. Width 22.50".

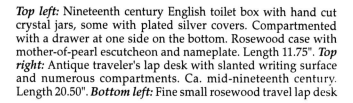

Top left: Nineteenth century English toilet box with hand cut crystal jars, some with plated silver covers. Compartmented with a drawer at one side on the bottom. Rosewood case with mother-of-pearl escutcheon and nameplate. Length 11.75". *Top right:* Antique traveler's lap desk with slanted writing surface and numerous compartments. Ca. mid-nineteenth century. Length 20.50". *Bottom left:* Fine small rosewood travel lap desk with brass bound corners and nameplate; elephant ivory escutcheon. Ca. mid-nineteenth century. Length 14". *Bottom right:* Rare whaleship agent's box for the New Bedford Whaleship "L.C.Richmond." The Richmond was part of the Stone Fleet sunk by the Federals to blockade the Rebels during the Civil War. Length 16.50".

Outstanding ship's carpenter's tool chest with compass rose inlays on the inside of the lid and on the inner folding cover. Ca. late nineteenth century. Length 36"; width 24.50"; height 20.50".

Exceptional scrimshaw watch holder with drawer; a beautifully designed and built piece. Dovetailed construction with inlays of whale ivory and baleen; engraved with an abundance of colorful flowers. Other inlays of plain whale ivory and abalone shell. Curved scrolled supports at the front, with a single drawer at the bottom. Ca. nineteenth century. Width 9'; depth 6.38"; height 10".

Rare early camphor wood sea chest with superb dovetailed construction, slanted both front and back; complete with original beckets and carved handles. Probably American sailor made of camphor wood obtained on a voyage to the Orient. Ca. mid-nineteenth century. Length 40".

Exceptionally fine large walnut sea chest with wonderful dovetailed construction and a painted whaling scene filling most of the inside cover. Outstanding heavy brass hinge, carved handles and original beckets. Interior has a ditty box with hinged lid and a smaller secret compartment underneath. American, ca. mid-nineteenth century. Length 42".

Ship's carpenter's chest, with the inside lid painted with a riverscape of a bridge spanning the river upon which various vessels are plying their trade. The scene is very reminiscent of the area around the Piscataqua River, which separates New Hampshire and Maine near Portsmouth. Signed "E. Bowman" in the lower right. Ca. mid-nineteenth century. Length 38".

Early inlaid document or bible box with large inlay of a whale in the cover, iron bound corners and iron bail handles. Ca. eighteenth century. Width 20.50"; depth 20"; height 8.50".

Extremely rare brass-bound mahogany document box, once the property of Captain Francis Allen of New Bedford. Elaborately brass bound, the box has three removable trays inside. There is a unique device with a clock key that enabled him to fasten the box to the desk, cabinet or counter top in his cabin that it would not slide off while on the rolling sea. Ca. mid-nineteenth century. Length 17.50"; width 11.50"; height 6.25".

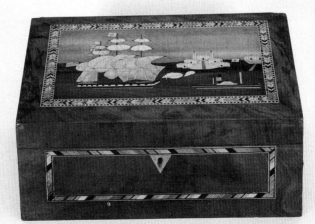

Top left: Rare burlwood sewing box with inlaid full-rigged ship on the cover. English, early nineteenth century. Length 9.75". *Top right:* Burlwood sewing box with inlaid wood lighthouse and schooner on the cover. English, nineteenth century. Length 10". *Bottom:* Exceptional burlwood sewing box; large inlaid wood scene on the cover depicts a paddle wheel tugboat with a ship in tow and a shoreline with many buildings. Elaborate interior features a lift-out tray with pincushion in the center and eight lidded compartments, each lid decorated with pairs of colored flags, also of inlaid wood. English, ca. nineteenth century. Length 13".

Top: Sailor-made mahogany scrimshaw ditty box, made like a sea chest with whalebone molding around the top and a whale ivory heart escutcheon on the front. Complete with handles and beckets. Ca. nineteenth century. Length 16.50"; depth 10"; height 7.25". *Bottom left:* Small sailor-made ditty box, dovetailed, with four diamond inlays and a star inlay. Crudely initialed "KML" on the top; lock with whale ivory escutcheon, complete with key. Ca. nineteenth century. Length 11.25"; width 6.50"; height 4". *Bottom right:* Sailor-made box with molding and inlays of whalebone and precious woods, plain interior. Ca. nineteenth century. Length 14"; width 9.25"; height 4".

Left: Sailor's ditty box, complete with pewter soap dish, mirror and provisions for razor and other personal items. Length 8.75". *Center:* Fine baleen ditty box engraved overall with foliage and a building, complete with the original cover. Length 6.50". *Right:* Rare small scrimshaw sewing box with slide-out looking glass and turned ivory finials. Width 7".

SHIP'S FIGUREHEADS, STERNBOARDS, AND BILLET HEADS

Figureheads and carved sternboards, as well as billet heads were practically the only decorations allowed aboard many of the early sailing vessels, reflecting the stern austerity of most of the ship masters-owners of the period. Many of these carvings were works of art, as can readily be seen when one views today's surviving pieces. Most of the sailing museums scattered throughout the world actively search for and acquire examples like those shown on these pages. The popularity of sternboards and figureheads is such that many of the old models are today being reproduced by machine in order to satisfy the demand. Most assuredly, these in their turn will become tomorrow's collectibles!

Top: Architectural rococo carving of a mermaid reclining in a gilt shell amidst green and gold waves. Ca. late nineteenth century. Length 51.75". *Center:* Half of a sternboard carving with foliate scrolls, American flag and Liberty Cap on a pole. Ca. nineteenth century. Length 67". *Bottom:* Large section of a ship's sternboard with foliate and floral carving. Ca. nineteenth century. Length 59".

Portion of the keel of the USS Constitution, given to the designer of the ship, Col. Claghorn, a distant ancestor of the author. This piece is in the form of a bound book, and has been in the author's family since it was originally received.

Rare Chinese carved billet head, identified as "Billethead Carved at Whampoa Anchorage,/China for the Clippership Antelope-Built Camden, ME. 1851/& Owned by the Prince Family of Boston." Height 12.50"; length 14".

Left: Very rare, early ship's billet head elaborately carved in scroll and acanthus form. American, ca. early to mid-nineteenth century. Length 21". *Right:* Exceptional carved ship's billet head, similar to the piece on the left. Ca. early to mid-nineteenth century. Length 23".

Pair of fine antique ship's trail boards from a nineteenth century schooner or sloop. Beautifully sculptured with scrolls, wheat and flowers. Length 56".

Fine late eagle carving of a stern board showing an eagle with trophy of flag and branch, holding a banner in its beak. Ca. 1940s. Length 80".

Extremely fine period eagle carved bow-sprit with eagle's head at the front and relief carved foliate work trailing behind. Length 44.50".

A collectible ship's trailboard from the ship "A.W. Cook." A delicate piece with tassels, cannon, cannonballs and foliate carvings. Ca. 3rd quarter nineteenth century. Length 92.25".

Very rare tradesman's figure of a sailor holding a spyglass. The figure wears a white shirt, gray trousers, gold vest, and red neckwear, black jacket with brass buttons, and a sailor's stovepipe hat. American, ca. 3rd quarter nineteenth century. Height 39.25".

Early ship's figurehead in the form of the upper torso, head and shoulders of a gentleman with long sideburns. Carved from a single block of solid oak, ca. nineteenth century. Height 30".

Fine early relief carved plaque of the head and shoulders of a gentleman. Polychromed in flesh tones with black jacket, red scarf, and brown hair. Thought to be a sea captain. Ca. nineteenth century. Height 19"; width 15".

Extremely rare carved eagle figure of the type used on early
steamboats. This superbly carved example has full spread wings
and individual feather carving. American, ca. 3rd quarter nineteenth century. Wingspread 48.50"; height 28"; overall length 42".

Large flat eagle carving, quite possibly a ship's gangway board.
American, ca. early nineteenth century. Width 29"; Height 35.50".

Outstanding early eagle carved ship's figurehead. A fine example with fiddlehead at the bottom. Probably American, ca.
early nineteenth century. Height 51".

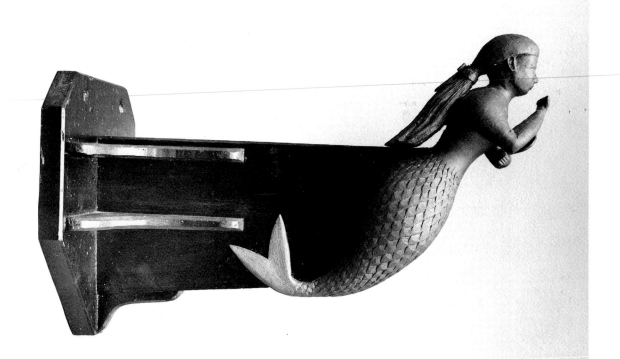

Miniature carved figurehead of a mermaid; possibly mounted over the door of a captain's cabin on board ship. Ca. late nineteenth century. Overall length 18.50".

Left: Fine ship's figurehead in the shape of a young dark-haired woman. Ca. mid-nineteenth century. Height 31". *Right:* Much weathered early figurehead of a young woman with a garland in her hair. American, ca. nineteenth century. Height 46".

SHIP'S JOURNALS

Most often kept by the captain or first mate of the vessel, ship's journals were an accurate, if sometimes ungrammatical account of the day-to-day progress of a ship's journey, recording daily events for the owners and posterity. Whales sighted and captured, barrels of oil obtained, deaths, ships sighted, landfalls made and ports entered, all these became a living part of the life of a ship. Often illustrated in a primitive manner, many journals are quite colorful and show that there was an appreciation of art, as well as for the written word. Often overlooked in the past, ship's logs or journals have become highly collectible, especially over the last twenty years, often commanding fantastic prices. Journals are truly a most important part of the sea-going heritage, reflecting the noble aspect of men, as well as the less-than-noble transgressions of the human species.

Very important illustrated whaling journal, on board a voyage of the Bark "Sea Fox" which commences at New Bedford, Mass. on April 18, 1871, and finishes near the end of the voyage with the last complete entry on Tuesday, May 31, 1874. The journal was kept by Thomas McLane, and the vessel was under the command of Captain William Wells Eldridge. Contains 357 drawings and a substantial number of whale stamps, many of which are colored. Nearly all the drawings are in color and the entries are lengthy and full of information. The journal, which is leather bound, retains the original label from Barbados, indicating that it was acquired there.

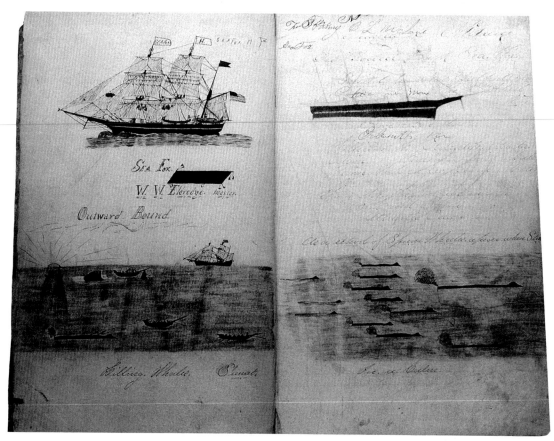

A view of some further color illustrations in the journal of the
"Sea Fox."

Very rare and important journal log book of a whaling voyage on board the Whaleship "Richard Mitchell" of Nantucket and kept by John Conant. The journal begins with the departure of the vessel from Edgartown on November 7, 1831, and concludes on November 17, 1834 with the docking of the vessel at Edgartown. This is one of the most complete and interesting journals one could hope to include in a collection. Among its unusual features are the log book stamps used, including those of whales, half whales, ships, porpoises, a whaleboat, and a possibly unique stamp in two different sizes of a sailor looking through a spyglass. In addition to this, the "Richard Mitchell" spoke to at least 57 different vessels during the voyage. One interesting entry concerns a burial at sea. Altogether, the journal contains 62 whale stamps (2 types), 69 stamps of the sailor with the spyglass (2 sizes), 116 ship stamps, 27 one half whale stamps, 9 porpoises, and 2 whaleboats. In addition, there are two large pen and ink and watercolor portraits of the ship and several interesting small drawings. On the last page of the journal is a verse entitled "Reflection on Home," signed by John Conant.

Opposite page, bottom:
Important Civil War whaling journal of the ship "Milo" of New Bedford. Kept daily by Augustus G. Jenny of Fall River, Massachusetts on a voyage to the North Pacific beginning November 26, 1863 and ending July 20, 1865. The "Milo" was taken by the Confederate Raider "Shenandoah" on June 23, 1865 and was bonded to bring crews of five whalers to San Francisco, and was thus spared destruction. On that date, a portion of Jenny's entry reads "employed in getting provisions from Ship Sophia Thornton. 8PM got through set fire to the ship...the Pirate lay by us till 7 1/2 oclk when she raised sail in pursuit of other whalers." Folio, 116 pages.

July 1843. Cruising for Whales.

July 1843. Cruising for Whales.

Rare journal log book including the personal journal of George W. Riley. The journey begins in October, 1842 with Mr. Riley taking the train to Albany by way of Troy, and thence to New York by steamboat. On the 30th of October, he secured a job on a New Bedford whaleship, and left New York on the steamship "Massachusetts" for New Bedford. On November 25th, Riley signed aboard the Ship "Caroline" for a whaling cruise to the Northwest Coast. Departing December 15, 1842, he maintained a day-to-day journal of the voyage. On October 6, 1843, Riley and several other seamen from the "Caroline" deserted ship in San Francisco by stealing a ship's boat and sailing south towards Santa Cruz. The remainder of the journal describes the adventures that followed and ends abruptly at Acapulco.

Journal log book of the ship "Oregon" of Fairhaven, Massachusetts while on a whaling voyage to the Pacific Ocean. The voyage commenced on July 12, 1841 in company with another New Bedford ship, and concluded on March 31, 1845, a voyage of 44 months and 08 days. The yield was 1397 barrels of sperm, 1207 of whale oil, and 14,500 pounds of bone. A very complete and detailed journal with many whale stamps in blue.

Remarks on board of Bark Canton

January 1876.

Monday 17th Commences with cloudy weather and a moderate breeze from the WSW bark cruising off bald head saw grampuses and other target fit for use.
Latter part fine weather and a light breeze from the WSW Employed in painting some so ends this 24 hours struck a porpoise and lost him

Tuesday 18th Commences with fine weather and a moderate breeze from the SSW. bark steering to Employed in painting the Starboard boat and scraping the mast.
Latter part much the same saw porpoises So ends this 24 hours. Land 30 miles off

Wednesday 19th Commences with fine weather and a moderate breeze from th SW one sail and the bond to th NofW Employed in filling the fore topsail yard and breaking out bait and beef.
Latter part fine at 2 PM the chief mate took the Leeboard boat and boarded the English Roberts Cleopatra 19 days from Melbourn & sent two letters to my wife and got two socks of potatoes So ends thirty

Thursday 20th Commences with a strong breeze from the SE took in the fore topsail at 5 set it again Bark steering N W W & W and W. Chatham Island. and white top rocks in sight. Engaged in mending the main topmast staysail
Latter part fine weather and a whale sail breeze from the S at 3.20 PM Mr Hoaland chief mate saw a breach ahead dis 4½ miles bearing S saw it again at 4 PM bearing S E proved to be Sperm whale going S E S Saw them until 6.45 PM So ends this 24 hours.
Lat 85.35.3 Lon 15.43 East

Friday 21st Commences with fine weather and a light breeze from the Eastward two sails in sight
Latter part fine Employed in washing the forecastle
at 5 PM semmored Bark Watch Watch 130 sperm and eight

January 1876.

Saturday 22nd Commences with fine weather and a light breeze from the SSW saw grampuses porpoises and two sails
Latter part much the same employed in white washing the forecastle saw killers So ends this 24 hours.

Sunday 23rd Commences with squally weather and a strong breeze from the SW. Bark cruising one sail in sight to the S Latter part much the same caught a porpoise So ends this 24 hours two sails in sight.

Monday 24th Commences with fine weather and a light breeze from the SE bark cruising saw porpoises and algerines Latter part the same so ends this 24 hours

Tuesday 25th Commences with thick squally weather and a strong breeze from the SSE. Bark cruising to Merchant ship to the SW Latter part weather the same. Saw algerines So ends this 24 hours a dying head ach all day t tone sick. porpoise for dinner porpoise for supper

Wednesday 26th Commences with cloudy weather and a moderate breeze from the SSW. bark cruising off bald head.
Latter part much the same the mate caught 6 days weather. saw grampuses. and porpoises So ends.

Thursday 27th Commences with cloudy weather and a strong breeze from the SE bark off bald head at 10 PM one sail bearing NW of us saw porpoises grampuses
Latter part much the same engaged in painting So ends this 24 hours off Bald Island

Friday 28th Commences with cloudy weather and a moderate breeze from the from the E. Bark cruising off Bald Island. Employed in mending the jib sail. Latter part comes the same So ends this 24 hours clouds mak in neon.

Very rare journal log book of a whaling voyage in the bark "Canton," Captain Peleg L. Sherman, Master. Kept by William Wells Eldridge, Chief Mate. The log contains approximately 500 small colored drawings plus a number of whales and other scenes in black ink. Included are whaling scenes, ships met, lands sighted, great varieties of sea life and snakes. Nearly every event worth recording is illustrated with a small drawing. This was an obviously successful voyage. Recording started on December 13, 1874 and temporarily interrupted on December 14, 1876 when Mate Eldridge was discharged at Albany, Australia due to severe heart pains. After a lengthy recuperation, Mate Eldridge continued to record his adventures during the long trip home, finally arriving in New York on March 3, 1877. A remarkable record!

NAUTICAL EPHEMERA

This section of the book gives the reader an appreciation of those items that, while not sea-going in and of themselves, have to do with the sea and the ships and men who sail it. Seaman's papers, ship's chandlers signs, broadsides for a trip to San Francisco, whale oil receipts, voyage mementos...all these and more are part and parcel of the lore of the sea. Readily sought after by collectors, they are tantalizing personal glimpses of the past, deserving of our attention.

Fine Chinese silk embroidered memorial to Samuel Adams with the American flag to the right and the American Naval flag to the left; an eagle at the top and Adams' portrait in the center. Portrait is an early aquatint engraving. Excellent bird'seye maple frame. Ca. nineteenth century. 16.38" x 15.38".

PROTECTION.

No. 338.

United States of America.

STATE OF MASSACHUSETTS. DISTRICT OF NEW-BEDFORD.

I W. H. Taylor Jr. Collector of the District aforesaid,
Do hereby Certify, That William Finch
an AMERICAN SEAMAN, aged 25 years, or thereabouts, of the height of
5 feet 6 1/4 inches, light complexion, brown hair, grey eyes,
born at Plymouth
Massachusetts

has this day produced to me proof in the manner directed in the Act, entitled "An Act for the relief and protection of American Seamen," and pursuant to the said Act, I DO HEREBY CERTIFY, that the said William Finch is a CITIZEN OF THE UNITED STATES OF AMERICA.

In witness whereof, I have hereunto set my Hand and Seal of Office this 13 *day of* June *in the Year of our Lord one thousand eight hundred and* thirty two

Wm. H. Taylor Jr.

Collector.

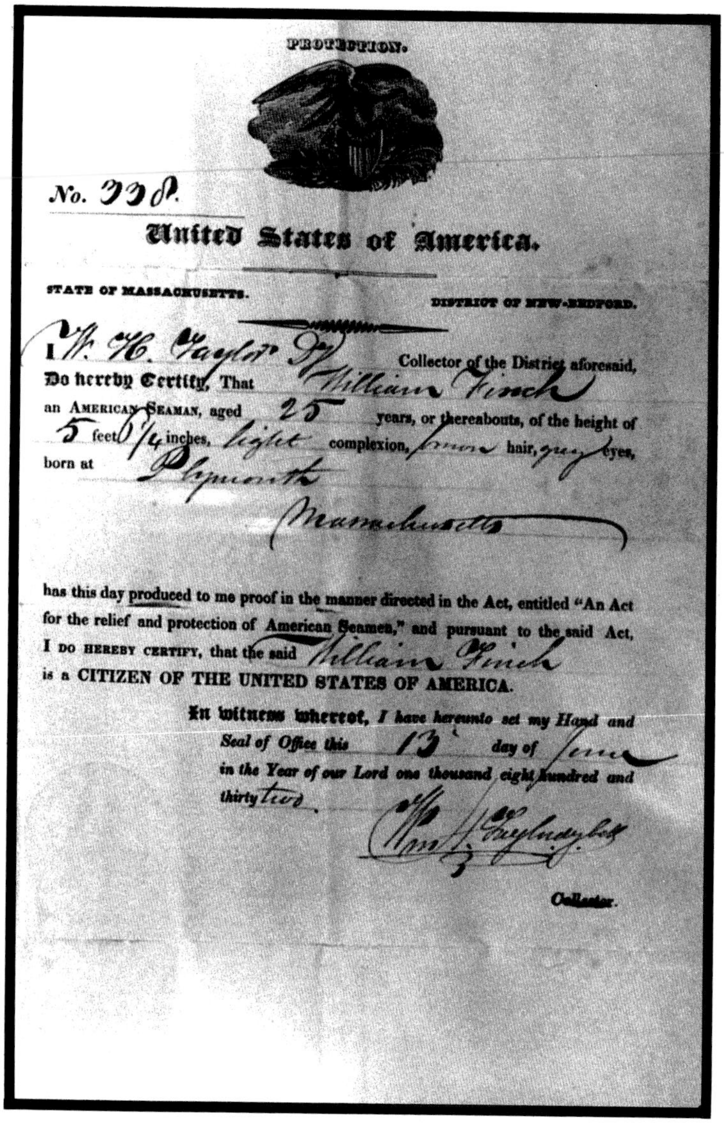

Seaman's papers testifying to the fact that the bearer is a United States citizen. Issued to an ancestor of the author, William Finch, aged 25, born in Plymouth, Massachusetts received his papers from a Mr. Taylor, collector of the District of New Bedford, Massachusetts on the 13th of June, 1832.

Receipt received by William Finch, ancestor of the author, for his share of 1/130th of the sale of 1200 barrels of whale oil, the results of the fruits of his labors on a whaling voyage.

Dr William Finch in Acct Curt with Andw Robeson Cr

1827 2 Mo	To Amt of Capt. Worth's Bill supplied on voyage	45	91	1827 2 Mo 27	By Amt of his voyage in Ship Roscoe 1/130 of 1200 Barrels of oil	201 68
	" Amt of sundries he bot from D. Sawyer's effects	17	42			
	" Amt of his proportion of discharg. Ship	9	"			
2 Mo 27	" Cash in full	129	35			
		$201	68			$201 68

New Bedford 2 Mo 27th 1827

Andw Robeson

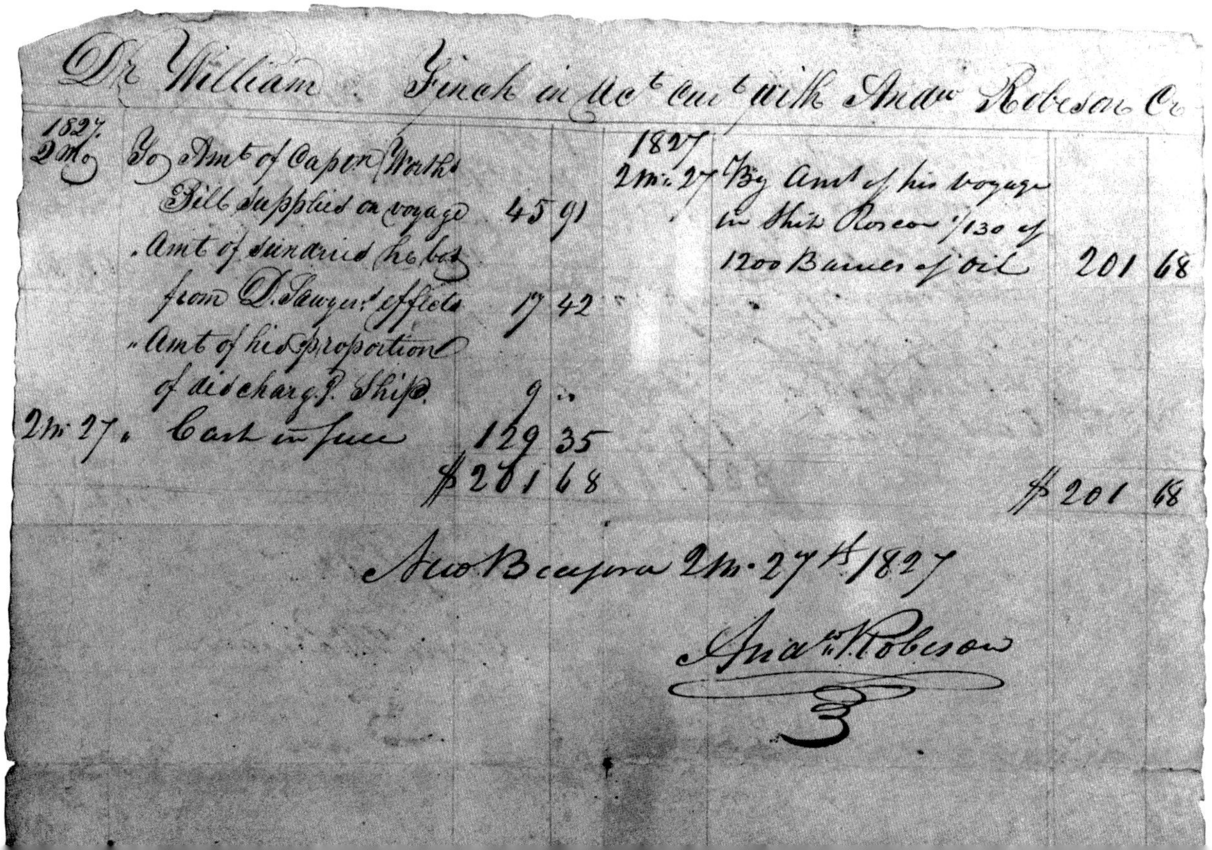

Outstanding large Chinese silk needlework portrait of an American eagle clutching a flag shield and arrows with a trophy of American flags behind him; banner with "E Pluribus Unum" and stars fill the background. nineteenth century. 26.50" by 32".

Large commemorative silk embroidery commemorating the visit of the Great White Fleet to Japan. Embroidery contains the portrait of the sailor for whom it was made, with a scene of the Fleet steaming in line astern, together with the portrait of a sea captain. Crossed cannon with cannonballs at the bottom, then a colorful trophy of flags above which is an eagle, stars and an anchor. Ca. turn of the Century. Measures 36" by 25.75".

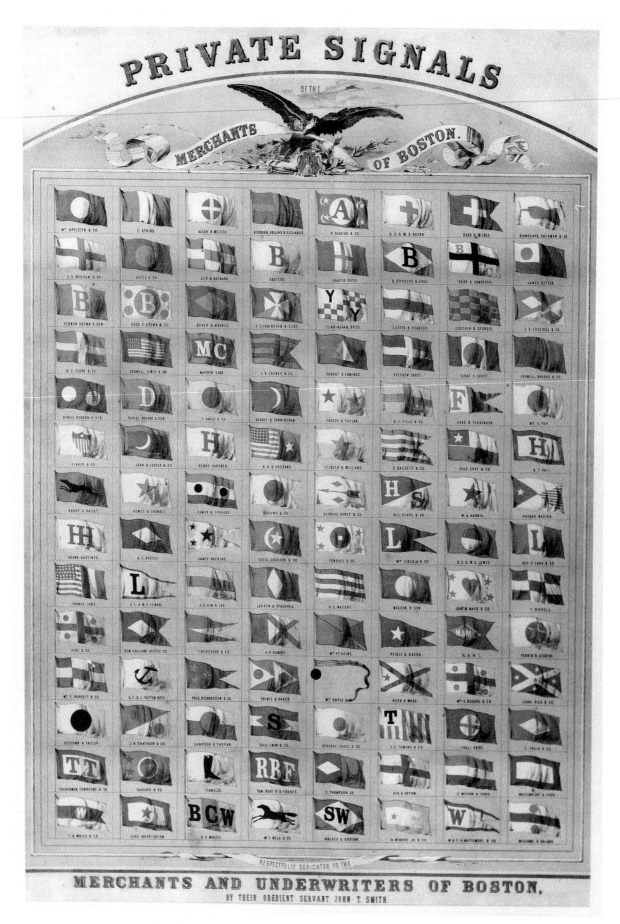

Rare large folio lithograph by Kramer Brothers, Boston. Entitled
"Private Signals of the Merchants of Boston." 39" by 36.25".

Rare large folio lithograph of the "Private Signals Of The Whaling Vessels & C. Belonging To The Port Of New Bedford." Published by Charles Taber & Co., New Bedford, 1857.

Extremely rare advertising broadside for the Eben Pierce Co. of New Bedford, describing their harpoons, bombs, and guns. Stamped twice with a rubber stamp that reads "From F.E. Brown/New Bedford, Mass." On the reverse are two large whale stamps, one a sperm and the other a bowhead. Complete with measurements, yields of oil and other notes. Ca. 1870-1880. Measures 12.25" by 5.13". Pronounced "Purse," these New Bedford Pierces are ancestors of the author on his maternal grandmother's side.

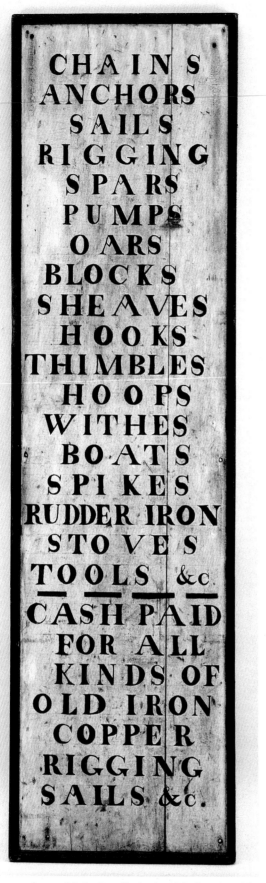

Rare advertising card for the "Splendid A1 First Class Small Clipper Ship 'Florence,' F.D. Wadsworth, Master...." 6" x 3.25".

Rarely seen large ship's chandler's sign, black painted lettering on a greyish-white background; made of pine, it advertises virtually all of the major needs of a shipmaster. Ca. mid-nineteenth century. Height 85", width 23.50".

NAUTICAL PAINTINGS

Successful men of any period have generally welcomed the challenge of ensuring their own immortality, along with a record of the means by which they achieved it. Once well established in the shipping trade, most shipmasters could afford to commission a portrait of themselves, their wives and families, and most often, paintings of the ships on which they sailed, not necessarily in that order. Thus, they were provided with the comfort that something of themselves would live on long after they were gone. How right they were! Today these artistic renderings offer yet another means of bringing the period to life. Profitable voyages were often celebrated with a painting of the ship proudly flying the house flag, entering or leaving foreign ports, with sails furled or unfurled. These seafaring images, along with the portraits so highly prized by collectors today, provide us with a deeper appreciation and understanding of the life and times of these hardy folks. Each is a record of the past...and each fulfills the wish for immortality that inspired them.

Painting. Oil on canvas. "Shanghai." A very rare view of Shanghai; Chinese signature on the stretcher, original Chinese Chippendale frame. Chinese School, nineteenth century. 17.50" x 30".

Painting. Oil on canvas. "Hong Kong." An exceptionally detailed view of the Port, ca. 1860-1870, with eleven large vessels in the foreground. Unsigned. Chinese School, nineteenth century. 17.50" x 31".

Painting, oil on canvas, entitled "Boca Tigris"(Tiger's Mouth). A panoramic view of the fortified passage. Chinese school, nineteenth century. Height 18.25"; length 19.50".

"Shipping Off the Coast," by Frederick Schiller Cozzens, American, 1856-1928. A long, flat beach, presumably Long Island, with aqua-tinted water and six sails in sight at sea. Signed "Fred S. Cozzens,'07." 13.25" by 23.50".

"Richard Morse of Bath. S.B. Dinsmore. Comd Passing Flushing. 1856." Oil reverse painted on glass. Attributed to Petrus Weyts (Belgian 1799-1856) A full portrait of a large black and white hulled vessel with all sails set, flying eight flags including her name pennant and the Belgian and American flags.

Painting. Oil on canvas. Entitled "Portrait of The Ship Temperance Entering Hong Kong Harbor." A large black-hulled British ship enters Hong Kong under full sail, a large junk and other vessels off to her right. Chinese School, nineteenth century. 18" x 23.50".

Painting. Oil on canvas. "Fishing Schooner On Her Way To Sea." Two-masted Gloucester-type schooner sails through a blue-gray sea towing a dory. Three men are on deck, pink sun-touched clouds above. Signed lower right "T.V.C. VALENKAMPH. 1906." American, 1868-1924. 20" x 30".

Painting. Oil on canvas. "View On Long Island Sound." A panoramic view of at least sixteen fairly large vessels in sight, including paddlewheel steamers, tug boats, a steamship and coastal schooners. An important recording of nineteenth century coastal activity. Signed lower left "H.B. Jewell. '87." American School, nineteenth century. 22" x 36".

Painting. Oil on canvas. Entitled "Clipper Ship Staghound At Anchor In Hong Kong Harbor." Portrait of a black-hulled ship with red stripe along her side, flags flying, resting at anchor with a large Chinese junk forward on her port side. Chinese School, nineteenth century. 17" x 23.50".

Painting. Watercolor. "Bark Emma Cushing of Wiscasset A.S. Tibbetts Master Entering The Port Of Palermo Mar - 1857." Black-hulled ship with green waterline, many of her crew visible on deck observed as she enters the port. Flying the American flag with blue field of 18 stars around its border and a single large star in the center. The lighthouse and fortifications are visible off her bow with ship's masts flying the flags of many countries in view beyond. Italian School, nineteenth century. 22" x 28".

Opposite page, top:
Painting. Oil on canvas. "Fishing Schooner Off The Coast Of Maine." A large fishing schooner sails past a buoy and a point of land, while another schooner drops her sails nearer to shore. Blue-green water, puffy white clouds fill the sky with traces of blue showing. Signed lower right "M. Johnson '79." American School, nineteenth century. 20" x 30".

Opposite page, bottom:
Painting. Oil on canvas. "British Ship-Of-War At Anchor In Hong Kong Harbor." An early Hong Kong view with one opium ship and several other vessels at anchor off Hong Kong. This unusual painting shows the warship at anchor with her spars overflowing with men in blue uniforms facing shoreward, a view depicting some unrecorded event. Chinese school, nineteenth century. 20" x 26".

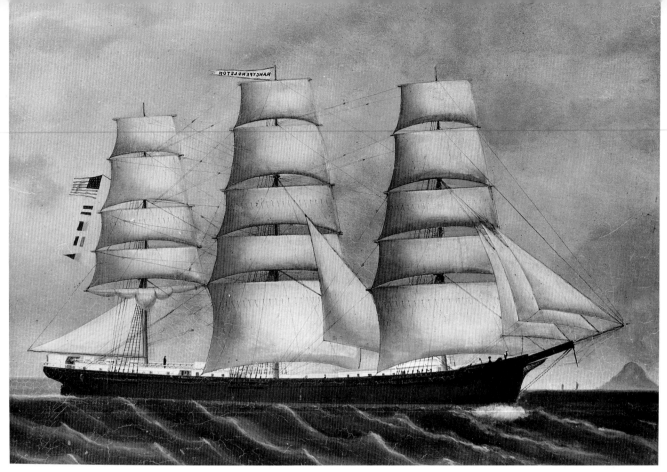

Painting. Oil on canvas. "Portrait Of The American Clipper Nancy Pendleton." Black-hulled clipper under full sail. Chinese School, nineteenth century. 20" x 25".

Painting. Oil on canvas mounted on wood panel. "A Blackball Line Sailing Ship." A black-hulled sailing ship under full sail in a light sea, another ship in the left background showing its stern while under full sail. American School, nineteenth century. 64" x 105".

Painting. Watercolor. "Topsail Schooner Resolute Approaching Land." A fine ship portrait with a wonderful crisp primitive style, excellent deck detail, pilot boat off her stern, red and white lighthouse off her bow. British School, nineteenth century. 24" x 33.50".

Painting. Watercolor. "Pocahontas." A view of the whaleship approaching a harpooned whale with stove boat nearby. Signed and dated "L.A. Briggs, 1851." American School, nineteenth century. 17" x 23".

Ship John Bryant of Boston, A. C. Gardner Master, passing Heligoland Sept. 18. 1860.

Painting. Watercolor. "'Hebe' Of Boston, David Cushman Jr.,
Mate, entering in the bay of Smyrna." The black and white-hulled
ship is seen reducing sail as she approaches the anchorage. Titled
on the bottom edge of the picture. Turkish School, 2nd quarter
nineteenth century, possibly the work of Rafael Corsini. 16.50"
x 22".

Opposite page, top:
Painting. Oil on canvas. "Portrait Of The Clipper Ship Reaper."
A grayish-white-hulled vessel with full set of sails flying the
American and her owner's flags. Signed "W.H. Yorke 1878." (Brit-
ish, Working 1858-1903) 24" x 36".

Opposite page, bottom:
Painting. Oil on canvas. "Ship John Bryant Of Boston. A. Gardner,
Master. Passing Heligoland Sept 1the, 1860." A full-rigged black-
hulled American ship flying many flags passes the island with
other shipping in the distance. Attributed to L. Peterson. 21" x
31".

Painting. Watercolor on paper. "Marcella, Capt. L. Swift, 1828." A rare port painting, showing the ship leaving port and bending on full sail. Signed lower right "H.re Pellegrin a Marseilles au 1828." Honore Pellegrin, French School, nineteenth century. 13.50" x 19".

Painting. Oil on canvas. "Captain Levi Swift." Captain of the "Marcella," subject of the accompanying painting. Captain Swift is shown in a half figure portrait with his left hand tucked into his waistcoat and his right hand holding a pair of dividers on a marine chart. American School, nineteenth century. 27.25" x 23.25".

Painting. Oil on canvas. Entitled "A Young Sea Captain."; half-figure view of a young, bearded sea captain wearing a dark coat with brass buttons, dark green background. American School, nineteenth century. 30" x 25".

Paintings. Oil on canvas. "Captain Benjamin Dyer, Jr. and His Wife." Half-portraits, with Capt. Dyer seated in a red plush chair, a chart and books on the table before him, a pair of dividers in his hand; a handsome youngish man with long sideburns, red drapery to his left, with a ship at sea viewed through the window. His wife is seated in a red plush chair, a kerchief in her left hand, a small book in her right, red drapery to her right with a view of mountains beyond. American School, nineteenth century. 36" x 24".

As a point of history, Captain Dyer served in several different vessels during the Civil War, and was appointed to the Pacific Squadron in 1866. Both he and his wife were aboard the "Fredonia" when swallowed up by the earthquake in Arica Bay, Peru, August 25th, 1868, aged 44 years. Their two children were on shore at the time of the earthquake.

Painting. Oil on canvas. Entitled "American Sea Captain and His Ship." A fine half-figure portrait of a stern-faced young sea captain seated on an empire sofa with his wood-cased telescope resting across his left arm. His ship, the Brig "Eleanor," sails proudly past the window over his right shoulder. Attributed to William Hare (American, working Baltimore 1842-1859). American School, nineteenth century. 37" x 28.50".

Painting. Oil on canvas. Entitled "Portrait of a Sea Captain." A young sea captain poses wearing a black coat with a white shirt, black tie and fancy brown vest, holding a telescope in his right hand against red drapery, a ship and lighthouse visible through open window to the left. American School, nineteenth century. 33" x 27".

OTHER NAUTICAL ANTIQUES

This section encompasses the many make-work projects, hobbies and projects-for-pocket-money undertaken by most sailors, even after they retired from the sea. Hand-made items for their loved ones are cheek-by-jowl with the erotica, hand-woven Nantucket lighthouse baskets, knot boards and ditty boxes. These and much, much more are to be found in the author's "slop chest" of memorabilia.

Left: Large carved pine log book stamp of a ship with a sperm whale on the left side, and a whale's tail on the right. American, ca. nineteenth century. Length 3.75". *Top center:* Carved pine whale stamp for a log book, with a whale's tail. American, ca. nineteenth century. Length 2.13". *Bottom center:* Carved hardwood whale stamp, with the figure of a sperm whale. American, ca. nineteenth century. Length 2.25". *Right:* Small pine whale stamp, with the figure of a right whale. American, ca. nineteenth century. Length 2".

Left: Rare whale stamp with a metal stamping of a baleen whale applied to a wood block; whale shown spouting. Ca. late nineteenth century. *Right:* Sculptured wood log book stamp of an anchor.

Top: A primitive wooden ladle made of maple. Ca. nineteenth century or earlier. Length 22.13". *Bottom left:* Rare oak or ash caulking mallet, used for caulking the seams of a ship. Ca. nineteenth century. Length 12". *Bottom right:* Adjustable scribe of the type used aboard ship. Ca. nineteenth century. Extends to 6".

Complete diving suit with helmet, boots, weighted belt and hanger. By A.J. Morse & Son, Boston, Mass. Ca. early twentieth century.

Left: Rare Liverpool jug with American ship on one side; on the opposite, a figure of "Hope" and a ship. The Great Seal of the United States and the date 1804 appears under the spout, the angel Gabriel under the handle. Height 10". *Right:* Rare Buffalo pottery souvenir pitcher of New Bedford, ca. 1907. Views of "The Capture," "The Niger," and various other views of New Bedford. Inside the spout is "The Whaling City/Souvenir of/New Bedford Mass." Height 6.50".

Center: Fine antique bronze cannon sundial signed "Lamy S. Simon." The cannon and mount appear to be eighteenth century. Diameter 13". Ends: Pair of superb antique beckets, old red and green paint. American, early nineteenth century.

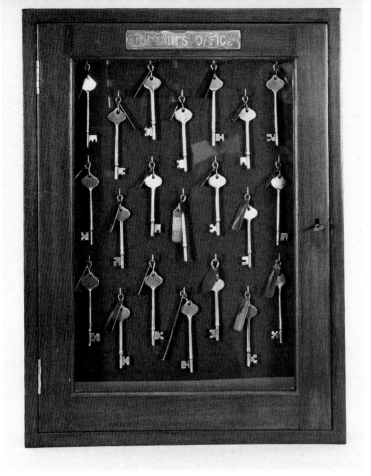

Fine walnut hanging cabinet with lock and brass label titled "Captain's Office." Contains 21 brass keys, each with its own tag identifying the cabin or door it unlocks. Ca. nineteenth century. Height 25.75"; width 19.50"; depth 3.50".

Top left: Nineteenth century double barrel percussion pistol with scrimshawed whale ivory grips; on one side, an engraved eagle, on the opposite, a fouled anchor and banner that reads "James Austin Boston Mass. 1874." Length 10". *Top right:* Rare multiple-use scrimshaw tool holder in the shape of a handle that accepts different tools, such as screwdriver blades, chisel blades, drills, etc. Mahogany handle is inlaid with whale ivory hearts and a star. Ca. mid-nineteenth century. Length 5". *Bottom left:* Pair of fine early whale's teeth, as prepared for engraving many years ago. Length 4.50". *Bottom right:* Very rare scrimshaw ditty box beautifully made from panbone with whale ivory handle on the cover, wooden top and bottom. Ca. early to mid-nineteenth century. Length 6.38"; height 4.25".

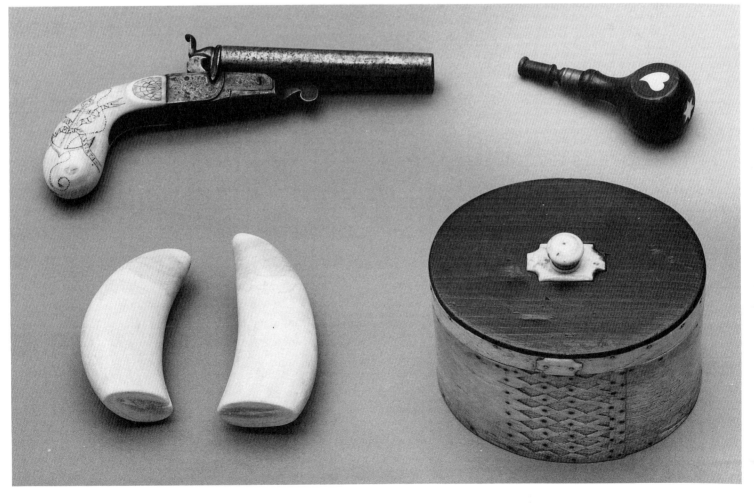

Top left: Early prisoner-of-war straw-work box, an unusually detailed example with carefully inlaid and colored trays, as well as scroll work around the sides. English, ca. early nineteenth century. Length 12.75". **Top center:** Fine Nantucket Lightship basket, ca. last quarter nineteenth century. Diameter 10:". **Top right:** Mast alarm used aboard ship to call the crew to battle stations. Made of walnut and brass mounted. Ca. nineteenth century. Height 13".

Bottom left: Rare sailmaker's kit as used aboard ship. Con-tains a carved cattle horn filled with greased sailmaker's needles, three sailmaker's leather palms, a spool for holding heavy line, and a rare "Sticking Tommy" miner's light holding a candle that could be stuck into a ship's beam to provide light below decks. Complete with the original canvas bag. Ca. mid-nineteenth century.

Bottom right: Cased sailmaker's kit containing an assortment of needles, wax, fids, and other devices, including scissors and leather palms. Ca. nineteenth century.

Opposite page, top:
Elaborate sailor's knot board prepared by noted New Bedford artist and illustrator Clifford V. Ashley, ca. 1920s. Approximately forty different knots mounted on an antique pine panel made from a 19.50" pine plank beveled at the edges. Length 33.75"; width 19.25".

Opposite page, bottom:
Top left: Fine scrimshaw coconut bowl dipper with turned whale ivory handle. Ca. nineteenth century. **Top right:** Small early wooden ship's block with whalebone shiv. Ca. nineteenth century. Length 3.50". **Center left:** Coconut shell dipper with pewter connector and turned hardwood handle. Dipper also has a pewter lip. Ca. nineteenth century. **Center right:** Whalebone double ship's block with whalebone shivs and metal mountings. Ca. mid-nineteenth century. Length 4.25". **Center:** Sailor-made rolling pin of hardwood with whalebone ends and inset whale-bone and baleen rings. Ca. mid-nineteenth century. Length 20". **Bottom:** Rare patent model harpoon complete with the origi-nal, made-to-scale carved form, from which it was constructed. Ca. mid-nineteenth century. Length 12.50".

Left to right: **1.** Heavy iron and brass lamp in the shape of a lighthouse; probably Minot's Light near Boston. Height 20". **2.** Captain's speaking trumpet with original protective red paint inside. Ca. nineteenth century. Length 16". **3.** Fine Captain's speaking trumpet, ca. nineteenth century. Length 18.25". **4.** Outstanding Captain's speaking trumpet, ca. nineteenth century. Engraved "L.W. Merrill/1836." Length 20".

Brass bound Royal Navy oak rum cask with heavy brass hasp used on early British Men-of-War to hold the crew's daily rum ration. Ca. early nineteenth century. Height 30.50".

Two large framed sailor's valentines, mounted in the original octagonal shaped frames, the one on the left with an anchor in the center, while the one on the right has a star design. Ca. nineteenth century. Diameter 16" across the flats.

Very rare stand with whale oil samples by the William A. Robinson Co. of New Bedford. The Robinson Company operated a whale oil reducing plant at New Bedford for 75 years. The plant was demolished and replaced by a parking garage in 1930. Length 15.25".

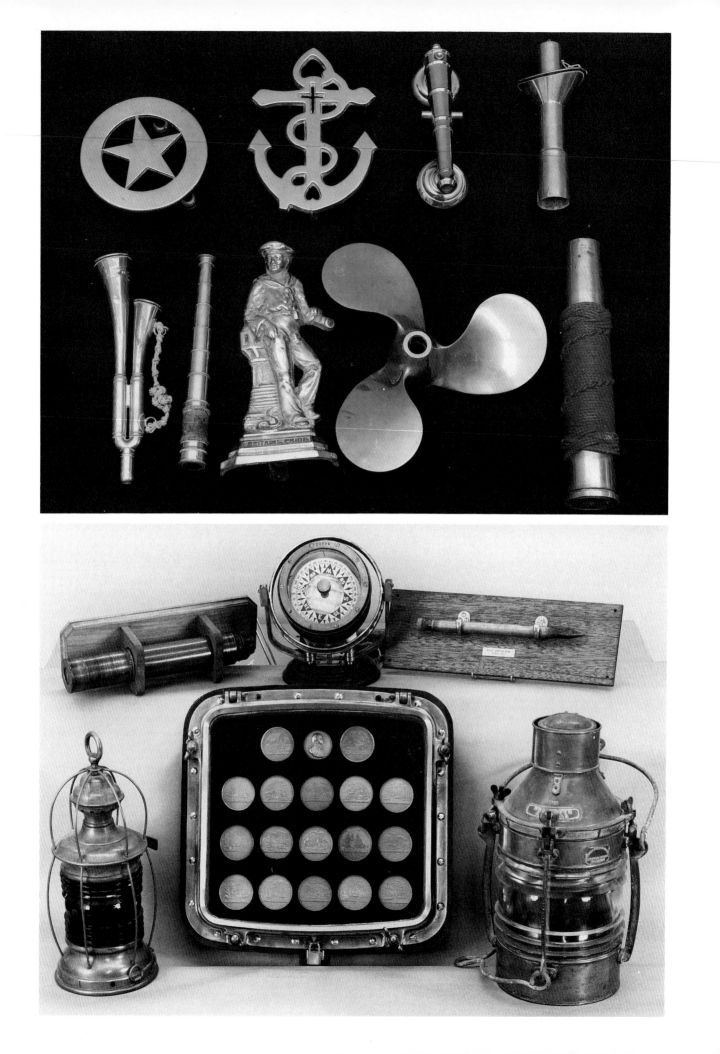

Top: **1.** Early small circular Nantucket basket with side handles. Diameter 6.50". **2.** Early circular Nantucket basket. Diameter 8.75". **3.** Very early circular Nantucket basket with bail handle. Diameter 7.88".

Center: **1.** Fine old circular Nantucket basket with bail handle. Diameter 10". **2.** Early circular Nantucket basket with bail handle. Branded "G.P. Coleman" on the bottom. An extremely early example with the name also branded on the handle. Di-ameter 9.25". **3.** Early eskimo basketry vessel with hinged lid and carved walrus ivory bird finial. Diameter 9.25"; height 8".

Bottom left: Exceptional parquetry inlaid sewing box of multi-wood construction, sailor made. Ca. 1870-1880. Length 12.50".

Bottom right: Exceptional marine architect's drafting set; multiple sections, pull-out feet to support upper lid, secret locking drawers and removable tray. Width 16"; depth 11.25"; height 4.25".

Opposite page, top:

Top, left to right: **1.** Circular brass ship's trivet, with star in the center. Diameter 6". **2.** Anchor shaped brass trivet. Length 9". **3.** Brass door knocker in the shape of a cannon. Length 9". **4.** Early brass steam whistle for a launch. Length 8".

Bottom, left to right: **1.** Small boat's brass hand-held whistle. Ca. nineteenth century. Length 10.50". **2.** Small early six-draw brass telescope. Length 10". **3.** Lovely nineteenth century brass doorstop in the form of a sailor. Height 11.25". **4.** Fine brass small boat's propeller. Diameter 11". **5.** Brass cased World War I naval artillery shell with sailor ropework. Height 12.25".

Opposite page, bottom:

Top, left to right: **1.** Early two-draw telescope with mahogany case, shown on a recent wall mount. Ca. early nineteenth century. **2.** Fine ship's "Telltale" compass by T.S. and J.G. Negus. Diameter 7". **3.** Mid-nineteenth century brass harpoon bomb on a recent wall mount. Length 13".

Bottom, left to right: **1.** Ship's port lantern, almost identical to one recovered from the U.S.S. Monitor. Made by Boesch Lamp Co., San Francisco. Height 17.25". **2.** Collection of 18 bronze medals commemorating American Naval hero John Paul Jones and his many naval feats, together with other famous American Naval battles. Primarily in Latin. Collection is mounted in a large square port light. **3.** Ship's copper "Not Under Command" light. Height 18.50".

Top to bottom: **1.** Rare decorative sword, complete with basket guard and blade made from the bill of a swordfish. Decorated with a swordfish, an eagle with flags, foliate decoration, the initials "C.F.S.", the date "1904", "Cape Ann," and signed Higgins Painter. Length 42.50". **2.** Unusual throwing knife with heart-shaped blade and wooden handle, complete with two-piece wooden sheath crudely carved with the name "A.E. Ellis." **3.** Rare ropework locking device with brass bar and padlock. Used to secure a sea chest. Ca. late nineteenth century. Length 11". **4.** Extremely rare Iron brand bomb harpoon gun, complete with original orange protective paint and fitted with a scrimshaw whale ivory and whalebone ramrod. Ca. last half nineteenth century. Length 36". **5.** Old caulking mallet with crosshatched handle bearing the name "G.G. Gifford." Ca. late nineteenth century. Length 18.50". **6.** Rare lignum vitae caulking mallet with crosshatched handle. Ca. late nineteenth century. Length 13.50".

Top to bottom: **1.** Iron Brand percussion bomb harpoon gun, skeleton metal stock. Ca. nineteenth century. Length 36". **2.** Rare Brand percussion bomb harpoon gun with wooden stock, ca. nineteenth century. Length 36". **3.** Rare carving from a whaleship once commanded by Captain Edward Coffin, reputed to be the last whaleship master to live and die on Nantucket. Ca. nineteenth century. Length 50". **4.** Another piece of carving from the same whaleship belonging to Captain Coffin; this piece bears a silver plate with the name "John P. Whitten." Ca. nineteenth century. Length 43.50".

Ship's Captain's liquor chest containing 8 quart size and 2 half-pint bottles, all of which are matching. The chest also contains a pair of cut glass tumblers and 2 wine glasses. English, ca. late eighteenth century.

Rare burl wood and solid gold lined and mounted snuff box, engraved in gold, with inset in the cover reading as follows: "3.1.54/Lightning/Boston." Probably a presentation made to the captain or owner of the Clipper Ship "Lightning," as this is the date on which she was launched. Length 3.63"; width 2"; depth.88".

Top, left to right: **1.** Oval brass bound oak cask of the type used on British ships for rum or water. Ca. nineteenth century. Height 24". **2.** Sculptured oak small vessel sternboard for the "Royal Sovereign." Ca. last half nineteenth century. Width 46". **3.** Cast bronze lighthouse, ca. late nineteenth century. Height 14.50".

Center: Rare depth sounding instrument in original box marked "Bassnett's Patent Sounder" (Liverpool, England). Ca. nineteenth century.

Bottom: Cased Brand iron bomb harpoon gun with two bomb harpoons, all in the original case. Ca. nineteenth century.

Top, left to right: **1.** Circular Nantucket Lightship basket, ca. late nineteenth century. Diameter 10". **2.** Early Nantucket Lightship basket, circular shape with swing handle. Ca. late nineteenth century. Diameter 7.50". **3.** Scrimshaw ditty box made of baleen with cutout geometric designs, plus animal and bird figures. The cutouts were once backed by red paper. Signed inside "Nancy Cummins, March 14, 1819." The initials "NC" are also carved on the pine lid. Diameter 6".

Bottom, left to right: **1.** Miniature ship's figurehead of a man wearing a feathered headpiece; made either as a miniature, or possibly for a small vessel. Ca. nineteenth century. Height 13". **2.** Fine small ebony quadrant. Ca. late nineteenth century. **3.** Royal Navy Crown Mast Jack, made entirely of metal on a wood base. Height 11".

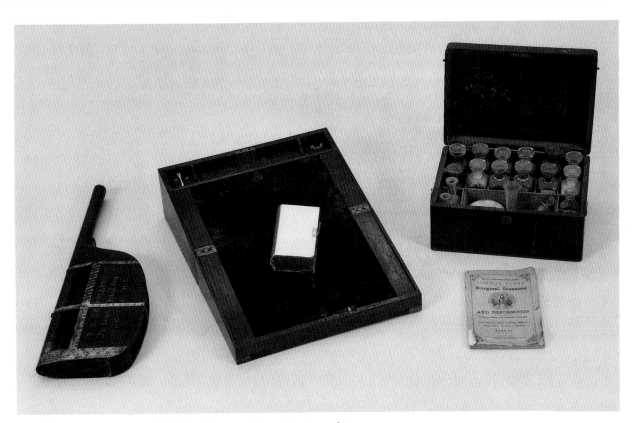

Left: A rare patent model of an improved rudder issued to Nicholas D. Le Pelley of Cleveland, Ohio on March 14, 1865, Patent No. 46807. Model is made of wood and brass and bears the designer's name and patent date on the piece. Length 19.50".
2. Three pieces of memorabilia of Mrs. Amos C. Baker; they are a solid brass bound rosewood folding travel desk with compartments, together with a small copy of the Holy Bible with embossed morocco leather spine, solid ivory covers and gold bronze hasp. The bible is inscribed "Presented to/Mrs. Amos C. Baker/By the First & Second /Officers of the Barque/ 'A.R.Tucker,' with/their best wishes.-/Bermuda/30 May 1877." Also included is a lignum vitae fid with Capt. Baker's initials. Desk width 12.88". **3.** Ship's medicine or apothecary chest containing 19 bottles, small measuring beaker, a porcelain mortar and pestle, together with a book entitled "Surgical Diseases and Deformities." Ca. late nineteenth century. Width of chest 19.50".

Left: A pair of brass crow's nest binoculars, together with their original stitched sail canvas bag with spliced lanyard. French made, ca. 1850. *Right:* A small boat's water cask with mounted whale ivory whale figure, and branded "Brig Diviola." American, ca. mid-nineteenth century. Diameter 8"; height 5".

Left: Two small unopened bottles of pure sperm oil, each bearing the label of "W.F. Nye Inc., New Bedford, Mass." Height 3".
Right: An unopened packet of early sail maker's needles, made by James Smith & Son. Ca. mid-nineteenth century. Measures 2.75" by 4".

Top left: Rare nickel plated ship's bell clock by Seth Thomas, time and strike movement. This clock is unusual in that it has a traditional style bell mounted atop the clock. Diameter 6.25".
Top right: Brass signal cannon mounted on a mahogany naval carriage; uses black powder. Ca. nineteenth century. Barrel length 17". *Bottom:* Nest of three matched Nantucket baskets, Ca. late nineteenth century. Diameters are 5.75", 8.75" and 11".

Top left: Fine early Nantucket basket with a pair of handles. Diameter 10". *Top right:* Very nice Nantucket basket with hoop handle. Diameter 10". *Bottom left:* Exceptional large Nantucket basket with hoop handle. By Folger, with his stencil on the inside bottom. Diameter 14"; height 9.25". *Bottom right:* Early Nantucket basket by Folger, a near mate to the preceding basket.

Left: Fine small nineteenth century Nantucket lightship basket. Diameter 6". *Right:* Low circular Nantucket basket, ca. nineteenth century. Diameter 9.75".

Top: Very early scrimshaw baleen ditty box engraved around its entire side with a panorama of buildings. Beautifully executed in great detail including willow trees and a man with a walking stick. Mahogany cover with whalebone and wood knob. Ca. 2nd quarter nineteenth century. Length 7". *Bottom left:* Fine early baleen ditty box with elaborate chain-like fingers. Ca. 2nd quarter nineteenth century. Length 7.88". *Bottom right:* Rare small oval baleen ditty box with red plaid pincushion top. Ca. 2nd quarter nineteenth century. Length 4.50".

VALUE GUIDE

Values vary immensely according to the condition of the piece, the location of the market, and the overall quality of the piece of work. All these factors make it impossible to create an accurate value list, but we can offer a guide. These values reflect what one could realistically expect to pay at retail or auction. It is, however, only a guide, and the author accepts no responsibility for any gain or loss the reader may experience as a result of using this guide.

The left hand number is the page number. The letters following it indicate the position of the photograph on the page: T=top, L=left. TL=top left, TR=top right, C=center, CL=center left, CR=center right, R=right, B=bottom, BL=bottom left, BR=bottom right. In photos where more than one object are identified, the prices follow the order of the caption. The right hand numbers are the estimated values.

10	BL	3000, 1200
11		13000
12	T	85000, 3500, 6000
12	B	4000, 4800, 3500
13	L	19000, 5000, 8500, 4500
14	T	2300, 2800
14	B	3500
15		1600, 900, 450
16		26000
17		1400
18	T	500, 300
18	B	1500, 800
19		1000, 1500
20	T	2400
21	T	1700, 500, 800
22		1200
23	T	2000
23	C	3000
24	T	700, 800, 500
25	T	700, 1000, 1300, 700
26	T	19000
27		150, 250, 200, 400, 600, 2700, 2800
28	T	500, 1000, 700, 600, 600
28	B	2000, 150, 1000, 1500, 400
29	T	27000, 18000
30	T	300, 350, 250, 300, 400, 400
30	B	500, 700, 500, 350, 400, 500
31	T	2000, 1000, 1400, 4200
31	B	3500
32	T	5000, 5500
33	T	2000, 1600, 2000
33	B	2400
34		700, 1100, 1300, 1800, 550, 500, 1700, 1300, 800, 1600
35	T	32000
37	T	35000
38		1800, 1600, 1200
39	T	3700

40	T	7000, 6500, 4500, 3000
40	B	45000
41	T	2000, 3500, 1500
41	B	1500, 1000, 500, 1200
42	T	3000, 3600
43	T	1100, 900, 800
43	B	1600, 700
44	T	30000
45	C	21000
46	T	12000, 10000
46	B	4000
47		9000, 4000, 5000, 5000, 2500
48	T	1050, 900, 400
48	B	1700, 2000, 500
49	T	600, 600, 250
49	B	1000
50	T	450, 450, 250, 440, 550, 450
50	B	3500, 600, 120, 300
51	T	650, 100, 400, 200, 100, 150, 100, 100
51	B	7000, 600, 800, 950
52		600, 900, 600, 650, 200, 700, 450
53	T	1500, 1000, 575, 1400, 900, 600, 450
53	B	1100, 700, 250, 900, 500, 275
54		18000
55	T	6000
55	B	900, 2500, 900
56	T	2100
56	B	2000
57		4500, 4800
58		850, 900, 700, 650, 550
59	T	800
59	B	3000, 700, 700, 1800
60		900, 800, 800, 4000, 700
61	T	450, 300, 550
61	B	900, 950, 750, 950
62		1300, 1300, 1400
63		750, 400, 850, 200, 600,

		600
64	T	Average 200 each
64	B	300, 250, 2100, 400, 900
65	T	800, 450, 750, 200, 175, 150, 200, 150, 200, 300, 300
65	B	700, 800, 900, 300, 300, 300, 350
66	T	450, 400, 250, 200, 100, 150, 400, 350, 200
66	B	250, 2300, 400, 700, 500
67		2300, 700, 600, 500, 200, 800, 500, 300, 200
68		300, 300, 200, 250, 350, 250, 400, 450, 375, 500, 400
69	T	1200, 650, 1100, 600, 300, 600, 400, 1000, 400
69	B	600, 600, 1600, 400, 300, 300, 300, 250, 250, 150
70		3500
71	T	500
71	B	100, 450
72		750, 600
73		4500
74	T	600
74	B	200, 1000, 400, 400, 400, 200, 200, 200
75	T	200
76	L	800
76	R	850
77	TL	2800
77	TR	3400
77	B	1200
78	T	800, 350, 75
78	B	600, 1600, 1200, 700, 900, 300
79	T	5500
79	B	3300
80	T	5500
80	B	1000, 700, 600
81	T	500, 1500, 500, 200

81	B	2000
82		14000
83	T	1200
83	C	1600, 800
83	B	900
84	T	1200
84	B	700
85	T	400
85	B	500, 200, 350, 200, 150, 100, 200, 200, 200, 150, 150, 200, 150
86	T	Average 50 each
86	B	70, 200, 90, 200, 40, 125, 70, 90
87		1100, 700
88	T	3500
88	B	4000
89	T	275, 125, 60, 25, 30
89	B	250, 275, 600, 300, 500, 250, 300, 100, 200, 450, 250, 275, 200, 150, 125, 150
90	T	275, 150, 600, 400, 200, 150, 300, 300, 200
90	B	2800, 700, 2600
91		700, 500, 500, 1500
92	T	2700, 600, 1100, 300, 500, 600
92	B	1100, 300, 1000, 900, 300, 200, 400
93		1500
94	T	900, 400, 100, 300, 100, 250
94	B	2600
95		2800
96		1400, 1100, 1000, 700, 450, 900, 700, 1000
97		950, 550, 1100, 950, 700, 400, 750
98	T	1400, 250
98	B	400, 500, 650, 450, 650, 200
99	T	450, 175, 200, 150, 300,

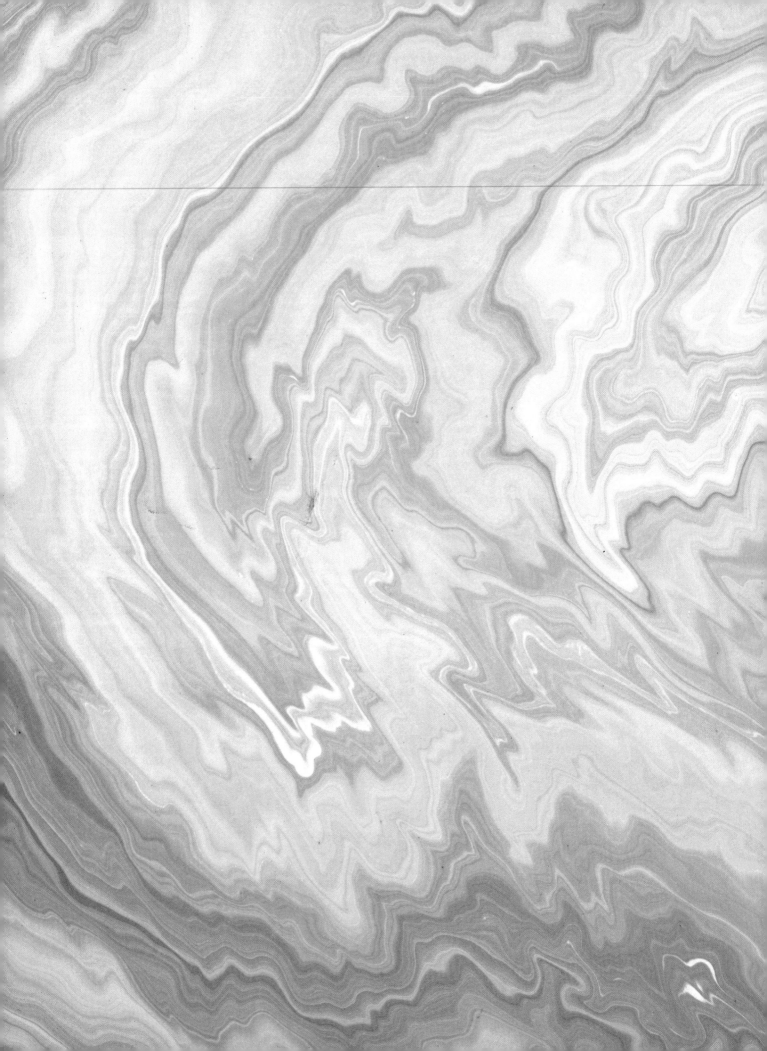